Zen Meditat
Psychotherapy

Zen Meditation in Psychotherapy

Techniques for Clinical Practice

C. Alexander Simpkins
Annellen M. Simpkins

JOHN WILEY & SONS, INC.

Published by John Wiley & Sons, Inc., Hoboken, New Jersey.
Published simultaneously in Canada.

Library of Congress Cataloging-in-Publication Data:

Simpkins, C. Alexander.
   Zen meditation in psychotherapy : techniques for clinical practice / C. Alexander Simpkins and Annellen Simpkins.
      p. ; cm.
   Includes bibliographical references and indexes.
   ISBNs 978-0-470-94826-2; 978-1-118-15934-7; 978-1-118-15933-0; 978-1-118-15932-3; 978-1-118-15568-4
   I. Simpkins, Annellen M.   II. Title.
   [DNLM: 1. Buddhism–psychology.   2. Meditation–psychology.   3. Mental Disorders–psychology.
4. Mental Disorders–therapy.   5. Psychotherapy–methods.   6. Religion and Psychology.   WM 425.5.R3]
   LC classification not assigned
   616.89′14–dc23

                                                                                2011029118

Printed in the United States of America

10 9 8 7 6 5 4 3 2 1

We dedicate this book to all the unknown people who deserve a dedication and never receive one. We really appreciate you and all you do in the world.

Contents

Part IV
Facilitating Therapists

Introduction

Although the sun and moon are shining brightly, the floating clouds cover them. Although the cluster of orchids flourish, the autumn wind wilts them. . . . No matter how much evil arises, if we steadfastly practice meditation over many long years, the floating clouds will disappear, and the autumn wind will stop.

—(Dogen, in Masunaga, 1971, p. 66)

Like the sun and moon shining brightly, each of us has the potential to be healthy. But problematic behaviors, thoughts, and feelings get in the way of expressing this positive potential. Psychological disorders are real and devastating, obscuring potential so completely that it seems like the autumn wind will never end. We have many helpful forms of therapy to deal with the problem level of disturbance by addressing troubling thoughts, behaviors, and feelings. These methods help people solve their problems, change faulty attitudes, and resolve emotional conflicts. Therapy has been shown to be effective (Frank & Frank, 1991), getting people out of problems to feel better and stop engaging in destructive behaviors.

So, why do we need meditation? Recent research has shown that meditation can sharpen awareness, regulate emotions, and promote deep relaxation and calm. We need it because the entire course of therapy unfolds more easily as clients gain invaluable skills. Resistance is bypassed through bottom-up processing that activates the natural instincts for healing. The stress reaction is quieted while maintaining alert attention to help meet needs more fully. Impulses are moderated as people become aware and in touch. And with the freedom gained from meditation's clear perception, moods, fears, addictions, and anxieties lose their suffocating grip. The mind, brain, and body function optimally, paving the way for recovery.

But beyond just resolving problems, meditation brings wisdom. People wake up to living in the present moment. They find satisfaction in whatever they do. Life becomes an art that can be lived fully. Enlightenment is wisdom's fulfillment.

ABOUT THIS BOOK

Zen Meditation in Psychotherapy teaches meditation and shows how to work with it as a therapeutic tool. With the awareness meditation fosters, people can do what they need and express themselves as they truly are, beyond psychological disturbance and problems, fully and uniquely.

We address both helpers and sufferers. Therapists will find definite methods to follow for a broad range of psychological disturbances. They will also find ways to enhance their own life, to feel and do their best, unified with life's tasks, both professionally and personally. These methods can be seamlessly integrated into the treatments they already do. Those who are suffering from psychological problems will find clear practices that they can follow to overcome difficulties. And with sound science behind the meditations included here, everyone can have confidence that these meditations will facilitate the brain-mind-body system at many levels.

This book is organized into four parts with 12 chapters and an appendix. Part I is devoted to research on meditation. Chapter 1 gives the latest research findings about meditation, its efficacy, and its psychological effects. Chapter 2 provides the neuroscience findings about how meditation changes the brain. Part II reveals the development of the meditation tradition in Chapter 3, key themes in Chapter 4, and fundamental practices that can help you and your clients in Chapter 5. Each chapter in Part III deals with common psychological problems. Chapter 6 offers a general protocol for integrating meditation into treatments at every phase. Chapter 7, Regulating Affect, gives the latest models of emotion with the brain science behind them, and shows why meditation is helpful and then how to apply it for problems such as depression and anger. Chapter 8 deals with anxiety and trauma. Chapter 9 addresses impulse problems, including addiction and weight management. Chapter 10 shows how to help clients foster healthy relationships. Part IV is for the care and enhancement of therapists.

Chapter 11 presents meditative ways to reduce stress and burnout. Chapter 12 gives meditative training to enhance therapeutic sensitivities. The conclusion is a culmination, so that you and your clients can discover clear, awake awareness in every moment. We also include an appendix that covers brain basics, to help those who are unfamiliar with the brain to better understand how meditation influences the nervous system as well as thoughts, emotions, and behavior.

Many of the chapters provide protocols to follow with specific exercises to do. We speak directly to those doing the exercises so that therapists have scripts to follow and clients can use these methods themselves. We encourage you to creatively individualize any of these methods, however, to suit your personal therapeutic style and the unique situation and needs of your clients. Please use these methods as guidelines, but always trust your own sensitivities and instincts.

We have also included traditional stories throughout the book. Zen was often taught through teaching stories with the idea that unconscious insight can be tapped more readily when communicating indirectly through stories. Allow yourself to notice any associations you have. And we hope you enjoy having new learning, as many Zen students have over the centuries.

May you find in meditation a helpful tool to enhance your own life and add new dimensions for your work with clients!

I

Research and Efficacy

We are living in exciting times, when science shines illumination on enlightenment!

—(C. Alexander Simpkins & Annellen M. Simpkins)

People have been talking for millennia about the profound effects of meditation on the mind, body, and spirit. But it is only in recent years that the West has been listening. We are now applying our most advanced scientific methods to explore meditation and, as a result, our understanding of this seemingly ineffable practice is coming into focus. Today we see a flood of high-quality studies that reveal what meditation does and how helpful it is for therapy. We now have a better sense of some of the psychological mechanisms and the impact on the nervous system. We bring you the latest research findings about meditation, its efficacy, and its psychological effects in Chapter 1. Chapter 2 provides the neuroscience findings about how meditation changes the nervous system.

With Zen's long tradition of meditation practice and science's recent research supporting its use, you can be confident in adding the meditation methods provided in this book for a powerful set of tools to help yourself and your clients develop to the fullest potential!

1

The Psychology of Meditation and Its Efficacy for Clinical Practice

Just turn on your mind's inner light, and its glow will show you the way. Then you will immediately dispel all the troubling thoughts of imperfection that take away your peace of mind. And effortlessly, you will become perfect and whole, with many open gates to truth before you.
—(Paraphrased from Bodhidharma's Breakthrough Sermon)

Zen offers a way to overcome psychological disturbance and become healthy and happy, to live well. The method is based on concentrating the mind in particular ways. Zen teaches these methods through the practice of meditation. Contrary to our Western perspectives that are based in doing something with a goal in mind, this practice centers on a special way of doing things that is goal-less, referred to as emptiness. This story about one of Buddha's disciples, Subhuti, introduces the concept.

One day Subhuti was meditating under a flowering tree, experiencing a calm and quiet consciousness, empty of thought, present in the moment. A gentle breeze shook the tree and its flowers began to fall down all around him.

The breeze seemed to be saying, "We are praising you for your clear statement about emptiness."

Figure 1.1   Cherry Blossom Nature

Source: Photographed by C. Alexander Simpkins, Jr., Washington, DC, Spring 2011

"But I haven't said a word," answered Subhuti.

"You have not said anything about emptiness and we have not heard anything about emptiness. This is true emptiness."

The blossoms showered down on Subhuti as he smiled (Figure 1.1).

This book opens you to the practice of emptiness. As Western healers, we are not content to simply experience a helpful method to use with our clients. We also need to place it under the watchful eye of science to ensure that the experience does indeed help people in measurable ways. And yet, how can you measure emptiness and the wordless experience of meditation that brings it about? Obviously there is something happening, because people have been discussing it for millennia. And intuitively, we feel the importance of such experiencing since some of our greatest insights have come in a flash.

Now, a large body of research has revealed repeatedly that the wordless, empty experience found in meditation has healing effects. Meditation can truly move people, opening possibilities for new potentials to emerge, and these changes can be measured. This is enormously important for psychotherapy, because now we have a whole new set of tools to add to our practice, tools that can truly help clients to benefit fully from the therapeutic treatments we provide.

Jennifer was a hospice nurse who used meditation as a pivotal part of her therapeutic treatment. She was tall, heavy-set, and large-boned, with curly brown hair softly framing her round face. Her gentle blue eyes and soothing voice emanated warmth. She was a caring and compassionate person who believed in helping others, which was why she had chosen to be a hospice nurse.

Jennifer had been overweight all her life, and now she carried at least 60 extra pounds. Her family doctor had recently warned her to get serious about losing weight. As a nurse, she was well aware of the health benefits of weight loss, but had never been able to do anything about it. Following her doctor's warning, she tried again to lose some weight on her own, but couldn't make any progress. Frustrated, she decided to seek therapy. She had heard about the benefits of meditation, and so she came to us for treatment. A meditational approach seemed an appropriate choice since it would use her compassionate nature to help others to help herself.

As she began therapy, she revealed a number of weights she carried besides pounds. Working at the hospice, she had to face death on a daily basis. She told us that she grew close to her patients, and then they died. She could literally see death creep up on them. Watching people she cared about waste away deeply disturbed her. Grief weighed her down. Then, when a patient finally died, she found it difficult to stop thinking about that person.

Therapy involved her practice of several forms of meditation. First, she learned how to use her attention meditatively by practicing focus meditations. She was surprised to learn that she could direct her attention at will. As she gained skills with her attentional focus, she said, "Wow! I never knew you could do that!"

We also taught her mindfulness meditations: to follow her experience moment by moment and nonjudgmentally, which she was encouraged to practice between sessions as well. Her mindfulness practice set a process in motion. And it helped to moderate the strong emotions of sadness that she experienced. Research shows that meditation helps to balance affect, lower reactivity to negative emotions, and foster better self-regulation as later sections of this chapter describe. But still, she was not losing weight.

Next, she learned Zen meditation, to simply be empty of all thought. When a thought or feeling arose, we told her to notice it, think about it if needed, and then let it go as soon as possible. This was helpful to her in learning another important lesson from meditation: how to let go and allow nature to take its course. As she practiced this form of meditation, focusing on nothing and letting go of any thoughts that might intrude, she found that thoughts and feelings of death kept interrupting her meditation.

The thoughts seemed to be about her hospice patients. But then, one night she had a frightening dream. She saw her parents dying at the hospice, shriveled up, and deformed, like frightening monsters. She felt intense grief and horror. She told us that she was surprised about these feelings, because she thought she had gotten over their death long ago. Her parents had both died from cancer in Eastern Europe when she was a little girl. Following their death, she had been sent to the United States to be raised by an aunt, and lived here ever since.

Mindfulness had revealed that she had deep emotion about their death. She recognized feelings of anger that arose, since both had contracted cancer from carcinogens they had been exposed to from living in a polluted industrial city in Eastern Europe. Meditation allowed her to recognize that these feelings were still unresolved. And every time she lost a patient at the hospice, she was living the horror, all over again.

Using the sensitivities and objectivity she was gaining from meditation, she began to recognize a distinction between her love for her parents, her sadness from losing them, and her anger about why they died. Even though these feelings felt strong and real, they were just her reactions. She could sense how the painful emotions of anger and sadness that seem so intractable were not her love for her parents, but were her reactions to their death. And through meditation, she was learning that she *could* do something about her reactions.

In a certain sense, these painful emotions were no more than passing fantasies, fleeting moments. And yet, even though they were impermanent, for that moment when they did exist, they were real, solid, and enduring enough to require that she find some personal resolution of them. Jennifer took a hard look at the nature of life itself, with its inevitable death. She had to recognize that her parents had been victims of their country's mistakes, and that she could do nothing to change that now. She learned to accept her grief as a natural response, and in its acceptance, she found the feelings comforting and even helpful.

She discovered ways to celebrate the lives of those who passed, including her parents. She started a garden in her backyard, since her mother had loved gardening, as a way of honoring her mother's memory. We discussed how gardening could be done as a Zen art. She experienced her time spent gardening mindfully. She particularly enjoyed being able to nurture growth. She observed the natural opening and closing of flowers, the living and dying of plants as they passed through the seasons of their lifespan, perennials with their inevitable return, and annuals with their birth-death cycle. She found comfort in nature's order of eternal recurrence. Increasingly, the garden became a hub for her heart, not just the kitchen. As she stood in the midst of the flowers and plants, she experienced empty moments of joy and peace. As Jennifer's tensions eased, the pounds began to shed. She found that now she felt differently about life and death. And with that change, she fully embraced and enjoyed her life.

Insights are sometimes outside the range of conscious thought. Reaching for them rationally, we miss them. Meditation stimulates irrational, unconscious processes. You initiate the process by your meditation practice. As it begins to unfold, the formless takes form. You can bring a profound transformation on a deep existential level. Once felt, change happens. Then, all our useful therapeutic methods become easier to implement. Attitudes shift in healthier directions, behaviors become more optimal, and people find deeper happiness than they have ever known.

THE PSYCHOLOGY OF MEDITATION

What are the psychological factors involved in meditation? Researchers have investigated the effects of meditation on attention and emotions, two key psychological factors so crucial for psychotherapy. You may want to refer back to the sections that follow after you have read Part II, where you can learn more about meditation and try doing it. We encourage you to keep referring back to your own experience, because this is where verification of many of these psychological principles is found.

Meditation as Special Qualities of Attention

Researchers (K. W. Brown & Gordon, 2009) have pointed out that meditation can be characterized as the turning of sustained attention toward an object. The quality of this attention is sometimes referred to as *bare attention*, meaning that it is not intertwined with abstract thoughts about the past or future or engaged in judgments and assessments about the quality of the attention. Researchers have also called this kind of attention *meta-attention* (Kornfeld, 1993) because, in a sense, it is attention to attention. In fact, mindfulness instructions direct practitioners to keep bringing awareness back to the present moment, and reflect on attention while attending, thus giving it a *meta* quality.

The focal point for attention can be narrow, as when attention is directed to breathing or to body sensations. It can also be broad, sometimes referred to as *open monitoring,* as in mindfulness, where attention is maintained on whatever is occurring in the present moment. Mindful attention is free to move to whatever emerges, and this skill, allowing attention to move flexibly, is a hallmark of mental health. When people are suffering from problems, attention often becomes stuck in redundant patterns of thought and emotion, out of step with what is actually happening, and thus unable to respond to the potential for something new that might be needed to solve the problem.

In both of these forms, attention is directed to *something.* But Zen includes another kind of meditation, also found in Daoism and Transcendental Meditation, a kind of attention that is directed to nothing—the empty moment without thought. This meditation is practiced by first noticing any objects that appear in the stream of consciousness, and then, letting them go. Usually, we are accustomed to thinking about something. Our consciousness is filled with thoughts, feelings, and sensations, along with our secondary interpretations and concepts about them. But the ability to focus on nothing can also be developed with time and practice if practiced correctly. We have had many clients tell us how surprised and pleased they were that they were able to learn these skills and sustain quiet moments without thought.

All three forms of meditation have healing benefits, as this chapter shows. Chapter 2 on neuroscience describes how these different ways of directing attention correlate with different patterns of brain activation. Each of these methods gives you a unique ability to work with your own consciousness, an invaluable skill for bringing therapeutic change.

Psychology of Emotions and How Meditation Affects Them

One of our mentors, psychotherapy researcher Jerome D. Frank (1909–2005), said that psychotherapy takes place in the realm of meanings. We would add that psychotherapy also takes place in the realm of emotions and the meanings we give to them. In general, emotions can be thought to involve an elaborate signaling system, tuned both to the external world and to our internal experience. The evolutionary theory of emotions is that they are important for our survival. We have automatic reactions to situations that are threatening to us, which bring automatic responses of fear, sadness, anger, or disgust that move us to action for self-preservation (Williams, 2010). This evolutionary theory gives us a helpful partial picture, but it does not explain the human capacity for symbolic processing that allows us to assess the level of threat and reinterpret the situation more realistically.

Labeling Emotions

Researchers have proposed that affect labeling could be a key component in many mental disorders, and that therapy helps by intervening with this process. One study showed that mindfulness meditation affected the key areas of the brain that are involved with affect labeling, concluding that this may be how meditation, which radically alters the process of labeling, is helpful (Creswell, Way, Eisenberger, & Lieberman, 2007).

Interpreting and Accepting Emotions

For decades, psychology has been exploring the interaction between the interpretive process and the instinctual response, and much of modern cognitive therapies are based upon the important effects of attuning our instinctual emotions realistically to the world.

In recent years, a three-step process for dealing with emotions in psychotherapy has added mindfulness as a meaningful step. When people first feel an emotion, they experience arousal accompanied with certain body sensations. Therapy helps them to first become aware of these sensations and body experiences. Next, they identify, label, and appraise their emotions. Cognitive therapies help people take an objective look at what they are feeling and how they are conceptualizing and appraising their emotions. Finally, mindfulness offers a way to accept emotions without judgment. Awareness, along with acceptance of what is experienced just as it is, has been developed in acceptance and commitment therapy (ACT), (Hayes et al., 1999, 2004; Hayes & Feldman, 2004) and dialectical behavior therapy (DBT) (Linehan & Dimeff, 2001) to add an important mindfulness dimension that makes cognitive-behavioral treatments more effective and lasting. Making the practice of meditation an integral part of the therapeutic process builds skills needed to regulate emotions well.

Regulating Emotions

Emotional problems develop when people ignore or misinterpret the arousal, or if they do not find a way to come to terms with the emotions and their interpretations. Modern theories have conceived of such problems as involving the regulation of emotions. The process is often referred to as affect regulation to represent a brain-mind-body system of interaction of arousal and its successful management (see Chapter 7).

People regulate their emotions differently. For example, some people dissociate from their emotions by narrowing their perceptual field. Others have trouble noticing or even knowing what they feel. And of course, many people will avoid their feelings, especially when they are uncomfortable (Braboszcz, Habnusseau, & Delorme, 2010). The intensity varies as well, which means that some people experience emotions strongly and others only weakly. People take on certain attitudes and fears about their emotions, such as being afraid the emotion will never end, fearing that they will lose control, dreading the judgment of others, and worrying that the body sensations they feel could be a disease. These emotional styles often become expressed in the different psychological disorders we treat in therapy. In fact, most mental disorders have a component of these styles and attitudes toward emotions.

Meditation can help people develop a realistic and aware emotional adjustment that paves the way for healthy functioning. The methods offer helpful ways to intervene with all of these emotion disorder styles even when strong emotions emerge. The methods are not interpretive—in fact, forming judgments is something the meditator learns to set aside. Rather, experiencing is to be noticed, with awareness but without assessment. Secondary thoughts about the experience are also to be suspended. So, the usual conceptualizing that we typically do is put on hold. What people find is that through this acutely aware but nonjudgmental and nonconceptual experiencing, strong emotions are quieted, troubling feelings are frequently soothed, and balance is found.

The empty focus form of meditation helps people let go of stress and suffering, and in this way, emotional reactions ease of themselves. Much of the suffering that we have is self-induced, or at least, certainly adding intensity to an already difficult situation. Learning to be in the empty, open moment, new options and solutions emerge, leading to therapeutic change.

Researchers have found that meditation does indeed help people to better regulate their emotions (Lutz, Brefczynski-Lewis, Johnstone, & Davidson, 2008). We discuss these and other findings in Chapter 2, with their interesting effects on the brain.

EFFICACY RESEARCH

Zen meditation brings enhancement of attention, better affect regulation, increased empathy, and compassion, along with overall feelings of calm. These skills are essential for being an effective therapist. A great deal of research has been done and is ongoing to test whether meditation added to treatment gives better outcomes. We offer a brief overview of some of these studies.

General Effectiveness

Countless studies have shown that Zen offers effective treatment methods for a variety of psychological and psychiatric problems. For example, research has shown that mindfulness improves immune response and reaction to stress, while also giving a general feeling of well-being (Davidson et al., 2003). Another researcher investigated mindful learning (Langer, 1989) and found that mindful awareness improves learning ability. The capacity to learn is helpful in psychotherapy, during which we often encourage our clients to be open to learning something new.

Enhancing Therapeutic Effectiveness

Researchers have investigated whether therapists who practice Zen meditation may be more effective with their clients. In one study, psychotherapists in training were assigned to one of two groups: those who practiced mindfulness meditation, and those who did not. The meditating therapists in training received better evaluations for their work, and their clients had more symptom reduction. The study provides evidence that teaching meditation to therapists can lead to measurable improvement in their work (Grepmair, Mitterlehner, Loew, Bachler, Rother, & Nickel, 2007). These findings make sense, since good psychotherapists need to be more open to their clients. It helps when we can be nonjudgmental of bad habits and negative emotions. Like the lotus flower that blooms in a muddy pond, we find the early buds for potential change lying hidden in murky waters of psychological disturbance. Therapists are always trying to be aware, to notice even the smallest details that may help them better understand their clients. Zen meditation teaches these skills, and the skills can be learned and do improve with practice (see Chapter 2 for research).

Depression and Bipolar Disorder

Researchers have done extensive research on how negative thinking affects mood. But another line of research turns that around and looks at how mood affects thinking. Teasdale (1983, 1988) induced a sad mood in subjects by playing sad music or reading a sad story. Those who had a history of depression were more deeply influenced than those without any depression in their background. Other researchers found that those suffering from major depression had reduced capacity to sustain positive emotions. This was reflected in reduced activation of the fronto-striatal brain pathways (Heller et al., 2009). This pathway connects the frontal lobe to the basal ganglia (motor areas) and receives inputs from neurotransmitters such as dopamine and serotonin, both involved in regulating moods.

Meditation has been shown to help the overreactivity to negative emotions found with depression and bipolar disorder. One theory about how meditation does so is based on the ability to become detached. Kabat-Zinn, one of the early researcher-clinicians to create therapeutic mindfulness programs, believes that meditation helps people put some distance between themselves and their sad thoughts and feelings (Kabat-Zinn, 2003). A recent study uncovered a possible mechanism of this process: the reduction of self-focus. Depressed individuals have an increase in self-focus. They tend to ruminate about themselves and their problems, and yet research shows that they are less capable of reappraising negative emotions than controls (Johnstone, van Reekum, Urry, Kalin, & Davidson, 2007; Ressler & Mayberg, 2007). This is reflected in more left-hemisphere activation in the language areas and lowered activation in somatosensory areas such as the parietal lobe, insula, and anterior cingulate, involved in the appraisal of emotion.

Mindfulness subjects expressed feeling sadness, but their brains responded differently. Attending to the present moment in mindfulness meditation showed distinct neural activity that changed how people responded to sad stimuli. Meditators had less activation of the left-hemisphere reappraisal areas of self-focus and a shift toward brain areas that correlate with sensory integration. Thus, the researchers concluded that meditators' brains were less involved in self-focus and more engaged in a somatosensory experience (Farb et al., 2010). Meditation may offer depressed individuals an alternative to simply trying to reinterpret their situations in a more realistic or positive way. They can use other parts of their brain instead that involve sensory awareness to shift the neural balance and start feeling better. Meditation brings feelings of well-being, which may help with recovery.

When combined with cognitive behavior therapy (CBT), meditation not only reduced depression, but it also prevented relapse. Researchers found that when mindfulness meditation was combined with cognitive therapy, patients who had suffered from three or more episodes of major depression reduced the risk of relapse from 66% to 37% (J. D. Teasdale et al., 2000). This study was replicated again several years later (Ma & Teasdale, 2004) and performed by other research groups (Michalak, Heidenreich, Meibert, & Schulte, 2008; J. D. Teasdale et al., 2000).

Clearly the research has shown that meditation is helpful for depression, stress, and anxiety. Bipolar disorder also includes periods of depression, stress, and anxiety, and so meditation in conjunction with CBT is becoming increasingly used for bipolar disorder. According to Harvard Medical International findings, mindfulness improves a number of factors involved in bipolar disorder, including decreasing medical symptoms of pain and high blood pressure, reducing anxiety and stress, improving sleep, enhancing the immune system's functioning, fostering self-awareness, increasing the ability to tolerate disturbing thoughts, and fostering feelings of well-being (Harvard Medical International, 2004).

Impulse Control and Substance Abuse

Substance abuse disorders (SUD) are on the increase. We are always looking for treatments that clients can take with them and use when the craving strikes. Meditation offers helpful tools that can be used on the spot when most needed. The use of all the forms of meditation used in Zen, focus, mindfulness, and emptiness meditation, have been studied and found to help people overcome substance abuse.

Stress is one of the by-products of substance abuse, and meditation training has been shown to help people reduce their stress, thereby making it easier to give up the harmful substance and handle withdrawal better. One study compared mindfulness training to empirically validated CBT for helping alcohol and cocaine abusers lower their stress and maintain their sobriety. The study found no differences between the groups, suggesting that meditation can be an effective treatment that helps recovering abusers keep their stress levels low (Brewer et al., 2009).

Mindfulness-based stress reduction programs have been used to help with addiction. One exemplary project (Bowen et al., 2006) taught Vipassana meditation, a form of mindfulness training, to subjects who were in jail. Upon their release, they had a significant reduction in their use of marijuana, crack cocaine, or alcohol as compared with those who had the typical treatments. They also had a decrease in psychiatric symptoms and an increase in an internal locus of control around the substance. They felt increased optimism as well.

Focused meditation has also been shown to help with substance abuse. In an impressively large study of more than 1,800 subjects, early researchers in meditation, Herbert Benson and Robert Wallace, showed that a form of focused meditation, transcendental meditation, was measurably helpful for overcoming substance abuse (Benson & Wallace, 1972).

Cravings are one of the difficult challenges that addicts need to overcome. Another factor involved in addiction is impulsivity. Focused meditation on breathing was shown to bring stronger activity in the prefrontal cortex and particularly in the attention areas of the anterior cingulate cortex and parts of the prefrontal cortex, which are involved in impulse control (Hotzel, 2007). These findings suggest that part of how meditation helps is that it enhances the ability to control impulses even when people are feeling strong cravings.

The different forms of meditation described in this book have been tested for relapse prevention. As therapists know, relapse is a difficult problem, and statistics show that around 40 to 60% of those treated for drug addiction will relapse (McLellan, Lewis, O'Brien, & Kleber, 2000). In fact, many abusers will relapse numerous times before quitting, or may even never quit. Witkiewitz, Marlatt, and Walker (2005) found support for mindfulness meditation as a treatment for preventing relapses for alcohol and substance abuse.

Anxiety, Fears, and PTSD

The effectiveness of treating anxiety with meditation has been known for several decades (Kabat-Zinn et al., 1992). In more recent years, meditation has been tested with many different types of anxiety. As we know, one way to establish efficacy is to compare a new treatment with a proven method. A meditation-based stress management program was compared to an anxiety disorder education program as an adjunct to pharmacotherapy. The meditation group showed significant improvement in scores on all anxiety scales over the education group. These researchers concluded that meditation could be effective in relieving anxiety symptoms in patients with an anxiety disorder (Lee et al., 2007).

Mindfulness practice appears to be a promising alternative technique for social anxiety when individuals are too shy to seek help or as an adjunct to psychotherapy (Arana, 2006). Research on worry, one of the components of anxiety, indicated that detached mindfulness training helped to decrease worry-proneness (Sugiura, 2004).

A 20-week meditation-relaxation treatment program for elderly women suffering from anxiety and depression resulted in a measurable decrease in anxiety symptoms (DeBerry, 1982). Focus on breathing has been applied as a public intervention to alleviate posttraumatic stress disorder (PTSD) in survivors of mass disasters (R. P. Brown & Gerbarg, 2005).

Many studies have been done to determine why meditation is so helpful for anxiety. Anxiety and fear engage a wide range of neural circuits involving the hippocampus, amygdala, and the stress pathway (see the appendix for the details of the stress pathway). Researchers (Goleman & Goleman, 2001) suggest that meditation is effective because it helps to moderate the amygdala's emotional responses. The amygdala responds quickly with an emotion, whereas the prefrontal cortex takes slightly longer, acting as a thoughtful mediator of emotions. Since many studies have linked meditation to increased activity in the prefrontal cortex (see Chapter 2), skilled meditators may be able to intervene with the amygdala's split-second emotional response by providing a more constructive, realistic response.

Zen meditation teaches thinking without thinking, a paradoxical and yet helpful activity. One researcher found that the regular practice of Zen meditation helps reduce distracting thoughts. The study compared 12 people who had been meditating for 3 years with 12 novice meditators. All subjects were measured by functional magnetic resonance imaging (fMRI) while meditating. The scans showed that the Zen meditators had different brain activity, particularly in what the researcher called a default network that activates when people have bursts of thoughts and mind wandering. The study concluded that regular practice of Zen meditation can reduce distracting thoughts and could be helpful with anxiety disorders, PTSD, and attention deficit/hyperactivity disorder (ADHD) (Pagnoni, Cekic, & Guo, 2008).

One interesting study analyzed the changes in electroencephalogram (EEG) using Zen meditation in association with trait anxiety assessed by Spielberger's State-Trait Anxiety Inventory. Research on meditation has consistently showed the dual effect (described in Chapter 2) of increased attention with increased relaxation. All 22 subjects showed the dual effect of meditation. Their EEG results also indicated the following correlation: Subjects with lower trait anxiety more readily induced meditation with a predominance of internalized attention, while subjects who had higher trait anxiety more readily induced meditation with a predominance of relaxation (Murata et al., 2004).

The effects of meditation on anxiety improve with time. Beginners who meditated for one month or less, short-term meditators who practiced from one month to two years, and long-term meditators who practiced for more than two years were compared. As the length of time meditating increased, attentional absorption increased while trait anxiety decreased (Davidson, Goleman, & Schwartz, 1976). Thus, the longer one engages in the practice, the larger the effect on anxiety.

But even brief meditation sometimes has an effect. One large study with 387 undergraduate students found that a single 20-minute session did result in reduced state anxiety after exposure to a transitory stressor (Rausch, Gramling, & Auerbach, 2006). Another study used a mindfulness-based stress reduction program over eight weeks. They found reduction in anxiety and related symptoms (Tory, 2004). So, even introducing a short course of meditation into your treatment of anxiety can be helpful.

Relationships

Recent research has revealed that meditation increases empathy and benevolence, and therefore, meditation should be helpful for relationship therapy when these qualities are so vital for success. As we would expect, researchers have found that feelings of empathy are associated with meaningful relationships (Kerem, Fishman, & Josselson, 2001). But the link works both ways:

When we feel compassion for others, we also feel better emotionally. The neurobiological studies of attachment show that having loving relationships is fundamental for our emotional health (Johnson, 2008). In a study using fMRI, researchers measured how experienced and novice meditators would respond to sounds that typically provoke an empathic response, such as the sounds of a laughing baby and a woman calling out in distress. The subjects also heard neutral sounds of background noise at a restaurant. Both groups showed greater brain activation during meditation than when not meditating in the areas that have been linked to empathy in the insula and cingulate cortices of the limbic region. During meditation, the activation in the insula was higher in experts when negative sounds were presented than when positive sounds were presented. These subjects also reported a deepening of their meditation when they heard the negative sounds. This study also made comparisons between meditation and states of rest between experts and novices. Their findings suggest that expert meditators were more capable of detecting emotional sounds than novices and that activation is higher while meditating than not (Lutz et al., 2008).

A study of a mindfulness-based meditation technique for couples therapy enhancement found that meditation favorably affected couples' satisfaction in their relationship, autonomy, relatedness, closeness, acceptance of each other, and relationship distress. Following treatment, the couples felt more optimism, spirituality, relaxation, and less psychological distress. They maintained the benefits after a 3-month follow-up (J. W. Carson, Carson, Gil, & Baucom, 2004). Another researcher performed a focus meditation for couples to "help heal and bring a greater depth, dimension and growth to a committed relationship." He found that both partners felt a closer and deeper bond following treatment (Shannahoff-Khalsa, 2006, p. 294).

CONCLUSION

As we learn more about the psychology and efficacy of meditation through scientific investigation, we can refine our use of meditation for treatments. Research is helping to clarify that meditation works with attention, sensations, and affect to bring about targeted changes in thinking, emotions, and behavior, as well as facilitating a more generalized sense of well-being. New evidence is emerging every year, and so we can look forward to deepening our understandings over time.

2

Neuroscience Findings: How Meditation Can Change the Brain

Anatomy is destiny, but it does not seal our fate
So let us meet contingency hopefully
As we step through destiny's gate
(C. Alexander Simpkins &
Annellen M. Simpkins)

Freud (1856–1939) proclaimed long ago that anatomy determines our destiny (Gay, 1989). And although the physiological structures of the body do determine much of who we are, neuroscience is finding that there is more malleability in the structure and functions of the nervous system than was previously thought. The brain is dynamic, with changes going on all the time. Whether we are awake or asleep, a balance of activation and deactivation is occurring in our brain. The location and patterns of this activity change as we move through the day, depending on what we are doing, thinking, and feeling, and as we sleep through the night, with different levels of brain activity. Zen meditation allows us to observe and deeply experience each moment in this ever-changing flow of activity. In meditation, we can attune to our anatomy to influence our destiny for the better.

Neuroscience has developed different ways to measure this activity. Electroencephalograms (EEG) and magnetoencephalograms (MEG) record patterns of electrical activity and can tell us how different electrical patterns correlate with the types of consciousness as they occur in time. Neuroimaging technologies such as functional magnetic resonance imaging (fMRI), positron emission tomography (PET), single-photon emission computed tomography (SPECT), and computed tomography (CT) measure other alterations in the brain, such as blood flow, glucose, oxygen metabolism, or receptor density of neurotransmitters in certain brain regions. These changes are correlated with different mental activities. Although these measurements are not as accurate in time as the EEG, they are far more precise in spatial location in the brain, telling us where the activity is occurring. By combining time-sensitive with location-sensitive measurements, we can begin to piece together typical brain patterns that correspond to experiencing. Advanced statistical techniques help to translate these patterns into pictures of the brain that we can view and analyze.

Clinicians are always looking for ways to understand how people think, feel, and behave so as to better help their clients. Neuroscience has added new information in these pictures of typical brain activity that correlates with different kinds of human activity. We use the word *correlate* deliberately. Keep in mind as you read the results from research that the findings are correlations, not causes. We still do not know exactly how mental experiences relate to brain activity. The precise nature of the mind-brain relationship is still being explored and has spawned many fascinating theories. In one of our recent books, the *Dao of Neuroscience,* we explored the different mind-brain theories and proposed a synthesis: Mind and brain form an interconnected unity, intimately interrelated together into a system (Simpkins & Simpkins, 2010a). The system can be activated by brain activity that affects experience or from experience to alter brain activity. Practitioners who understand these interactions and the patterns that typically correlate with certain experiences can use interventions that foster healthy brain patterns and thereby facilitate better functioning.

MEDITATION'S EFFECTS ON THE BRAIN

Meditation traditions have claimed that its practice relieves suffering and bring feelings of well-being. Many studies have revealed that meditation practice correlates with healthy brain patterns. Findings show that meditation correlates with brain patterns found during calm, relaxation, healthy affect regulation, focused attention, and alertness—all helpful qualities for psychotherapy.

Neuroscientists have been investigating the brain activity that occurs during Zen meditation and mindfulness practices, and have found distinctive and measurable effects. They have discovered specific and general ways that the regular practice of these methods changes the brain and mind, with real and lasting alterations in brain structures and mental functions. These changes can be extremely helpful for therapy, providing a more favorable brain-mind balance that is known to reduce stress and help in overcoming psychological problems. This new information encourages us to use treatments such as meditation to foster brain patterns that correlate with better functioning or improved problem-solving ability as an additional means to facilitating change in our clients.

EARLY SCIENTIFIC STUDIES

Scientists have been fascinated with Zen meditation for more than 50 years. One of the pioneers in the scientific study of meditation was Tomio Hirai, a psychiatry professor at Tokyo University School of Medicine. He performed some of the earliest careful studies of Zen meditation, using electroencephalography (EEG) (Figure 2.1), electromyography (EMG), and galvanic skin response (GSR) (Hirai, 1974).

Subjects and Findings: Zen Meditation Changes the Brain

Subjects were experienced monks from both Soto and Rinzai, the two main forms of Zen practiced today. The subjects were placed into four groups:

Group	Number and Type of Subject	Years of Zen Experience
I	42 disciples	1 to 5 years
II	31 disciples	6 to 10 years
III	25 disciples	11 to 15 years
IV	48 monks	22 to 55 years
Controls	18 healthy men	no experience

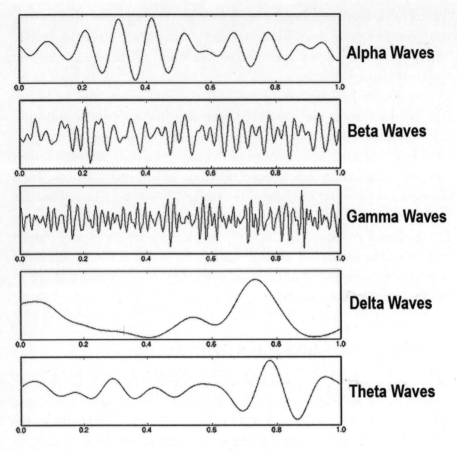

Figure 2.1   EEG Brain Patterns

The results from the seasoned monks in Group IV showed that before meditation began, they had the typical beta brainwave patterns found when people are awake and alert. As they began meditating, their brainwaves changed into well-organized alpha waves in the frontal and central regions of the brain, even though their eyes remained open. Their respiration slowed while their heart rate became faster. After around 9 minutes of meditation, the alpha waves became larger, slower, and more organized. Twenty minutes into meditation, the monks produced rhythmic theta wave patterns.

Overall, during meditation, the greater the alpha and theta waves, the more the respiration rate decreased and the heart rate increased. Interestingly, the effects were most pronounced when the monks felt that they had had a good meditation session (Hirai, 1974). The longer the subject had been involved in meditation, the more pronounced were the effects. Controls had no change in their EEG. Group I, practitioners from one to five years, showed alpha waves even with eyes opened, but they did not produce alpha consistently, nor did they have theta. Group IV, the experienced monks, had consistent alpha with decreasing frequency and eventual rhythmical theta. The researchers concluded: "The degree of EEG changes during Zen meditation parallel the disciple's proficiency in Zen training" (Hirai, 1974, p. 31).

EEG in Response to a Clicking Sound: Each Moment Is New

A clicking sound was presented every 15 seconds during the alpha phase of meditation. The alpha pattern was blocked each time the click occurred, just as it had the first time the click sound was heard. Alpha blocking occurs when sensory stimuli are presented. People typically manifest waking beta waves when awake. As one might expect, at first the controls produced alpha blocking. But after repeated clicks, they stopped responding, a phenomenon known as habituation. This data gives evidence for the idea in Zen that each moment is new, and each thing is experienced just as it is, every time. So, the monks had alpha blocking each time, and habituation did not occur during Zen meditation (Hirai, 1974).

MODERN NEUROSCIENCE RESEARCH

Modern studies have incorporated some of the newer technologies and measurement methods such as measuring sensory evoked potentials (EP), cognitive event-related potentials (ERP), and brain coherence. Also, neuroimaging technologies such as fMRI and PET scans have helped researchers isolate what parts of the brain might be affected by meditation (B. R. Cahn & Polich, 2006). All of these innovations have led to new understandings about the nature of meditation practice and how it influences cognition, emotions, and behavior (Figure 2.2).

Meditation Takes Distinct Forms

Meditation is not just one practice. Many different practices derive from a rich and varied tapestry of traditions found in yoga, including Transcendental Meditation, Daoism, Buddhism, Christianity, and Zen. Even within Zen

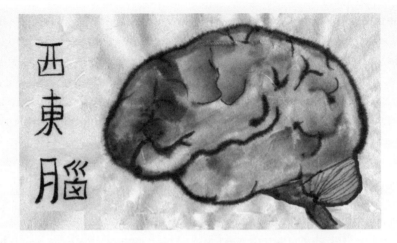

Figure 2.2 East-West Brain

itself, we find varied forms of meditation. Researchers have measured meditators from a number of different meditation traditions and compared the effects using EEG and neuroimaging technologies.

Many studies have shown that distinct groups of brainwave patterns occur, depending upon the meditative practices that are performed. We describe the forms of meditation practiced in Zen, and you will learn how to practice and apply these in later chapters.

Focused Meditation

Meditation that controls the directed concentration, such as focusing on breathing, a common practiced in Zen, engages an active use of the attention (Lutz et al., 2004). Meditators measured with EEG recorded gamma and beta waves in the 20 to 50 Hz range. Gamma is typically found when people are attending to something rather than when they are not paying attention (Jensen, Kaiser, & Lachaux, 2007) and beta waves are correlated with everyday consciousness when we are awake (Zhang, Chen, Bressler, & Ding, 2008). Thus, this form of meditation activates the attention centers of the brain.

Nondirected Meditation

Several types of meditation are nondirected and open, such as mindfulness and Zazen. Researchers have called these forms of meditation open monitoring (R. Cahn, Delome, & Polich, 2010; Lutz, Slagter, Dunne, & Davidson,

2008) and nondirected meditation (Lagopoulos et al., 2009). Here, the object of focus is continually changing and free to move, as in moment-by-moment mindfulness meditation. Attention is open and changing.

One study compared simple relaxation with nondirected meditation. Results showed an increase in theta waves in the frontal and temporal-central areas as compared to the posterior areas. While meditating, subjects also had an increase in alpha waves, whereas when these subjects performed simple relaxation, their brain waves did not show increased theta or alpha (Lagopoulos et al., 2009). Theta waves correlate with relaxed attention that monitors inner experiencing, and with creativity, deeply relaxed tranquility, and restful alertness.

Meditators practicing zazen showed frontal lobe theta and occipital lobe gamma, with the more experienced meditators having the strongest theta (Chiesa, 2009). Vipassana meditators practicing mindfulness also showed frontal midline theta waves (R. Cahn et al., 2010). Frontal midline theta originates in the medial prefrontal cortex and in the anterior cingulated cortex (Vinogradova, 2001). It makes sense to find theta waves correlated with these nondirected forms of meditation whereby people are monitoring their ongoing experience in a relaxed, flowing, and open way.

Automatic Self-Transcending

More recently, Travis and Shear (2010) have distinguished another form of meditation known as automatic self-transcending that is characterized by its absence of both focus and control or effort. Here, meditators transcend their own activity, letting go of the experience and responding automatically. The EEG associated with self-transcending meditation was shown to correlate with higher alpha frontal coherence. Alpha tends to occur when people are involved in relaxed attention (Shaw, 1996), while also remaining alert (Takahashi et al., 2005). Alpha waves accompany passive awareness and experiences of well-being and comfort.

Meditation's Effects on the Nervous System

Many different studies explain the varied effects of meditation. Regular meditators experience relaxation, alertness, improved attention, and better self-regulation. These findings can help therapists understand what meditation methods are best to use to facilitate what the client needs.

Rebalancing of the Autonomic Nervous System

The sympathetic nervous system prepares us for action. Under stress, this system mobilizes a fight-or-flight response with an increased heart rate, restricted flow through blood vessels, and quick breathing so that we can take speedy action. After the stress has passed, or during peaceful times, our parasympathetic nervous system facilitates rest and inaction by slowing down breathing, dilating the blood vessels, and lowering the heart rate. You might expect that meditation would activate the parasympathetic nervous system, and this does occur. These changes during meditation have been understood for quite some time (Gellhorn & Kiely, 1972) and help explain the feelings of calm and relaxation that people experience during its practice. But meditation does more than enhance the parasympathetic nervous system: It also activates the sympathetic nervous system. These findings have been confirmed by fMRI and EEG studies (Hugdahl, 1996). So, meditation tends to bring about a balance in the nervous system. These findings explain why meditation is so helpful for clients who are working on overcoming PTSD or addictions, when the nervous system needs to find its way back to a calmer activation level.

The Dual Effect

Not only were the brains of meditating subjects in a more relaxed state, but their brains were also activated in helpful ways at the same time. A number of recent studies have elaborated on this interesting dual effect. Normally, when people are relaxed, their brain activity is in a relaxed state and when they are attentive, their brain shows a corresponding stimulation. But in meditation, people seem to be able to remain calm while at the same time being highly aware. Maintaining alertness without a corresponding tension can prove helpful for handling stress and challenge well.

A study by Lutz et al. (2004) added more information about the alertness achieved during meditation. They found that EEG was at the high end of beta waves, known as gamma waves, ranging from 26 to 70 hertz. Furthermore, the gamma waves were highly synchronized across the brain. This finding could account for their heightened powers of perception.

Lazar et al. (2005) proposed that meditators sustain a highly alert state that directs attention to behaviorally relevant stimuli while at the same time maintaining deep relaxation. What can be seen is a dual action of both relaxation and alertness. Typically, when people are paying close attention, they are not relaxed. Instead, they tend to be physiologically aroused. But Lazar's meditation study has shown that meditators stay highly aroused and focused while also maintaining a low heart rate and slow breathing, which are qualities of relaxation. These researchers interpreted their results as indicating that meditators have a decoupling of attention from arousal that makes it possible for them to maintain both states simultaneously.

Enhanced Self-Regulation

Researchers have used fMRI to show that meditation brings about a relaxation response (Lazar et al., 2000). These neural effects developed slowly as the subjects meditated, with the second brain scan showing increased effects over the first scan. These results suggest that meditation is dynamic, with effects increasing through the meditation session as the individual gradually produces a calming effect over time.

These benefits can assist in developing better self-regulation over physiological reactions, such as those that occur with strong affect. A recent study measured the physiological and brain changes of subjects before, during, and following 5 days of an integrative mind-body meditation training. They were compared to a control group that practiced relaxation. The meditation group had significantly better physiological reactions than the control group. The neuroimaging data revealed more activity in the anterior cingulate cortex (ACC). The ACC is involved in a network that helps in self-regulation. The increased activity in the ACC of meditating subjects correlated with better self-regulation of the autonomic nervous system on the physiological measures than the relaxation group (Tang et al., 2009). In a more recent study, this research group found that structural changes had occurred from a brief meditation course. They found increased white matter connectivity between the ACC and other structures in the meditating group (Tang et al., 2010). Thus, meditation might literally enhance the neural networks involved in self-regulation, making it more likely that clients will have the brain structures they need to self-regulate more effectively and easily.

Affect Regulation and Stress

Our emotional reactions play a complex and key role in most of our motivated behaviors. People vary in their affective style, how they react emotionally and regulate their reactions under stress (Davidson, 2010). The neural substrates of emotional control and affect regulation involve an interaction between the prefrontal cortex and the amygdala. Most therapists would agree that these processes vary greatly between individuals. In fact, researchers have discovered plasticity in the neural circuitry involved in emotions between the amygdala and the prefrontal cortex (Davidson, Jackson, & Kalin, 2000). Animal studies have also shown that early nurturing experiences from rodent mothers had measurable and lasting effects on the rodent offspring that enhanced their emotional circuitry. These mice had increased receptor density in the amygdala, hippocampus, and prefrontal cortex (Francis & Meaney, 1999).

These animal studies led researchers to ask, could certain kinds of experiences help shape the emotional circuitry of humans? Research has shown short-term changes occur when we are deliberately regulating our emotions (Davidson et al., 2000), and so Davidson researched whether an 8-week meditation course using Kabat-Zinn's mindfulness-based stress reduction program could alter the neural circuitry. They found that subjects who underwent the training had an increase in the left side anterior activation, while the control group, who were on a wait list, showed an opposite change. When they exposed all the subjects to a flu virus, the meditators produced more antibodies than the control group, thus indicating an improved ability to cope with the stress of the illness.

Improved Attention

Meditators showed greater gamma band EEG synchronization across more of the brain, which correlates with improved attention and cognitive functioning. Subjects were long-time practitioners of meditation, performing an open, objectless form of compassion meditation. They produced high-amplitude gamma-band oscillations in phase synchrony during meditation. And the effects grew stronger as they meditated. The researchers suggest that these findings indicate that attentional skills might be able to be trained by the practice of this form of meditation (Lutz et al., 2004). As practitioners, we know that clients often lack the ability to be appropriately attentive, and so meditation may provide a corrective.

Another group of researchers found that meditation practice enhanced three distinct subcomponents of attention: alerting, orienting, and conflict monitoring. These skills involve being ready to put attention on something, to be able to direct attention to that thing, and then to stay focused on it even when there are distractions. One group of subjects had never meditated before, but underwent an 8-week course that included 30 minutes per day of meditation training. A second group was composed of experienced meditators who attended a 1-month, full-time intensive meditation retreat. A control group with no meditation was also included in the study. All subjects were tested before and after. The pretest showed that the experienced meditators had better conflict monitoring skills than both of the other groups who had no previous meditation experience. The results of the posttests indicated that the 8-week mindfulness-trained subjects significantly improved in their orienting, alerting, and conflict monitoring. The retreat group also enhanced their alerting ability. These results indicate that people can learn to improve their attention, and they can do it quickly and easily. As their experience deepens with years of experience, people continue to enhance their attentional skills (Jha, Kropinger, & Baime, 2007).

How we allocate our attention is important, especially when attentional resources are limited. The fact that attention is limited results in diminished capacity when dual tasking (Pashler, 1994). This has led to the need for laws prohibiting the use of cell phones when driving, or the importance for safety of not being distracted when cutting with a sharp knife. Researchers investigated whether mental training from meditation could enlarge the allocation of attention. They used a well-known psychological test known as attentional blink, in which two tasks are presented quickly in sequence, T1 and T2. Before training, subjects tended to allocate most of their attention to T1 and neglect T2. Following 3 months of training in meditation, subjects were better able to distribute their attention between both tasks (Slagter et al., 2007).

Brain Areas Involved and What This Means

We have seen in the sections on affect regulation that meditation activates the prefrontal cortex along with the cingulate gyrus. This activation occurs particularly in the right hemisphere (Newberg & Iverson, 2003). These areas are key for attention and alertness.

Other areas that are activated proportionally with the prefrontal cortex are certain subnuclei of the thalamus. The thalamus is the gateway for the flow of sensory information into the cortex. One of the thalamic nuclei that activates is the reticular nucleus, involved in global attention (Portas et al., 1998). When this area becomes activated, it secretes the inhibitory neurotransmitter gamma-amino butyric acid (GABA), which cuts off input to a part of the parietal lobe (the posterior superior parietal lobule) involved in processing higher order sensory information (Elias, Guich, & Wilson, 2000). With more GABA being released, (and thus more inhibition of sensory information sent to the cortex), meditators will literally have less sensory stimuli arriving at the cortex, leading to the experience of empty mind and enhanced focus (Newberg & Iverson, 2003).

For example, the information that the parietal lobe receives from the thalamus generates a 3-D image of the body that helps us locate ourselves in space and distinguish between the self and the world. The decrease of information sent to this area in meditation may be facilitating the meditative experience of oneness. Further research has found that these quieting effects might actually be a reduction in neural noise, thus enhancing the signal-to-noise ratio on certain tasks. Such a reduction in neural noise could make learning easier (Davidson & Lutz, 2007).

Another result from the prefrontal cortex activation involves activation of the hippocampus, important for attention and memory. The hippocampus becomes activated through the nucleus accumbens, a primary part of the reward pathway. This hippocampal activation in turn stimulates the amygdala. The fMRI study by Lazar et al. (2005) confirmed an increase in activity in the amygdala and hippocampus during meditation. The hypothalamus-limbic system interconnections alter the autonomic nervous system by increasing parasympathetic activity associated with relaxation and a reduction in heart rate and breathing rate, all of which take place during meditation. Truly, meditation is rewarding!

Insula and Empathy

The role of the insula was largely neglected in studies of the brain, but it has more recently become a topic of interest in neuroscience for helping us understand emotion regulation, decision making, and even addiction. Sometimes referred to as the insular cortex, this area is located in the cerebral cortex (one in each hemisphere), and is folded in the deep grove called the lateral sulcus located between the temporal and frontal lobes. The insular cortex is important for social feelings of empathy, compassion, fairness, and cooperation. This area also helps to monitor and be aware of current internal states, known as interoception, something which meditation activates. And it has been found to be involved in processing decisions when there is uncertainty (Singer, Critchley, & Preuschoff, 2009). Researchers believe that the insular cortex is involved in understanding emotions and helps us handle uncertain emotional environments (Lamm & Singer, 2010).

Regular practice of meditation has been shown to prevent the usual thinning of cortical areas that usually occurs with aging. Older meditators had thickness in their insular cortex comparable to younger nonmeditators. These findings may help explain how meditation can help people better understand and assess their own and others' emotions. The study also found thickness in key attentional areas of the prefrontal cortex, accounting for the ability to focus attention well in meditation (Lazar et al., 2005).

Using More of the Brain: Coherence

Meditation brings about increased EEG coherence between and within the cerebral hemispheres. EEG coherence is a quantitative index of the degree of long-range spatial ordering of brain waves. That these gamma waves fire rapidly were also found in the study cited earlier (Lutz et al., 2004). Higher gamma wave coherence means that more of the brain is being used and is associated with improved quality of attention. For meditators with 2 years of meditation experience, coherence began to spread before the meditation session. Halfway through the meditation period, coherence spread to high and lower frequencies. High coherence continued into the eyes-opened period after meditation. During meditation, even new meditators' EEG showed an increase in coherence (Badawi, Wallace, Orme-Johnson, & Rouzere, 1984). This activation could help people improve their mental development in general. Oneness takes place in the brain itself.

CONCLUSION

Neuroscience has provided evidence for some of the ancient claims about meditation. Clearly, meditation does bring about measurable changes in the brain and nervous system, and these changes can be helpful for clients. Thus, along with the positive experiences that people get from regular meditation, you can be confident that these real effects will facilitate your therapeutic interventions. As the research continues to blossom, we encourage you to explore the findings of new studies as they are emerging, even as we are writing this book. It is an exciting time to be practicing psychotherapy, with so many of our intuitions about human potential now being verified by scientific research!

II

What Is Zen?

Be a lamp for yourself.

—*(Paraphrased from the Buddha)*

Zen comes from a beautiful tradition, woven in a tapestry of rich and varied meditative practices. As you come to understand the context of these practices, you begin to partake in the traditions as you experience meditation yourself. Through the process, you gain a present-moment framework to view psychological problems and their treatment. Based in meditation's unique foundations, the traditions open opportunities to perceive intractable problems in a fresh light, illuminating the darkest recesses with hope in human potential. This section provides the development of the meditation tradition in Chapter 3, key themes in Chapter 4, and fundamental practices that can help you and your clients in Chapter 5.

3

Zen Traditions

The translation of the Sanskrit word buddha *is "awake and extraordinarily aware." Whenever you look with your eyes, speak from your mouth, reach with your arms, or take a step with your legs, you are awareness itself. And this awareness is your mind, and your mind is Buddha. And Buddha is the path, and this path is Zen.*

—(Paraphrased from Bodhidharma's Bloodstream Sermon)

The history of Zen chronicles the story of an inner experience. It has been given many names: enlightenment, satori, samadhi, and kensho. This experience involves an awakening to the idea that people can find happiness, peace, and harmony, even if they are suffering. This realization brings heart-felt and life-transforming change. Awareness is the key, and with it comes wisdom and serenity. Psychotherapy is devoted to bringing about change in clients by teaching them ways to be more self-aware. By understanding and incorporating these ancient methods of awareness into your practice, you will find new ways to help clients transform themselves. And in practicing these methods yourself, you may find your own enlightenment!

The Zen experience was communicated from one person to another, down through the ages. Influential Zen masters communicated the experience directly to their students through a process known as direct transmission. Zen's long history traces these transmissions and the teachings that were given as a vivid way to communicate the Zen experience, as it traveled through the ages for 2,500 years from the Buddha to you (Simpkins & Simpkins, 1998).

The direct transmission of Zen shares a core commonality with psychotherapy. We can think of therapy as a form of direct transmission, from therapist to client, that also overcomes suffering. Through the relationship, clients wake up as their awareness develops and deepens. Research indicates that the therapeutic relationship is one of the central vehicles for healing (Frank & Frank, 1991), and it is within that relationship that the transmission transpires. Much like the transmission of enlightenment in Zen, therapeutic transmission truly brings change when clients experience it personally and deeply. Famed Gestalt therapist Fritz Perls described therapy as bringing a mini-satori to the client (Perls, 1969). Thus, when therapy works best, clients awaken to their deeper nature. From the therapist's direct transmission, clients can be enlightened.

Buddha often said that his teachings were like a boat to take people across the sea of life and death. And once they arrived on the other shore, they could leave the boat to continue their travels on land, living an enlightened life. In a similar sense, psychotherapy provides a boat for weathering the storms. As the weather clears, therapy in the relationship with a therapist is completed, and then clients can continue the journey on their own. This sense of undergoing a transformation and then literally being that transformed, aware person is a key element in Zen and psychotherapy.

Zen evolved, moving from one country to another, through unique, individual personalities and cultural contexts, and in different time frames. During its long and fascinating travels, transformation of awareness always took place. Legends have recounted it, and practitioners through the ages have attested to deeply sharing in it. Now, modern neuroscience has shown and measured meditation's effects on the brain. As with psychotherapy, the essential quality, waking up, can be identified. Narratives of these exchanges have been recorded and passed along. It is our hope that by partaking in the narrative history of Zen presented in this chapter, you, too, will walk with the many who came before, awakening to your own awareness, transforming you and your clients.

ROOTS IN YOGA

The special transmission of Zen began in India with one man, the Buddha, but its roots can be traced back even earlier. The origins of Buddhism in India are found in the Indian practice of Yoga. India has always been a spiritually minded country, steeped in higher consciousness. At a time when many civilizations were only just discovering language and tools, India had an advanced civilization with complex systems of spiritual practice.

Yoga is a powerful method of personal discipline involving ways to regulate the mind and body. The eight limbs of yoga from Patanjali in the second century provided one of the earliest holistic approaches to health. Practitioners attained a peaceful state and achieved powers of knowledge and self-control. It teaches focusing of attention in such a way that perception can be honed and sharpened to a single point. Practitioners experience new insight that brings a feeling of intimate union with the universe. The word *Yoga* means *union*, and the practice has that effect, uniting the self with something greater. The enlightenment experience, known in Yoga as *samadhi*, brings a

Figure 3.1   Heart Chakra (wood on wood: tiger maple, walnut, mahogany, and makore)

Source: Created by C. A. Simpkins and A. M. Simpkins, 2010

feeling of peace and happiness, an understanding grounded in a larger per-spective: higher consciousness.

The influence of Yoga on Zen can be seen in its emphasis on medita-tion. Yoga is a generic name for the numerous forms of *dhyana* or meditation that were practiced throughout India for thousands of years. There are many paths of Yoga, such as Hatha Yoga, using postures; Bhakti Yoga, a devotional yoga of love and spirituality; Karma Yoga for work; Mantra Yoga with sound; and Kundalini Yoga, which activates chakra centers of our embodied being to move prana energy and consciousness for transformation (Figure 3.1). (For a more detailed description of Yoga and its use for psychotherapy, see Simpkins & Simpkins, 2010b.) Meditation as the pathway to enlightenment is the common thread that connects them all. Buddha was a practitioner of Yoga and incorporated yogic meditation methods into Buddhism.

CHINESE DAOIST ROOTS

As the seeds of Zen were planted in China, they were nourished by the indigenous beliefs that were already present in the minds and hearts of the people. The wellspring of Chinese thought was the belief in a single cosmic universe, with no beginning or end. Activity, expressed as yang, and inactivity, expressed as yin, were a primitive duality within the universe. The interactions between activity and inactivity formed everything we find in

Figure 3.2 Yin-Yang (wood on wood: mahogany, East Indian rosewood, and satinwood)

Source: Created by C. A. Simpkins and A. M. Simpkins, 2006

our world, represented as the famous yin-yang symbol (Figure 3.2). A vital energy known as *chi* is generated through the activity and inactivity of yin and yang. This vital force can be used in many facets of life, for example medicine, martial arts, and painting.

Chi guides us toward a deeper, universal spiritual principle of which we are all part, but which paradoxically lies beyond us: the Dao. Dao is the essence of things, the source, and the core. When we guide our actions by the Dao, matters resolve effortlessly. A balance can be found that includes both yin and yang, unified in the wholeness that is the Dao. In this union, we find harmony and peace (Simpkins & Simpkins, 1999a).

ZEN BEGINNINGS IN BUDDHISM

I teach only suffering and the transformation of suffering.
(The Buddha, in Thich Nhat Hanh, 1998, p. 9)

Most scholars agree that Zen was born from a spiritual interaction between the Indian and Chinese people. In a sense, one could say that Buddhism, with its roots in Yoga, was the father, Daoism was the mother, and Zen was the beautiful child. The interweaving of these two great traditions helped to create Zen.

The history of Zen is traced back to the enlightenment of one man, Siddhartha Gautama (563–483 B.C.), known to the world as the Buddha (Figure 3.3). Siddhartha was born to the Sakya clan of a small republic in northern India. During this time, India was divided into many small independent kingdoms, each ruled by clans. Siddhartha's father was the wealthy raja of the Sakya clan area. Young Siddhartha led the active and happy life of a child from privilege. He had a gentle-hearted nature, and so his father tried to protect him from anything unpleasant. He was given the best tutors, who taught him the Hindu classics. He rode his own horse, practiced martial arts, and played the popular sports of the day. When Siddhartha came of age, a marriage was arranged to the most beautiful girl in the kingdom. Siddhartha lived happily with his wife, never leaving the confines of his comfortable palace grounds.

One day he ventured outside the palace gates with his servant, Channa. First, he encountered an emaciated man, wracked with pain, calling out, "Alms for the poor!" Siddhartha stopped the chariot and asked Channa, "What is wrong with this man? Why does he suffer so?"

Figure 3.3   Buddha

Channa answered, "This man is ill, my prince. Many suffer from illness. This is the way of life!"

Siddhartha, who had only experienced good health, felt deeply troubled. They continued along and came to an old man, bent over, shaking, and leaning on a twisted cane. "Now what is wrong with this man? Why does he suffer so?" asked Siddhartha again.

"This man is old, my prince. We all grow old and die eventually. That is the way of life!"

Siddhartha returned to his palace, but he could not stop thinking about the suffering he had encountered. Now he could see that the beauty and joy of his privileged life was only transitory. Everyone grows old, often become sick, and die. Siddhartha wrestled with the problem of suffering. Despite his love for his wife and their baby boy, he resolved to leave the palace and seek answers to the problem of suffering.

At the age of 29, Siddhartha left the palace to join a group of ascetics, people who denounced worldly pleasures to seek higher truth through austere meditation practices. The ascetics viewed the human body as the root of suffering. They believed that by taming the body through absolute denial of physical pleasures, the soul would be free of suffering. Siddhartha thought these practices might hold answers, and so he experimented with many kinds of meditation. He restrained his body by reducing his food to one grain of rice per day. He suppressed his breathing to the point of convulsive pains. Day after day, he sat motionless in meditation. He endured heat, rain, wind, hunger, and fatigue without wavering in his self-denial. Seven years passed and yet, instead of finding truth, his mental powers were dimming and his life force was fading. If he continued in this direction, he would die without answers!

That night, Siddhartha decided to try something else. He took fresh milk and rice from a kindly girl. He sat down under a bodhi tree, a type of fig tree that has come to mean wisdom tree. With renewed strength and hope, he resolved to keep meditating until he found the answer to suffering. As the sun rose over the horizon, Siddhartha was illuminated by a wordless realization, an intuitive understanding of life and death that dissolved suffering. He arose radiant and strong, now fully enlightened. From then on, Siddhartha Gautama became known as the Buddha, the Awakened One.

For the next 45 years, Buddha spread his message of a middle way, moderation between abstinence and indulgence, and a method to tame the mind. Using meditation, people could learn to conquer their problems and find a true and lasting end to suffering. He gathered followers throughout India, and Buddhism took hold (Simpkins & Simpkins, 2000).

THE EVOLUTION OF ZEN: FROM FIRST TRANSMISSION TO MODERN DAY

The spirit of Zen began as a direct, wordless transmission from Buddha to one of his closest disciples, Mahakasyapa. The incident occurred one day when Buddha was teaching 1,200 students at Vulture Peak in India. Everyone sat quietly and listened intently, trying to grasp for deeper meaning in his words. But Buddha was not just trying to communicate meanings—he had a deeper experience in mind. He ended his lesson by quietly holding up a flower as he looked out into the audience. Only Mahakasyapa smiled. This silent exchange between teacher and student was the first direct transmission of enlightenment. This transmission expressed the essence of Zen.

The First Patriarch of Zen: Bodhidharma (440–528)

Buddhism was passed along, teacher to student, from Mahakasyapa and on through 27 direct transmissions in India to Prajnatara. Prajnatara was a great

Figure 3.4 Bodhidharma

Buddhist master who is best known for being the teacher of Bodhidharma, the first patriarch of Zen. Historians debate the authenticity of dates and details (Ch'en, 1973), but the narrative serves to communicate the spirit of this movement, and so we can use it as a learning tool.

Bodhidharma came from a Brahmin family in southern India (Figure 3.4). He was converted to Buddhism at a young age and spent many years studying with the Buddhist master Prajnatara, who gave him his religious name, Bodhidharma, "The Law of Enlightenment." Bodhidharma distinguished himself as a serious and talented student. He had a strong personality and is often pictured with dark, penetrating eyes that seemed to see directly into the soul.

According to legend, Prajnatara begged his student to bring meditation to China, and Bodhidharma promised to do so. After his teacher's death, Bodhidharma set out on the long journey from India to China. The classic story is that he walked alone for 3 years. As a Buddhist monk, Bodhidharma did not believe in harming any living creature, and so he carried no weapons. He observed how animals hunted and fought, and incorporated these movements into his own form of unarmed self-defense against wild animals and bandits he met along the way. He would later teach these techniques to the Chinese monks. Many styles of martial arts consider Bodhidharma their

legendary founder. Thus, in their origins, Zen and martial arts were intertwined. With Bodhidharma's arrival in China, Zen Buddhism, or Chan
Buddhism, as it was known in China, officially began.

During that time, Buddhists were contending over esoteric distinctions
and abstract philosophical issues. Bodhidharma offered an approach that was
grounded in the meditative experience. His methods pointed Buddhism back
to its original roots: the direct transmission of awakening. It was a transmission outside the scriptures, not based in words, concepts, or abstractions. It
pointed directly to the mind itself. And when people received this transmission, Bodhidharma claimed that they would achieve enlightenment.

Bodhidharma traveled around China, teaching his pure form of meditation. As his reputation grew, he was given an audience with Emperor Wu
(502–557), a devout and generous Buddhist. The dialogue is famous. The
emperor asked Bodhidharma, "I have built monasteries all over the country,
distributed scriptures, and been generous to the poor, so have I accumulated
merit?"

Bodhidharma replied, "None!"

Taken aback by this answer, the emperor asked, "Then what is true merit?"

Bodhidharma responded with an understanding that is central to Zen:
"Not external acts, only void." Asked who he was, he said, "I know not."

Annoyed by this answer, Emperor Wu banished Bodhidharma from the
palace. Bodhidharma despaired that anyone could ever receive the teachings
that he had traveled such a long distance to communicate. He made his way
to the Hunan province, the home of the Shaolin Temple. There, he turned
toward the wall of a cave and meditated in silence for 9 long years. Through
these years, Bodhidharma's enlightenment deepened and his reputation grew.

Bodhidharma Guides the Second Patriarch Hui-k'o (484–590)

Hui-k'o was a well-educated scholar. He studied Daoism in his youth and
was well read in Chinese classics and Buddhist literature. But despite all his
knowledge, Hui-k'o felt that something was missing. He heard about Bodhidharma's amazing capacity for intense meditation and decided to seek him out.

Hui-k'o tried to gain audience with Bodhidharma, who continued to
meditate at the cave wall, ignoring him. Day after day, week after week,
Hui-k'o came to him and asked to be taught. But Bodhidharma sat in
meditative stillness without answering him. The weather grew cold, icy snow

and whipping wind beat upon the two solitary figures, one standing, one sitting quietly, day and night. Finally, on a particularly stormy night, Bodhidharma was moved to compassion for this man who had endured so much for so long. For the first time in 9 years, Bodhidharma looked up and asked Hui-k'o, "What do you want?"

Hui'k'o said, "Please teach me, master."

Bodhidharma answered sadly, "No one is worthy."

Hui-k'o felt deep emotion sweep over him. According to legend, Hui-k'o cut off his own arm and handed it to Bodhidharma to prove his absolute sincerity. Without a moment's hesitation, Bodhidharma accepted him as his disciple. Hui-k'o received the bowl and robe from Bodhidharma. This gesture was the traditional symbol of direct transmission and made Hui-k'o the second patriarch of Zen.

Bodhidharma showed his students how to see into their own Buddha-nature directly. *Buddha* means awake, or aware. Bodhidharma guided people to wake up, to penetrate through the many layers of beliefs, concepts, problems, and social concerns that we construct. Only our mind can lead us back to the path of clarity and awareness.

Bodhidharma repeatedly emphasized in his sermons that one's own mind is the Buddha. He noticed how often people look outside themselves for answers: to gods, to holy books, to experts. He warned his students not to waste their time. Just know your mind, he encouraged, and you can be enlightened. Over the centuries, Zen has continued to emphasize meditation as the most direct way to know your own mind.

If someone is determined to reach enlightenment, what is the most essential method he can practice?

The most essential method, which includes all other methods, is beholding the mind.
But how can one method include all others?
The mind is the root from which all things grow. If you can understand the mind, everything else is included.
(Bodhidharma's Breakthrough Sermon, in Pine, 1989, p. 77)

Hui-k'o spent many years deepening his insight with questions to his master. Now that he had experienced enlightenment he wanted to know what method he should use to maintain enlightenment. Bodhidharma's answer was simple: contemplate mind. This one method dictated all practices. Meditation alone was all people needed.

Bodhidharma explained that the mind is the root from which all things grow. If you nourish a root, the plant grows. If you cut the root, the plant dies. He urged Hui-k'o to nourish his mind through meditation.

Hui-k'o stayed with his master until Bodhidharma's death. The religious climate began to change in China during the last quarter of the sixth century. The warmth and welcoming atmosphere that had nurtured Buddhism became cold and filled with enmity. Chinese authorities burned sutras and images of Buddha. Monks and nuns were returned to the lay life. Not only did Hui-k'o suffer from general Buddhist persecution in 574, but he was also faced with severe criticism and intrigues from traditional Buddhist monks who did not like this strange new Zen sect. Hui-k'o fled to the mountains, where he hid for many years. Not until he was quite elderly did he feel safe enough to return to the city, where he lived his last 10 years.

Hui-k'o carried on Bodhidharma's Zen meditation method of wall gazing. His disciples learned through an emphasis on intuitive insight, not sutras and rituals.

Seng-Tsan, the Third Chinese Patriarch

Seng-tsan, the third patriarch, became a student of Hui-k'o. He was known for his friendliness and gentle personality. He lived the monk life, homeless and without possessions, fleeing with Hui-k'o to escape the persecution of Buddhists. After his master's death, Seng-tsan continued wandering all over the country, carefully avoiding the Chinese authorities.

Seng-tsan is credited with having written the first Zen poem, entitled, "The Hsinhsinming, Inscribed on the Believing Mind." The poem shows how Daoism blended with Zen as the new sect began to take root on Chinese soil. The literal translation of the title, *hsin* (faith), *hsin* (mind), *ming* (record) refers to the meaning of Zen, a way to gain faith in the potentials latent in our own mind. The poem leads the listener to rise above the duality of yin and yang, to an understanding in which conflict no longer exists: Buddha mind: empty, peaceful, and complete. By transcending duality, we find clarity and

peace of mind. Here is a passage based on the wisdom in the opening lines
of this poem:

> The Enlightened Way is not difficult,
> Just stop picking this and not that!
> Go beyond right and wrong,
> And everything will become clear.
>   (Paraphrased opening lines of the
>   *Hsinhsinming)*

Tao-Hsin, the Fourth Chinese Patriarch

Seng-tsan first encountered Tao-hsin, who was to become the fourth patriarch, in 592. When they met, Tao-hsin immediately recognized the great
teacher and approached Seng-tsan with a bow. "I ask you to please teach me.
Show me how to be released."

Seng-tsan answered, "Who has bound you?"

Tao-hsin paused a moment and then answered, "No one."

Seng-tsan's reply was, "Then why do you ask me to release you?" Tao-hsin
became enlightened at that moment.

The previous three patriarchs had been largely itinerant, traveling around
to various established Buddhist monasteries or hiding in remote areas to escape persecution. They spent their time lecturing, begging, and meditating.
Their disciples were few, but always intensely devoted.

Tao-hsin made definite changes in the lifestyle of a Zen monk by establishing the first Zen monastery. His dynamic personality drew more than
500 disciples. There was no state support for Zen at this time, and begging could not bring enough sustenance for the large group of monks who
wanted to learn Zen. In response to this new situation, he set up a monastic community in which all the monks shared in household tasks as well as
in farming duties. Working, standing, sitting, lying down, all became integral aspects of the Zen experience. Here began the Zen tradition that maintained the inner spirit of meditation even in the midst of daily activities.
In this way, the monastery was able to survive independent of any outside
assistance.

Tao-hsin expressed the unity of thought with action, a primary characteristic of Zen that is carried through to this day. Like Bodhidharma, Tao-hsin

believed that Buddha is the mind, but he stressed how this awake mind must be maintained at all times, in movement and in rest.

Hung-Jen, the Fifth Chinese Patriarch

Hung-jen (601–674), Tao-hsin's successor, was remembered for his intensity. He spent a lifetime of devotion, beginning at age 6. He worked all day long and then meditated all night until dawn. After he was given the robe and the bowl, he moved to Mount P'ing-jung, now remembered as the Mountain of the Fifth Patriarch. He continued to follow the monastic structure initiated by his teacher, Tao-hsin.

He offered his disciples some helpful techniques for maintaining that quality of mind. This passage is from a set of instructions Hung-jen gave to his followers. It presents a method that can still be useful today:

> Look to where the horizon disappears beyond the sky and behold the figure One. This is a great help. It is good for those beginning to sit in meditation, when they find their mind distracted, to focus their mind on the figure One.
>
> (Doumoulin, 1988, p. 101)

The *figure one* in the Chinese language is a horizontal line, like the horizon. "One" has significance characterizing unity, and in Zen, the *one* is the single Buddha nature in us all.

The Sixth Patriarch: Hui-Neng

One of the most popular and inspiring Zen narratives is about the sixth patriarch. The story was chronicled in *The Sutra of the Sixth Patriarch,* also known as *The Platform Sutra* (Price & Mou-lam, 1990) and expresses the fundamental elements of eighth-century Zen. The sixth patriarch, Hui-neng, led Zen in a new direction, which helped to shape the Zen experience into what it is today. Although historians are not sure of the exact dates of this document, it remains a valuable teaching tool to open you to deeper understandings.

Hui-neng was an illiterate peddler of firewood. One day, when he was selling his firewood in the marketplace, he overheard someone reciting one of the classic Buddhist sutras, the *Diamond Cutter Sutra.* Diamonds are one of the hardest substances to cut, and the mind properly directed can cut to the truth. On hearing the stanza, Hui-neng was suddenly enlightened. He decided to join the Zen temple led by Hung-jen, the fifth patriarch, to learn more. Because he was uneducated, he was given a job as rice pounder in the kitchen. Even though he lacked schooling, Hui-neng showed exceptional intuitive understanding.

As Hung-jen grew old, he began looking for his dharma heir. He asked his students to produce an enlightenment poem. The senior student, Shen-hsui, was expected to be given the robe and the bowl, the symbol of transmission. He wrote a poem that expressed the idea that our mind is a mirror, and if we are diligent with our meditative practice, continually wiping the mind clean, we keep it dust-free and clear.

On hearing this message, the master knew that Shen-hsui had not reached enlightenment. Meditation is not just about trying to wipe away thoughts. Hui-neng realized this too and asked one of the monks to write down his poem, since he was incapable of doing it himself. His poem captured the deeper insight, that there is no mirror to dust, no mind to keep clear, since everything is void. Then, there is no place for dust to gather, no mind to keep free from thoughts. Return to emptiness!

Hung-jen recognized the enlightened wisdom in this stanza and gave Hui-neng his bowl and robe. But because Hui-neng lacked the distinguished background of Shen-hsui, the master feared the other monks would not accept him as their next leader. He instructed Hui-neng to leave the monastery and start his own temple, which he did. Hui-neng became the founding figure of the Southern School of Chan (Zen) lineage in China. Shen-hsui established a Northern school. The two schools disputed, and Hui-neng's understanding became the dominant perspective. His teachings made clear that the void of Zen was not a vacuum, which we know from our Western science cannot exist. Nature abhors a vacuum. The Zen void is different. The void is filled with the universe of things, people—everything in our world. So to understand correctly, we should keep our minds detached without suppressing thinking. He advised: "When you hear me talk about the void, do not at once fall into the idea of vacuity" (Price & Mou-lam, 1990, p. 80). By learning to remain unattached to the pushes and pulls of our judgments and concepts, we can become enlightened. By staying with the void, even in the midst of everything, problems drop away and we can live fully. Hui-neng not only freed meditation from being only for an elite, he also showed how anyone can wake up immediately. He returned Zen to a middle path that does not fill the mind with illusory thinking, but also does not empty it of thinking, either. In that alert, aware void between filling and emptying, we find enlightenment.

The T'ang Dynasty (618–907): Zen Evolves With Creative Masters

Zen became more widely practiced during the T'ang period with many great masters teaching all around China. These masters were individualistic and eccentric. Their innovative methods inspired their students as well as future generations of students who would learn from their stories of their actions. These stories would later become codified as a Zen teaching tool, known as koans. You will learn in later chapters how to work with koans, to help set clients on a personal path of discovery.

Ma-tzu (709–788) shouted loudly and used sudden, eccentric behaviors to teach his students. Taken by surprise, students would be drawn into a momentary gap in their ordinary consciousness that offered potential for enlightenment. Milton Erickson used this device in his famous "confusion technique" that helped people escape their limited perspectives, creating an opportunity for change (Simpkins & Simpkins, 2010c).

One of Ma-tzu's students, named Pai-chang (720–814), expanded the awake, aware attitude into life activities of working, eating, and sleeping. Everything we do, even such mundane activities as eating or working, can be an opportunity to be aware. Huang-po (d. 850), next in the lineage, taught his students to rid themselves of all concepts and beliefs, in order to create an openness that permitted the discovery of the radiant clarity already present in the mind. He became the teacher of one of the most memorable Zen masters, Lin Chi.

Lin Chi (d. 866), whose name translates as *Rinzai* in Japanese, became the leader of the Rinzai sect of Zen, one of the two main Zen schools today. Lin Chi made lasting contributions to Zen, taking it to a new level of clarity and universality. In his lifetime, he never wrote any of his ideas down and reached only a small number of disciples in his remote country monastery. Zen owes a great debt to the main compiler of Lin Chi's many teachings, Li Tsun Hzu (d. 1038), a lay disciple of the Rinzai school. The *Rinzairoku*, written down during the Sung period and based on Lin Chi's teachings, has profoundly affected Zen to this day. Thanks to this collection, the Rinzai school grew vigorously and continues to thrive to this day.

In many ways, Lin Chi's message embodies a psychotherapeutic person-centered spirit. He thought that the meaning of life is in the unconditional worth of human beings—that is, ordinary people. Lin Chi took the Buddhist belief that the Buddha mind is within everyone and went further when he said that nothing is missing. You are the Buddha patriarch just as you are. His words to his monks are just as relevant to us today as they were then:

> Virtuous monks, time is precious. Yet, you try by hurrying hither and thither to learn meditation, to study the way, to accept names, to accept phrases, to seek Buddha, to seek a patriarch. After all, do you have a father and a mother? What more would you seek? Turn your own light inward upon yourself.
>
> (Watson, 1993, p. 86)

Therapy carries a similar message: Anyone can overcome his problems, because deep down, we all have the potential for mental health. We hear echoes of Lin Chi in the encouraging life-stance from the humanistic movement in psychology beginning in the 1960s that claimed, I'm okay and you're okay (Berne, 1996).

Lin Chi taught that we are all ordinary people, all equal, or, as he put it, of no rank; depending on nothing, or, in other words, nondependent. As such, we are inherently wise and capable. Rather than seeking wisdom from an external source, we should recognize that we are well equipped to find wisdom within. Rank cannot be taken away because we do not have it.

Lin Chi also popularized the symbolic use by Zen masters of blows with a stick to bring about enlightenment. When students were struck suddenly, they experienced a momentary jolt out of everyday consciousness. In that split-second gap, they could find enlightenment. Lin Chi was an exceptional teacher who inspired many through his loud yells, sharp blows, but humanistic heart.

During the second half of the T'ang Dynasty, five schools of Zen evolved from dynamic masters, known as the Five Houses. They included the Lin Chi school, which became one of the main styles of Zen in Japan, Rinzai Zen, and the T'sao-tung School, which later developed into the other major style of Zen in Japan, Soto Zen.

Sung Dynasty Period (960–1279): Zen Expands

Zen became a prominent component of Chinese culture during the Sung dynasty, a renaissance period in China. A state system for organizing and teaching Zen, known as Five Mountains, Ten Temples, was created, training large numbers of students. The temples were also centers of learning as well as teaching children. Koans and narrative stories were introduced, giving the students a feeling of direct transmission from the earlier T'ang masters. Japanese and Korean monks journeyed to China to learn Zen firsthand and bring it back to their own countries, founding monasteries in which Zen would experience new creative growth and development.

Korean Zen

Korea received Zen directly from students of Ma-tzu and other Chinese masters. These Korean students returned to their country and founded remote mountain temples, known as the Nine Mountain Schools.

One of Korea's greatest masters was Chinul (1158–1210), a comprehensive thinker who helped to unify Zen with other forms of Buddhism in Korea. He believed in enhancing the sudden enlightenment of Hui-neng's school with gradual cultivation to deepen and integrate enlightenment fully within life. Although enlightenment can be a wonderful experience, working it into everyday living needs constant effort. This insight also rings true in psychotherapy, in which insights during sessions often take time to become integrated into life. This phase is referred to in traditional therapy as "working through." The unifying of sudden awakening with gradual cultivation is still practiced today in many Korean monasteries and has become part of Zen as it traveled around the world.

Japanese Zen

Japan received Zen from the Chinese more than 600 years after Bodhidharma, but they enriched its practice in multiple ways. It is thanks to the ingenuity of the Japanese that Zen has become intimately intertwined with lifestyle and practice.

Eisai (1141–1215) is credited with being the Japanese founder of Zen. Eisai went to China to gain deeper understanding from the Zen masters. He believed that Chinese Zen would help to reform Japanese Buddhism. He brought Rinzai back to his country, but was met with opposition from the conservative Buddhist establishment. He eventually succeeded in establishing the first lasting Zen temple in Japan called Kennin-ji monastery, located in Kyoto. Little did he know what a huge impact Zen would have on Japanese culture (Simpkins & Simpkins, 1999b)!

Dogen, Japan's Inspirational Soto Master

Dogen (1200–1253), a student of Myozen, one of Eisai's disciples, was the first to bring Soto Zen to Japan. Dogen would become one of Japan's greatest Zen teachers. Dogen and Myozen traveled to China to study Zen. Myozen went to the Ching-te-ssu monastery where Eisai had gone, and stayed there. But Dogen could not disembark from the boat for three months because of an immigration problem. At last, when he was able to leave the boat, he followed Myozen to the Ching-te-ssu monastery. But Dogen felt unfulfilled, so he journeyed throughout China in search of broader training. Finally, when he was about to leave, Dogen heard that a great Soto teacher named Ju-ching (1163–1228) had just become the new abbot at Ching-te-ssu. So, Dogen returned and became Ju-ching's student. He quickly attained enlightenment. Then he brought his style of Zen back to Japan with Ju-ching's approval.

From Ju-ching's teachings and the wise insights of a tenzo monk (monastery cook) he met on the boat, Dogen learned that the quality of practice is most important. This became a primary principle of Soto Zen: Practice is not separate from enlightenment; practice *is* enlightenment. Everything you do in your life is an opportunity to practice Zen and to be enlightened. There is no difference.

Dogen taught his students to devote themselves to sitting in meditation, which he called *Zazen*. Dogen was the first Japanese monk to rely only on Zen meditation. The prerequisite was to live an ethical life. Then, with the regular and sincere practice of meditation, nothing gets in the way of enlightenment.

Zen Integrates Into Japanese Culture

The Soto school that Dogen founded spread through Japan, as did the Rinzai School originally founded by Eisai. The government established a complex system to disseminate Zen, which was similar to the Five Mountains, Ten Temples system of China. The Japanese system had an elaborate hierarchy of temples and subtemples that reached out from the cities into the most remote rural villages. Zen monks educated children in monastery schools and advised the emperor and government leaders at every level.

Another Japanese innovation was the practice of Zen arts. Tea ceremonies, swordsmanship, archery, martial arts, painting, haiku, and gardening became a pathway to follow for a living experience of the true spirit of Zen. Practitioners of these arts mastered Zen as they developed extraordinary skills in artistic expression. The Zen Way became a highly developed approach to activity itself that could enhance every aspect of living. This is still practiced as a tradition today in some Zen schools.

Hakuin: Japan's Inspirational Rinzai Master

One of Japan's most influential Rinzai Zen masters, Hakuin (1685–1768), was put in charge of a tiny, dilapidated monastery in his hometown farming village of Hara, near the base of Mount Fuji. Hakuin chose to stay there so he could help out his mother and the people of his village. Despite his humble position, Hakuin had a lasting effect on Zen.

Hakuin pursued enlightenment with an unparalleled ardor. He encouraged his students to follow his lead and strive for enlightenment like a person running from a burning building. Nothing should interfere with the single-minded determination to penetrate your own true nature. A single enlightenment was only the beginning in Hakuin's view. The Zen path is a lifelong pursuit to be followed sincerely and passionately.

He believed that nothing could surpass meditation in the midst of activity. Although quietly sitting in meditation has its place, he felt it was far more important to be able to sustain deep meditation no matter what you are doing.

> I am not trying to tell you to discard completely quietistic meditation and to seek specifically for a place of activity to carry on your practice. What is most worthy of respect is pure koan meditation that neither knows nor is conscious of the two aspects, the quiet and the active.
>
> (Hakuin, in Yampolsky, 1971, pp. 15–16)

Hakuin and his disciples revitalized and organized koans into a progressive system of study to help guide students on their path. The first koan, Mu (nothing), was used to help students penetrate deeply into their true nature. He also created the famous koan, "What is the sound of one hand clapping?" This organized course of study had a broad appeal to both monks and laymen by giving a curriculum for teaching Zen.

Hakuin was also a prolific calligrapher and painter who created more than 5,000 works. Many of his pictures were amusing caricatures and poems with simple mottos, which he often generously gave to the townspeople, who enjoyed them. The picture of Bodhidharma shown earlier in this chapter (Figure 3.4) was painted by Hakuin. He was beloved by the everyday person as well as the many Zen practitioners he taught. Hakuin's influence continues to be felt today.

Zen Arts

One of Japan's lasting contributions to Zen was the development of Zen arts. Zen arts offer structure to follow and skills to gain. Yet mastery in a true Zen art cannot be achieved without going through a transformation. The master's instructions bring about a change in the student. The change involves more than simply adding new skills. It also brings about an alteration of consciousness, much like what is achieved through Zen meditation. In fact, Zen arts are a form of meditation, both for the artist and for the audience. Zen arts epitomize the relationship between form and emptiness (Figure 3.5). The Heart Sutra tells us that form is emptiness and emptiness is form—a central theme in Zen. Some of the most widely practiced Zen arts are archery, flower arrangement, martial arts, dry gardening, haiku poetry, and calligraphy.

Zen in the West

Zen was largely unknown to the West until its introduction at a groundbreaking gathering in Chicago in 1893, the Parliament of the World's Religions. D. T. Suzuki (1870–1966), a young man at that time, accompanied the Zen representative, Shaku Soen, as translator. Suzuki met an American publisher, Paul Carus (1852–1919) who brought Suzuki to the United States to translate a series of Eastern classics. Suzuki lived with Paul Carus for 10 years, working on numerous translations that helped bring the Zen Way to the West. This set Suzuki on a lifelong path of writing and teaching Westerners about Buddhism and Zen. His many books and years of teaching throughout the country and at institutions such as Columbia University influenced the

Figure 3.5   Circle Bridge, Japan

Source: Original photograph by C. Alexander Simpkins, Jr., Toyko, Japan

beatniks, modern artists, intellectuals, psychologists, and countless people who read his books.

Suzuki's approach to Zen came from Hakuin's Rinzai tradition, although he reinterpreted it to be more understandable to the Western mind. He often used Lao-tzu's Daoism to illustrate Zen concepts of enlightenment, which would be expected since Hakuin also drew from Daoist techniques and visualizations for healing.

Many other Zen masters came to the United States and Europe during the 20th century, founding Zen temples and teaching at universities. Most found Westerners to be avid learners who brought a fresh and open beginner mind spirit to Zen (S. Suzuki, 1979). For example, Shunryu Suzuki was a quiet master of Soto Zen, who founded the San Francisco Zen Center. And Korean master Seung Sahn formed a large organization of Korean Zen, Kwan-Um, that continues after his passing, actively growing in the United States and Europe.

Western Influence on Zen

As the West is becoming more involved with Eastern ideas, so also is the East opening up to Western thought. Visionary Japanese monk and intellectual

Nishida Kitaro (1870–1945) founded a theoretical school devoted to the interaction between Eastern and Western ideas. A friend of Suzuki, Nishida studied the great Western philosophers while becoming a Zen monk. Inspired by the existential philosopher Soren Kierkegaard (1813–1855), Nishida advised people to turn to faith as the ultimate solution to the human condition: "Faith is the depth of the self, at the foundation of ourselves" (Dumoulin, 1992, p. 23). He conceived of God in a way that blended Zen with Christianity. He said, "God is absolute nothingness and absolute being. God in St. Paul's words 'is empty himself'" (Dumoulin, 1992, p. 25).

One of his greatest contributions was the creation of a nondualistic form of logic. He developed the Zen Way of thinking into a nondualistic, concrete logic that holds the perspective of affirmation and negation together, not with synthesis like Hegel, nor Aristotelian subject-object logic, and not even with predicate logic like Kant. Instead, the tension between opposites is maintained. The usual logical position is that a thing either is or is not. We know by difference. Zen holds that the point between, where there is no difference, is the true center. The point of indifference is the center, the starting point of knowledge, in Zen.

Nishida believed that Zen was extremely relevant to modern people. He felt that Zen emphasized the power of the self, because the Buddha mind resides within each of us. Koans reflect our modern existential dilemmas. He reminded people of a koan about a student who asks his master a question in the presence of a dead man: "Is human existence life or death?" The master answered, "Neither life nor death." Nishida's interpretation is that we must live life knowing of impending death but also not knowing.

Nishida's ideas invited a dialogue between Eastern and Western philosophers and between Zen and Christian scholars. An affiliation of like-minded scholars formed and taught a philosophical approach to Zen at Kyoto University, which became known as the Kyoto school. This became a forum for philosophical debates about fundamental modern problems, based in Zen and yet embracing many Western ideas. The dialogue continues today, as more Westerners are meditating and experiencing Zen and, more generally, Buddhism firsthand.

Nishitani Keiji (1900–1990), another member of the Kyoto School, dedicated his life to enhancing this dialogue between East and West. He believed that fundamental to all human life is doubt. In a sense, this is the deepest form of nihilism. Our task as human beings is to overcome nihilism, because such negative thinking weakens the stability of the self. It forces us to reexamine the plea made by Socrates: "Know thyself."

Nishitani wrote an essay, "The Standpoint of Zen," in which he compared Eastern and Western conceptions of self. Westerners form their idea of the self from their rational minds. Through the stream of consciousness, people observe and experience themselves existing separately from the world. The Eastern concept of the self is seen as part of the larger universal Oneness. The self is not the stream of consciousness but exists as something prior. Nishitani thought that Descartes shared in this insight, and that when he said, "I think, therefore I am," he had experienced a Zen-like breakthrough to enlightenment. He speculated that Descartes named his book *The Meditations* to indicate that he was pointing to an experience different from normal, rational thought. Coming from the Eastern perspective, Nishitani thought Descartes went astray when he tried to use his intuitive breakthrough as a basis for rational reason.

Nishitani believed the essential character of modern civilization is nihilistic. People feel dehumanized because of the ever-increasing technology that is overpowering modern life. This is where Zen offers a solution: spiritual freedom in emptiness. Emptiness helps us transcend all the contradictions of modern life to discover something fundamentally true: our concrete humanity in immediate experience.

Masao Abe (1915–2006) was a Buddhist scholar, a professor at Nara University, and an active member of the Kyoto School. He served as one of the prominent contemporary emissaries of Buddhism to the West since Suzuki's death. He wrote many books that explain Eastern principles, using Western ideas as a springboard for deeper understanding of the Eastern thought. He believed the East and West had much to teach each other. The West, with its fully refined philosophical development of concepts such as *being* and *ought* could be integrated with Zen's deep conceptual grasp of nothingness.

> Just as Western notions of Being and Ought are being forced into a basic reexamination through present dialogue between Zen and Western thought, Zen, too, must internally embrace the standpoints of Western Being and Ought, which have been foreign to itself.
>
> (Abe, 1989, p. 120)

Together in dialogue, we as citizens of the larger world will find a broader and deeper understanding.

Today, scholars continue the Kyoto School tradition of bridging the gap between East and West through Zen. Always, the efforts have been to tackle the important human problems that affect our contemporary age. Zen masters from the past and continuing now in the present offer us alternatives relevant as long as human beings continue to search for fulfillment of the human spirit.

CONCLUSIONS

Thanks to the many Zen masters through the ages and in modern times, Zen continues to evolve. Now in the 21st century, therapists are discovering its usefulness for helping their clients make deep and lasting changes. With its accessible methods, we can all benefit from adding Zen meditation to our practice.

4

Zen Philosophy

If the gesture of a hand shows you the Way, follow the Way. Don't just follow the hand.

—(C. Alexander Simpkins & Annellen M. Simpkins)

Themes and concepts are often used to help understand a subject. For therapeutic practice, the philosophical principles expressed in these themes offer opportunities for reframing. Like the gestalt figure pictured in Figure 4.1, we might find that our therapeutic theories suggest that we look at the vase as the figure. But as we experiment with the new ideas expressed in Zen philosophy, we might find our perspective shifts to view the faces as figures.

For Zen, concepts can point the way, but as abstractions from reality, they are never the path itself. Zen meditation points us to direct experience, beyond our conceptualizations. Concepts tend to delimit experience to an interpretation. In the open felt moment without thought, we become attuned to our deeper, ever-changing and evolving nature, and from that as the foundation, we can find a natural, healthy, balanced way.

As you read this chapter, consider these concepts as guidelines to turn you in a new direction, found in the meditative awareness of direct experience.

Figure 4.1 (Wood on wood, walnut burl and maple burl)
Source: Created by C. A. Simpkins and A. M. Simpkins, 2009

Like a compass pointing a ship through uncharted waters, these themes will help guide you to new destinations, with all the potentials they contain.

This chapter gathers themes from Zen important for therapy: mental flexibility, emptiness, meditation, true nature, and enlightenment.

MENTAL FLEXIBILITY

The measure of mental health is flexibility. . . . The essence of illness is
the freezing of behavior into unalterable and insatiable patterns.

(Kubie, 1975, pp. 20–21)

Healthy people learn through experience. They respond appropriately to changing internal and external conditions and alter concepts and behavior when needed. But if people are suffering from neurotic and psychotic problems, they become inflexible, with rigid and redundant reactions. An important part of good therapy is helping patients return to a more natural mental flexibility.

Flexibility and spontaneity are hallmarks of mental health. Rigidity of the mind, with a notable accompanying redundancy of pattern, is associated with problematic functioning. When we can encourage healthy spontaneity in our clients, we help them with their difficulty. We open the potential for creative solutions. Creativity is not tied to neurotic patterns but rather is inhibited by it.

We seek flexibility for our clients, flowing moment to moment, with emotion, behavior, and cognition free of obstruction, healthy and flexible, adaptive to their personal and interpersonal world. But psychological problems tend to be redundant. People repeat patterns with little variation. They feel stuck and unable to change. Zen encourages naturalness and attunement to the nature of the world. Through the practice of meditation, rigidities soften as practitioners open to the ever-changing nature of reality. Inner nature flows, in correlation with outer nature, flexibly attuned and in touch.

Inflexibilities of Mind

Each individual accumulates a set of concepts, beliefs, and assumptions. All of these constructs help us make sense of everyday life. Some arise out of individual life experiences. Others come from family, school, work, and the shared concepts, beliefs, and assumptions held by the culture. Many of them tend to be taken for granted. Our experience of the actual world interacts with and is influenced by our assumptions and concepts about it (Frank & Frank, 1991).

Our assumptions may become so habitual, so taken for granted, that they come to feel very real and true. We may feel trapped, stuck, and unable to do our best at the time, little knowing that what holds us back are faulty concepts. What appear to be situational restraints could be illusions from narrow, limiting, or inaccurate concepts that have become habitual. If a new situation or person is presented, we may misrepresent it, and consequently not recognize the positive potential already there in a person or in our situation. Our reactions become inappropriate and rigid. We may need to change.

For example, we had a client who always came to the sessions with a notebook. He said, "Just please give me a structure to follow, and things to do." His self-descriptions were concrete and literal. His behavior and lifestyle were predictable, routine, and controlled. He felt unhappy and dissatisfied with his life, but couldn't imagine why. Another client who was unable to step outside of his own perspective said, "I can't switch roles; this is stupid." He responded by feeling awkward and unsure of himself. He could not think of himself outside of his fixed self-concept. Spontaneity was never considered by him to be personally achievable in a meaningful way. Change in this dimension was change that expanded his life dramatically.

Socrates asked, in Plato's famous dialogue, "Meno," can virtue be taught? We may ask then, can spontaneity and flexibility be taught? How is this possible? Zen, which has great respect for spontaneity, takes the position that it can be taught in the sense that this virtue is already there. We all have, in our deeper nature, the capacity to be spontaneous, flexible, and healthy. We obstruct our natural capacities with the faulty beliefs and assumptions we hold so dearly. Zen can be used for up-ending redundant expectancies, to loosen their tight hold and invite something new. Whether the troubling expectancies derive from interpersonal relationship concepts or self-concepts, they can get between you and the client and between your client and the world.

Deconstructing

We must learn to deconstruct, rather than construct. The process is not so much *what* you turn to, but *that* you turn. The turning of attention is the point. This becomes a challenging paradox. We train ourselves to use constructs in a flowing way. Science incorporates constructs, and one could argue whether it is even possible to experience and communicate without constructs. However, we know now that constructs cannot contain wisdom, even though they might point to it. Constructs are like a finger pointing to the moon, but they are not the moon itself. If we are too caught up in the constructs, we miss the heavenly glory.

The intricate complexities of analysis a language philosopher can perform on a simple turn of phrase demonstrates how even the simplest constructs can obscure rather than reveal. For example, this philosophical question is raised if we ask what Lois Lane knows about Superman. She knows Clark Kent and she knows Superman. She has experienced the man, Clark Kent, who is also in (fictional) reality the man Superman. She constructs two different people in her mind. Zen's solution is to deconstruct and get back to direct experiencing. Clark Kent and Superman are only separate in her mind, as constructs that hide the true identity. When we apply this to therapy, we use constructs in a specific way so that they will point us toward wisdom rather than away from it. Clark Kent and Superman are one.

Ancient Deconstruction Theory, the Middle Way

Nagarjuna (second century) was the founder of Madhyamika, the Middle Way philosophy. He was an Indian monk, philosopher, and logician, and also considered to be a founder of Mahayana Buddhism.

Nagarjuna stated logical propositions that demonstrated the self-contradictory nature of all possible assertions about the nature of reality. All pairs of opposites (being, nonbeing, neither, and both) can be negated, because they are all logically untenable concerning ultimate reality. Only the Middle Path offers a basis for true understanding.

Following Nagarjuna's logical discourse, the doctrine of Sunyata, or emptiness, was proposed, a concept that cannot even be called by name lest it lose its empty nature by being named! Nagarjuna demonstrated logically that since nothing has independent origination, everything has an inner emptiness of any individual self-nature. Since everything is relative to this inner emptiness, as well as being linked to everything else, logically nothing exists in and of itself. All is ultimately empty, devoid of outer existence or any inner nature. This was a forerunner of the modern philosophy of relativism and later deconstructionism, though with a different application.

Modern Deconstructionism

Like Zen's history with respect to Buddhism, Western philosophy has created deconstructionism to explain the paradoxes that arise for constructs. This modern philosophical theory arose in reaction to the intricate complexity of philosophy's constructs and arguments, evolved over thousands of years (Derrida, 1982). Rather than arguing only with specific concepts and assumptions while accepting others, deconstruction holds that all philosophical constructs need to be considered as lacking substantive truth, and analyzed to gain freedom from them. When all these false constructs are cleared out of the way, it will be possible to discover truth.

Deconstruction is central in Zen, using a different approach. Zen masters encourage their students to give up fruitless endeavors, to stop traversing the hopeless path of logic and reason so as to reach the goal of deeper understanding and oneness, similar to the state of affairs Socrates called true knowledge.

Bypassing Resistance

Logic is helpful, and we use it often in psychotherapy. Cognitive behavior therapy (CBT) and many other forms of therapy show the path to follow, just as with excellent logical arguments and sound behavioral and emotional methods, logic leads the horse to water. These methods approach change from the perspective that there is water, so to speak, and a clear path to it, seeking to link thought with conceptual clarity in method. But Zen holds that this is not a necessary condition for an enlightened perspective, which always transcends its roots. Concepts can lead one into a box from which there is no easy escape.

What about the client who turns her eyes away from the therapeutic experience you have so aptly pointed toward instead of looking? A neurotic horse, even though thirsty, may be led to a sweet, bubbling spring, and instead, stubbornly refuse to drink! Here is the place for Zen in therapy—a step beyond logic that shifts the whole being of that individual in such a way that she will naturally open her eyes and drink the water of therapy. This inner change is profound, and many problems will dissolve in the flow. Don't make your theory the object of therapy. Don't put it between you and the client. Look at the person. Zen is more than a theory. Like the finger pointing to the moon, Zen is a stepping-stone on a healing path.

MEDITATION

The purpose is to see things as they are, to observe things as they are, and to let everything go as it goes. This is to put everything under control in its widest sense.

(S. Suzuki, 1979, p. 33)

How can you get the client to experience himself and his relationships in a way that cuts through his troubling constructions? Meditation is a direct and experiential way to bypass this level of thinking, offering an opportunity to experience it firsthand.

Zen teaches that our actions and reactions are just that, no more. Preconceptions and assumptions need not be the center, nor are they the ultimate parameters of a situation. We can become more flexible by suspending assumptions. Regular meditation will bring moments of awareness without limitations from preconceptions.

Zen meditation is the method to use to bring about a unique experience: the stream of thinking quiets, consciousness becomes clear, empty; awareness is moment to moment, in the present. Zen is optimistic about human potential, since all people have the capacity to be aware, latent within. Huang-po expressed this when he said, "All sentient beings are *already* of one form with Bodhi [enlightenment]" (Blofeld, 1994, p. 144).

Meditation is a time for sitting quietly, seemingly doing nothing. In Western cultures, sitting quietly and doing nothing might be seen as a waste of time. How can anything significant be accomplished by doing nothing? Or are you really doing nothing? The answers to these questions require a shift in perspective. When we are willing to experiment with this shift, a new world of possibility opens up.

When we meditate, we take a break from all the usual thoughts and activities that fill our lives. As we learn how to quiet our thoughts, we begin to perceive clearly in a new way. We get in touch with a deeper part of ourselves. We are all endowed with a mind that is clear, pure, and deep. This is what the Zen masters call our true nature. It is already there, within everyone, but we usually don't notice because we are too busy being pushed and pulled by our thoughts and desires.

Meditation is a tool that can teach us how to return to our deeper experience to perceive clearly, resulting in a profound sense of calm and confidence that won't be shaken. As people get more accustomed to meditation, they realize that what seemed at first to be a nonactivity is its own kind of activity. Meditation lets us be immersed in our usual, everyday life while also remaining fully aware. For clients, it provides a way to attune to their best capacities for healthy functioning. The chapters of this book will guide us in how to do so.

TRUE NATURE

Psychotherapy is a quest for wholeness, higher integration. Getting in touch with our true nature is like getting in touch with a mirror in which one can see the reflection of the greater universe. To best reflect the ongoing, changing world as it is, the inner mind must be pure and clear.

In the West, we tend to think of nature as something external to predict and control. Science tries to understand the forces of nature and harness them for the benefit of humanity. Zen views nature as something to connect to, to

Figure 4.2 Nature Bird

become one with, and flow along with. Through nature, we experience our own natural being. When we are truly attuned to nature, we know ourselves.

Nature is always there, accessible and patiently waiting. Just walk out into the woods, climb a mountain, or visit the seashore and we instinctually feel something stir within (Figure 4.2). As Ralph Waldo Emerson said, "All natural objects make a kindred impression when the mind is open to their influence" (Emerson, 1965, p. 181).

Our relationship with nature is a kinship. Through meditation comes an acceptance and awareness of the intimate interrelationship of all things. By letting go of the self as a separate ego, each of us is no longer an isolated being living alone in our own skin. We are in an active partnership with the world. If we put a toe into a pond, we cause ripples. As we understand this relationship, we can be at peace and find tranquility wherever we are.

We can find stillness in the midst of continual movement. Singing birds, rustling leaves, a bubbling brook, all evoke quiet tranquility within. Stillness in motion and motion in stillness is nature's way and Zen's way, never choosing one over the other. Nature's way is our own inner nature. By becoming a part of nature's calm in the midst of activity, we become that calm in the midst of activity as we engage in our life. The true nature of the flow of consciousness is unencumbered and clear in its natural, continual flow. This clarity of mind can be there for us, always.

Zen masters teach people: Attune yourself to nature by attuning to your own awareness of what is all around you, in each passing moment. Then you discover the peaceful moment that is always there as a potential. You can be aware of the whole, experiencing the wonders of nature with your own wonder. You are no different: You are nature itself.

There is no external standard in nature. Each flower, every tree, expresses its own nature, complete and perfect. If you go out into a forest, you will see tall trees and short ones, wide ones and narrow ones. Even within species, there are individual differences. Yet, trees don't aspire to be taller or shorter: They just grow to the height they grow. This way of nature is our way, too. People become disturbed when they engage in comparisons or aspirations to be different from what they truly are. Meditation can help people to become aware of and then fully accept their true nature. Problems then fade away. Nothing is missing, and in this moment living in accord with our true nature, we are complete just as we are.

No Self-Nature

What, then, is this true nature? Zen teaches that our true nature is no-self nature. There is no lasting, enduring self that we can hold on to. As we go through life, we are continually growing and changing. The self that seems to endure is merely a mental construction, a concept of ourselves that can never capture all that we are. The concept of the soul described in Plato's dialogue, "Phaedo," offers a good analogy to begin to comprehend Zen's concept of no self-nature. The individual mind or soul is like the harmony created with a lyre, an instrument that can be played to express music. The music that it makes depends on the strings, their tuning, and how the musician plays the instrument. All these elements come together in each moment to bring about the harmony. Do the tones have any reality beyond what we experience when listening to the tuned instrument? Is the music just a functional expression of the interrelationship of tuned strings when they are plucked with a guitar pick or the fingers of the musician? Or does music also involve the listener's experience, with the anticipation of the notes that will come, the remembrance of what has been played, and familiarity with the music?

Similarly, our self-nature is an attunement to our being in the world, and we express ourselves in our responsive relationship to the world we experience, like music. We have a past, which is part of how we are in the present, and we anticipate our future, as well. Through the continuity of past to future, we build a sense of ourselves as having a fixed nature. But in truth, we are, like the melody, moving through time. The interrelationship we have with others and our world in each moment is how we create ourselves, but ultimately this self-nature is empty.

EMPTINESS

Emptiness is the wellspring of potential. To be empty is to be truly attuned to the world and one's true nature. To get there is not easy without comprehending the limitations of our usual attitude of mind. Emptiness does not mean a vacuum as we might think of it from a Western perspective; that something is lacking. Emptiness from the Eastern perspective refers to a state of no-thingness. Thus, it is not limited in any way.

Mahayana Buddhism's emptiness, known as *sunyata,* was the springboard for Zen. If originally "not a thing is" (Ma-tzu), then there is no reason to objectify or make an object of what we perceive or know. Words are not used as concepts in Zen. We can expand this understanding when we realize that objects are interrelated to our perceptions of them. The experience of perception is primary.

Cognitive therapy says we need something different—change your cognitions; and Zen therapy adds, make the empty space because then there is openness, with a potential for something different.

Emptiness as Process

In Zen, emptiness is not just a concept or goal. Nor is emptiness an ultimate state. This is different from the Western scientific concept, which defines emptiness as a state, a vacuum consisting of the absence of molecules. Emptiness is a process, a continuum, always in flux, for Zen Buddhists. The founder of Gestalt therapy, Fritz Perls (Perls, 1969, p. 57), noted that the void implies *no*-thingness, only process. Perls believed the void was a source of creativity and therapeutic change.

Zen masters discourage immersion in any kind of empty state. Instead, they help students discover the process. Hakuin strongly urged students of Zen not to get stuck in the swamp of nothingness. When the Zen master

Figure 4.3 Empty Square (wood on wood, wenge and walnut)
Source: Created by C. A. Simpkins and A. M. Simpkins, 2005

Yamaoka Tesshu (1836–1888) was a young Zen student, he searched for enlightenment by visiting one Zen master after another. He tried to show each teacher that he knew a great deal about Buddhism. Talking with Master Dokuon of Shokoku he said, "I know that the mind, the Buddha, all beings, and everything in the world does not exist. In fact, the nature of all things is emptiness." (Figure 4.3)

Dokuon watched the young student silently as he sat calmly smoking. Without warning, he lifted his bamboo stick and struck Tesshu.

Tesshu felt himself fill with anger.

Then Dokuon said, "If nothing exists, where did that anger come from?"

In that moment, Tesshu learned to let go of even the concept of nothing *as a thing.*

Zen doctrine holds that even emptiness must be emptied of its apparent content. Paradoxically, when emptiness is fully accepted, even emptiness is empty. There is nothing to empty when nothing is there. The Zen master says, "Empty your cup." But how can you empty an already empty cup?

ENLIGHTENMENT

It is the privilege of satori to be sitting in the Absolute Present quietly surveying the past and contemplating the future.

(D. T. Suzuki, 1969, p. 35)

Zen meditation brings about a unique experience: the stream of thinking quiets, consciousness becomes clear, empty, and present. In that empty moment, something can happen: enlightenment. Many different words are used to describe it: "one absolute thought," *sunyata* (emptiness), *canti* (tranquility), clear mind, everyday mind, unconscious, *prajna* (wisdom), *satori*, *kensho*, seeing into one's true nature . . . so many words to describe a wordless experience!

As we come to recognize our potential, discovered through meditating, we experience our own being differently. Feelings of uncertainty and confusion give way to clarity—Oneness, "Our original inseparability with the universe" (Watts, 1973, p. 86). The first steps, the root of the discovery of something greater begins with something smaller—turning toward our own mind. Voltaire's famous statement in *Candide*, "Cultivez votre jardin" (cultivate your own garden), points us in the correct direction (Voltaire, 1950, p. 144).

Enlightenment in Everyday Life

There is no separation between everyday life and enlightenment. A Zen master was asked how to enter the path to enlightenment. His answer was a question, "Do you hear the stream?"

"Yes," responded the student.

"Well then, you have found the entrance to the path!"

When we take a moment to truly hear the stream, letting go of any other thoughts about the past or future—being fully attentive to that sound in the moment, we can experience enlightenment. Even the simplest experience can be the doorway.

No aspect of life—career, family, leisure—is outside of enlightenment. All are intimately linked. Anything we do can become a place to begin a search for enlightenment, as well as helping to maintain it.

Many people might think, "My life is too boring for such an experience." They feel like they aren't good enough, and long for a different life to make them happy. Zen discourages this kind of thinking as dualistic, comparing yourself to something outside of yourself. Such dualistic thinking ultimately leads us away from the richness of what is there in each ongoing moment. By staying fully aware of what we are experiencing, whatever that is, we can have an intuitive leap of understanding.

Live every moment fully, letting each experience receive your equal and full attention. Here and now is where enlightenment can be found; here and now can be your paradise.

Nothing to Seek

Even though Zen students are seriously devoted to discovering enlightenment, it cannot be sought after. No particular outcome or effect should be expected. This seems paradoxical for our modern, goal-oriented lifestyles, and yet it opens potentials for deeper wisdom. If you practice meditation without expecting anything, then, as Suzuki said, "Eventually you will resume your own true nature, that is to say, your own true nature resumes itself" (S. Suzuki, 1979, p. 49).

In therapy, there is a difference between knowing what's going on, with no deeper insight into its inner meaning, and comprehension, when the client really understands, with personal insight, deeply grasping inner meaning. These discoveries come about spontaneously, sometimes after deep therapeutic probing, but other times in an effortless way. Then, the client can be gently guided from grasping the original meaning to letting go of it, for example, with a client's sudden recognition, "I don't have to do this anymore!"—And then she had a vivid experience of the moment, a therapeutic mini-satori.

CONCLUSION

Zen Therapy is concerned with turning the client away from conflicts and concerns that are redundant and have little to do with the real world, to reorient toward reality. We can live well and fully in the real world. Zen enlightenment involves an ineffable and total realignment of consciousness, a new way of experiencing the world and one's life. Therapeutic enlightenment is also an ineffable and total realignment of consciousness, and a new way of experiencing oneself and others, which paradoxically, Zen doctrine holds is empty of form or content. People can let go of illusions and be satisfied, leading to what a good life is really all about: living happily and fully, just as we are.

5

Zen Practices

Meditation
Better than anything
Can restore us
To inner wellsprings
Helps us shed all cares for now
Cools and soothes the soul
Clears the mind
Makes us whole.
(C. Alexander Simpkins)

One day a student knocked on a master's door. The student had heard of this master's great wisdom from other teachers and had traveled a great distance to learn. This student was knowledgeable about many forms of psychotherapy, and was always seeking to add to his understandings. The master answered the door and the student said, "I am an ardent student of psychology. I practice a cognitive form of therapy, but I also incorporate psychodynamics as well as neurobiological theories. I use a little behavioral technique, especially when I give homework between sessions. I have heard that you have a new therapy system. Will you take me on as your student?"

The master answered, "Only if you tell all the people you brought with you to leave."

The student turned around to see who had followed him to the master's house but saw no one else around. At first, he felt mystified and confused. But in time, he learned how to truly let go of "all the people he brought with him," to open himself for new learning, and be completely present in each moment.

Zen is the Japanese word that translates as *meditation*. You can read about it, learn the traditions from which it arose, and gain information about it. But ultimately, the way to truly know meditation is to do it personally. Meditation is an experience that can be especially helpful for therapy. This chapter guides in key meditation practices that you can use to enhance your own awareness and teach to your clients.

We opened the process with a classic story, which illustrates how to take the first steps on the path to learning Zen meditation. The methods do not involve the accumulation of new knowledge and information. Rather, they guide us to let go and become open to the present moment, without bias or preconception. Such a learning approach is different from our typical Western education methods. But it can become a valuable set of tools for you and your clients (Simpkins & Simpkins, 2009).

PREPARING FOR MEDITATION

Meditation can be done anywhere at any time, but when you are first starting, you will make it easier for yourself if you find a quiet place with subdued lighting where you will be undisturbed. Ideally, the temperature should not be too hot or too cold.

If you plan to add meditation as a regular part of therapy, you may want to create a simple and soothing atmosphere in a corner of your office: A small plant on a stand, an unadorned picture on an empty wall, and a few meditation pillows on the floor may help clients get in the mood for meditation.

When learning to meditate, pick a time when you don't have any immediate responsibilities. For clients, a short meditation at the beginning or end of the session can be added into the treatment hour. Begin by devoting a short amount of time to meditation, even as little as a few minutes. In fact, we usually have the first meditation last only 1 minute. Most people can find a few minutes here and there to spare between sessions, which makes it easier

Figure 5.1 Meditation Hall

to start a process. Longer meditation sessions at the early phases may discourage some people, especially if they find it difficult to do. But even those who have attention problems can manage a very short meditation. One ADHD man we treated could only sustain his meditation for 15 seconds. But this was enough to get him started. He felt pleased with his progress when he was able to sustain his meditation for 1 minute. And with practice, he was able to keep meditating for 30 minutes. Eventually, as people begin to feel the benefits, they usually feel more motivated to increase the time they spend meditating, and as their skills build, they are able to sustain it.

Meditation Postures

There is a traditional way to sit on the floor in meditation (see Figure 5.1), which is still followed today in many Zen temples. But don't let the conventions for positioning prevent you or your client from meditating. For those who can't sit on the floor, use a chair or a meditation cushion. If you can't sit in a lotus or half-lotus, just sit comfortably. Meditation comes from within, and body restrictions need not hold you back.

Figure 5.2   Cross-legged

Traditional Meditation Position

Place a pillow on the floor. Sit down and cross your legs into the lotus position by which the left heel rests on the right thigh and the right heel rests on the left thigh. If you don't have the flexibility for this position, sit with only one foot up, known as a half lotus (or simply sit cross-legged with both feet resting on the floor) (Figure 5.2).

Sit with your spine straight, aligning your head in the center without tilting. Relax your shoulders and keep your head straight. Don't strain. Your breathing passages should be free and unrestricted. Let your breathing be normal.

Place your hands on your lap with your left hand on top of your right middle joints of your middle fingers together and thumbs together, lightly touching (Figure 5.3). Your hands will be shaped like an oval. One reason for crossing your legs and hands is to make your body a unity, with no distinction

Figure 5.3   Hand Position, Complete Circle, Thumbs Lightly Touching

between left and right, no beginning and no end. You can also sit with hands resting comfortably on your knees (see Figure 5.2).

The classical Zen meditation eye position is half open. Traditionally, eyes were not entirely shut to prevent the monks from falling asleep. Remain relaxed, but alert. We often have people close their eyes. Closed eyes keep out visual distractions, making it easier to focus attention. If you have a client who is uncomfortable with either of these eye positions, allow him to keep his eyes open. Always listen to the needs of your client. He will tell you when he feels uncomfortable, and you should be sure to listen.

Warming Up to Meditation

We have taught meditation for many years and have found that many Westerners have never been exposed to the kinds of skills used in meditation. Some people may benefit from exercises that teach how to deliberately sit still, relax, and direct attention. Clients who have never done anything like meditation before may need to be eased into the experience. We offer a few exercises to help build the skills that will be useful for Zen meditation.

Warm-Up I: Just Sitting

Sitting quietly doing nothing may be a challenge for some people, especially those who are anxious. But the benefits of taking some time to sit quietly can be very helpful for learning Zen and for a calmer life in general. Try this for a few minutes when you are already feeling somewhat quiet.

Sit down in a comfortable place. Don't think about anything in particular, but don't try to stop thinking. Just sit quietly, breathing normally. You will probably notice that your mental activity slows somewhat as you sit. You may even find yourself becoming more relaxed.

Warm-Up II: Mindful Relaxation

We can all benefit from learning how to relax. Lie down on your back on a wooden floor, a carpet, or a couch. Place your feet flat on the surface, knees raised to allow your back to relax naturally. Breathe comfortably. Turn your attention to your body. Start at your head and scan down through your body. Notice if you have any tensions. People commonly hold tension in their necks, shoulders, or backs. As you continue to breathe gently and become aware, you may find that you can let go of any unnecessary tensions. Don't try to force anything. Just become aware of what you feel. This may take a few minutes. Continue to become aware of your body and allow relaxation wherever possible. Becoming aware of yourself, just as you are, is the beginning of meditation.

Warm-Up III: Counting the Breaths Concentration

Zen uses attention on breathing to help bring the meditator into experiencing here and now. Some people find awareness of breathing to be a natural inroad into meditation.

Begin by sitting quietly and turn your attention to your breathing. Count each complete breath, where breathing in and then out again is one breath. Count up to 10 and then begin again. Let your breathing be natural and relaxed. Keep your attention on your breathing as you count. Continue counting for several minutes.

Now that you have become more accustomed to working with awareness and inward focus, you will enjoy beginning Zen meditation. Keep in mind that when you meditate in the Zen way, you must let go of thoughts of attainment while at the same time trying hard to keep meditating. This probably seems like a contradiction: to try without trying, to have a goal without striving. But as you begin to experience meditation, you will eventually understand how they are not different.

The Japanese Zen Master Dogen often told his students that practice is enlightenment. Life is not getting ready for something else, the getting ready part is life itself, and here is where you will find the meditative moment. These classic meditations will guide you on this well-worn path.

FOCUSED MEDITATION

Focusing one's attention is a skill that develops with practice. Where you place your attention can vary. We offer two methods that activate different brain areas: first focusing on a body experience and then focusing on an image. You may find one seems easier for you than the other. Start with what feels most natural and gradually extend to what is more challenging.

Attention to Breathing

Sit in the traditional posture described earlier and direct your attention to your breathing. Try to relax your body and just breathe naturally and comfortably. As you inhale, notice how your ribcage expands slightly as you bring air in and down through your breathing passages. Pay attention as the air pushes out again. Keep your awareness on each new breath, in and then out as you allow the process to happen naturally. If you have any thoughts distracting you, gently bring your attention back to your breathing. Let yourself experience each breath anew, as a new moment. Continue staying with your moment-by-moment breathing.

Focus on a Color

Sit comfortably, close your eyes, and think about your favorite color. Keep all your attention focused on the color. You may want to think of something that is that color, such as a blue sky, a yellow sun, or a red car. But you might prefer to just visualize the color itself. Keep attention focused on the color and nothing else. If something else comes to mind, gently bring your attention back to the color as soon as you notice. Stay focused on the color until you are ready to stop.

MINDFULNESS

Mindful he breathes in, mindful he breathes out. Whether he is breathing in a long or a short breath, he comprehends that he is breathing in a long or a short breath.

(Mindfulness in Majjhima-nikdya I, in Conze, 1995, p. 59)

A Zen student had been studying for a number of years. He was considered an accomplished master who was scheduled to be promoted to teacher. One rainy day before his promotion ceremony, he made a visit to his first Zen teacher, whom he had not seen in many years. Before he entered the teacher's hall, he respectfully left his shoes and umbrella outside the door and entered barefooted. He bowed respectfully to his instructor and said a warm hello. His instructor smiled, visibly glad to see him, and then he asked, "Tell me, on which side of the door did you leave your shoes and umbrella?"

The student thought for a moment and then bowed his head in shame. He had been so excited to see his old teacher that his anticipation had interfered with his mindful awareness when he placed his shoes and umbrella. He decided to postpone his promotion and went back to his meditation until he could sustain his awareness no matter what the circumstances. Eventually he did become a true master, mindfully aware in whatever he did.

The word *mindfulness* implies its meaning: Mind *full* ness is a method for filling the mind fully and completely with each moment. Mindfulness is not just a matter of what you do, but rather how you apply your mental attention and involvement.

Mindfulness has many applications to psychotherapy, and so you will want to spend time developing these skills. We offer step-by-step methods for developing proficiency with mindfulness that will be most useful to therapy.

Taking a Nonjudgmental Attitude

Mindfulness offers a distinct approach for observing actions, thoughts, and feelings. But when people perceive more deeply, they do not always like what they see. And as a result, they often become tempted to pass judgment on themselves or others before the perception is fully understood. Conceptualizing about the experience interferes with direct perception. Therefore, mindful awareness should be nonjudgmental. Like a scientist who is gathering data, you should not jump to conclusions or use the new information gained from being mindful to form biased opinions. For the purposes of the mindful awareness, suspend judgment and allow the experience to unfold. Trust the process and cultivate an open mind.

We would like to add that sound judgment is a valuable cognitive capacity. We are advocating suspending a particular use of judging as it is applied to ongoing experiencing moment to moment. As people develop their skills in withholding judgment, they concomitantly develop a clearer reality sense from which sounder judgments will later follow, when appropriate. So, begin the process by suspending judgment with the understanding that the ability to discern clearly will be ultimately improved.

Mindful of Body

Put the nonjudgmental attitude into practice as you notice details of your body experience. One of the traditional Buddhist mindfulness exercises encouraged practitioners to focus on the negative and unattractive physical aspects of their body. This trained the student to accept the bad along with the good and cultivate detachment.

To apply this nonjudgmental attitude to mindfulness, survey yourself from head to toe and recognize all your different parts. Traditionally, Buddhism counted 32 body parts. Describe each part to yourself. Notice, for example, your hair, its color, texture, style; your eyes; and so on. But stay factual. For example, observe that your hair is, for example, long, dark, brown, and curly. But don't add evaluations, such as your hair being too long or too curly.

If you notice something about yourself that you don't like, take note of it. Know that you are noticing something you don't like. You may decide this quality should eventually be changed, but for the moment, observe that you would like to change it. Know that you want to do so, without self-criticism. Observing it, note the feeling that you want to change it as another experience. If you begin to pass judgment about it—this is a bad quality (ugly, stupid, and so on), notice that you are doing so. Whenever you can simply observe, you will find that perception opens. So, it is a two-part exercise in that you are free to allow your ongoing experience to flow, but you notice it as it goes along. Let yourself be aware in the situation. Keep your observations clear and descriptive. Learn to accept your experience of yourself, without making comparisons or criticisms to something outside of this moment. You will then be able to appreciate experiencing, just as it is.

Clients are often especially hard on their appearance. This exercise provides a good beginning for developing attitudes of self-acceptance and tolerance. Encourage them to embrace what they are and what they feel, without belittling themselves. The Zen Buddhist teacher Lin Chi often told his disciples that nothing is missing. Our problems occur because we doubt ourselves on a deep and often unconscious level. Everyone is fully equipped with everything they need to become mindfully aware. Even therapists may benefit personally from this exercise. Helpers are often more accepting of others than they might be of themselves. This exercise provides a good discipline for getting to know oneself deeply and discovering a profound level of self-acceptance that can provide powerful and subtle modeling for clients to learn from.

Body Mindfulness: Noticing Body Positions

Extend mindfulness with a generalized sense of body awareness. Notice your body positions and movements at times while sitting, standing, lying down, and walking. When you are going about your day, take a moment to notice your body sensations. We often pay very little attention to such fundamentals. But our body sensations are part of everything we do, an important and valuable experience to tune in with. They can give us clues about deeper feelings and even signal an impending disturbance that might be averted.

So, when you first wake up in the morning, begin by taking a moment to notice yourself lying in bed. Then as you get up, pay attention to how you sit up, step on to the floor, and slowly stand up. Take note of your body positions whenever you have a chance throughout your day.

Mindful Breathing

Once you have been able to notice your physical being, you have taken the first steps toward mindfulness. Next, delve into one of the most widely practiced meditation traditions: mindful breathing. We must breathe to live, but we often do so without paying much attention to the process. By consistently turning your attention to breathing, you have an accessible inroad into your deeper being. Many people find that paying attention to breathing is one of the easiest ways to begin the process of becoming aware.

Sit on a small pillow on the floor and cross your legs. If you have difficulty sitting on the floor, please feel free to sit in a chair. Let your hands rest comfortably on your legs. Keep your back relatively straight so that your breathing passages are free and unrestricted. Close your eyes and breathe normally.

Notice as you bring the air in through your nose. Feel the air in your nasal passages and then follow the sensation as the air travels down into your lungs. Notice the movement in your chest and diaphragm as the air enters. Next, follow the air as it moves out. Note how your diaphragm pushes down as the air travels up and out through your nasal passages. Feel the sensation of air pushing out as it leaves your nose.

Try not to alter your normal breathing. At first, you might feel tempted to take in deep breaths, but don't. Continue breathing mindfully for several minutes. If you catch your attention drifting away from your breathing, gently bring it back.

You may find yourself naturally relaxing. Your breathing may want to be a little deeper and slower. Allow this process to take place only as it feels natural. Over time, you will be able to develop a feeling of calm and ease from mindful breathing. Your sense of inner peace becomes a resource.

Mindful of Emotions

Emotions are an important component of living, and so mindfulness must include attention to feelings. Feelings can be categorized as pleasant, unpleasant, or neutral. People tend to cling to pleasant feelings and reject unpleasant ones. But this clinging and rejecting sets in motion a secondary set of reactions that interfere with awareness and cause suffering. You will be able to drop the secondary reaction as you become more aware of the feelings themselves, leading to more comfortable, aware, enlightened reactions.

Mindfulness of emotions begins when you can identify the feeling you are having. To start the process, sit down for a moment and close your eyes. Turn your attention inward. Try to put a name to your emotion or mood. Then match the description with what you feel. If it is not quite right, modify your label until you feel satisfied.

Let yourself become curious to know more about each feeling as you feel it, to sense where the feeling is felt in your body, how it changes through time, and what it becomes as you stay attuned and aware of each feeling just as it is.

Next, identify whether the feeling is pleasant, unpleasant, or neutral. As you identify it, try to remain calm. Be like a benevolent kindergarten teacher who watches over her students as they play on the playground. When two children begin fighting, she does not become angry with them. Instead, she tries to calmly attend to their needs. Benevolently observe all your different feelings, even the ones you have labeled as unpleasant. By eliminating the secondary aversion reaction to a negative feeling, you continue to develop a process of accepting what is.

The Impermanence of Feelings

People often feel like their feelings are permanent—something they can't escape. But in reality, feelings are changing moment by moment. Buddhism instructs that feelings are impermanent. Like every other aspect of human experience, feelings are actually a series of fleeting moments involving sensations, thoughts about those sensations, and a response. This classic story offers a lesson from Zen Master Bankei (1622–1693) about dealing with anger.

> A monk consulted Master Bankei for help with his short temper. The monk said, "I know I should do something about it, but I was born this way and there's nothing I can do!"
>
> Bankei asked him, "Show me your temper now."
>
> The monk replied, "I'm not angry now. My temper just pops out at unexpected times, when someone provokes me."
>
> Bankei said, "Well, if you aren't angry now and your temper comes and goes, you couldn't have been born with it. The only thing you inherited from your parents was your pure, original nature. Everything else you have created yourself!"
>
> The monk was very surprised and felt hopeful that maybe he could change his temper. Bankei went on to explain that the source of his feeling was that he took himself too seriously. People create their opinions, their tastes, and their insistence that things must be done a certain way. Then, if someone disagrees, they feel angry, sad, or frustrated. Let go of ego.

(Paraphrased from Waddell, 1984)

Clinging to a pleasant feeling will inevitably lead to frustration because the feeling always ends. Conversely, trying to avoid an unpleasant feeling will also bring suffering, since you cannot escape from your moment-to-moment experience.

Notice what you are feeling for a predetermined length of time, such as 10 minutes. Take note of the sensations, the thoughts that go with the feeling, and anything else that comes into your awareness. Without trying to alter anything, notice how the emotion gradually changes over time. Perhaps you become calmer, less unhappy, or less annoyed. Take note of how that change is experienced, such as cooling down of the cheeks, a change in the feeling in your stomach, or perhaps an overall loosening of muscles. As you pay attention to emotions mindfully, they typically tend to become less severe. As pointed out in Chapters 1 and 2, meditation has a moderating influence on emotions, making them easier to handle. So stay with the emotion if you can, alert and aware of each changing moment.

Mindful of Mind

Mindfulness of mind involves observing cognitive activity itself. Thinking takes on many different forms, filling our minds with one thought after another. At times, we think with clarity, while other times our thoughts are confused. Sometimes the mind is filled with emotion, and other times it is completely unemotional. But if you step back and look at the broader picture, you notice that these different states of mind are a series of transitory processes. For example, if you look at a flower, seeing this flower engages a combination of brain processes, including sensory information from the eye to the brain, cognitions about flowers and what they mean to you, and an emotional reaction, such as, "I like flowers!" Perception involves the meanings you have about flowers, both personal and shared with the culture, as well as your sensory experience of the flower. According to Buddhism, all the collected meanings, both cultural and personal, are stored in the store-consciousness. These processes are constructed by the mind in response to the stimulus of a flower. In fact, everything you perceive is mentally constructed in this sense. Through mindful awareness, you can observe the typical mental constructs that seem to fill each moment, and begin to recognize the complex ongoing series of ever-changing experiences.

Psychologists might take these understandings for granted, but many clients will not have thought about things this way. Careful guidance in mindfulness of mind can be helpful for clients in gaining objectivity even toward their most compelling thought processes.

Become Aware of Thoughts

Mindfulness of the mind begins by first recognizing what you are thinking as you think it. Sit quietly and close your eyes. Notice what you are thinking as you think it. Follow the flow of your thoughts. Be like someone sitting on the bank of a river who watches leaves and twigs flow down the river. Don't jump into the river, but stay back on shore observing. Keep observing and letting each thought drift past. If you find yourself drifting downstream with a thought, climb back on shore and resume your observing as soon as you notice.

Mindful of the Impermanence of Thoughts

Mindfully observe your thoughts. Think about this statement from a Buddhist sutra, "A thought is like lightning; it breaks up in a moment and does not stay on" (Conze, 1995, p. 163). You will see the fleeting nature of thoughts as they come and go. Stay with each moment of experiencing, and you will notice how every thought lacks staying power. Even if the content of your present thought resembles earlier thoughts, each actual momentary thought is brief and then gone.

Mindfulness of the Objects of Mind

Whenever we think, we are thinking about something. When we feel an emotion, it is directed toward something or someone. Similarly, sensory experiences are of an object or a person. Consciousness is filled with an object of mind. The Chinese word for perception is made up of two ideograms: sign and mind.

We have difficulty identifying an external world outside of our consciousness of it. How can we step outside our consciousness of the world to know the world? The objects we think are outside of ourselves in the world are connected to the objects of our own mind. Through the mind, a world of experience comes to be.

Mindfulness can get you in touch with this process. The realization can be liberating, especially with entrenched problems. Once there is a recognition of how thinking intertwines with the objects of the world, we can take steps to change the mind side of the equation, which inevitably alters the situation.

Sit quietly in meditation and bring your awareness to the flow of thoughts. What are you thinking about? In other words, what is the object of thought? Each thought has the *I* part, the thinker, and the *object* part, what is being thought about. Can you recognize how you are representing this object from your own perspective?

Practicing Mindful Thinking in Everyday Life

Expand mindfulness practice by turning your attention to your thinking at times during the day. Take a reflective moment here and there to observe beyond the content of thinking, to thought itself. Notice the thinking process, the objects of thought, and whether the thoughts are wholesome or unwholesome. Stay with this experience for a little while. By making a deliberate effort to be mindful through the day, thinking begins to clarify and entrenched habits become easier to change.

Bringing It All Together: Mindful in the Moment

Gestalt therapy founder Fritz Perls (1893–1970) said, "And I believe that this is the great thing to understand: that awareness per se, of and by itself, is curative" (Perls, 1969, pp. 15–16). These wise words can be put into practice with the regular practice of mindfulness.

Now that you have experimented with various ways of being mindful, bring yourself to the present moment whenever you can. Scan your body to raise your body awareness. To become mindful of your emotions, observe what you are feeling. Notice your mental activity. What are you thinking or perceiving? Pay close attention to the objects of your perceptions. These four qualities of mindfulness can be done quickly, centering you in the present. Once you are in touch with the moment's experiencing, can you let all this go and just be present without any thought?

Notice how your experience transforms moment by moment. Stay with each moment anew. Whenever you can, at various times during the day, turn your attention to your experience. Get in touch mindfully as often as you can. In time, mindfulness will feel natural. You will not only recognize when you are being mindful, but also know when you are not being mindful. Knowing the difference will be a helpful tool for attuning to the therapeutic process and can be helpful in bringing about real changes in everyday life.

Traditional Zazen

Please try releasing your hold. Open your hands. Just let everything go, and see: What is body and mind. What are daily activities? . . . Take a careful look at these things again and again.

(Dogen in Tanahashi, 1985, p. 31)

Mindfulness helps to become aware of what is occurring in experience, moment to moment. But clients can also develop skills they need to let go and move forward. Years of living with problems can be difficult to transcend, even when they are resolved psychologically. One of the great traditions in meditation, zazen, is known to help clear the mind and let go. Zazen teaches you how to let go of distractions that interfere with your clear awareness, a valuable tool for truly becoming free of difficulties.

People sometimes think the answer is to just get rid of their problems, like wiping the dust off a mirror. Even if we could take away problems like wiping dust off a mirror, doing so, nothing is learned and so much would be lost. Similarly, novice meditators sometimes think meditation will simply empty their mind of all thought. But such a goal is not only unrealistic, it would also be ineffective. Similarly, with meditation, the purpose is not to stop thinking. The effects are transformative. The following classic Zen story guides meditators away from superficial efforts.

A Zen student was trying very hard to make his mind clear like a mirror. He sat quietly and tried to think of nothing. But thoughts inevitably kept distracting him. Feeling in despair, he asked his master, "No matter how hard I try, I cannot clear my mind! What should I do?"

The master picked up a tile that was on the ground and began polishing it with his robe. Confused, the student asked, "Master, what are you doing?"

"I am polishing this tile to make it into a mirror."

Figure 5.4   Mirror Reflection (acrylic on paper)
Source: Carmen Z. Simpkins, American artist, 1975

"That's impossible! You cannot make a tile into a mirror," said the student. The master smiled. "Nor can you make your mind perfectly clear!"

Meditation brings out capacities that are already there, clearing away obstructions to let the deeper self shine through. In this sense, you don't have to change the mind you have or add anything new. Think of your mind as similar to a murky lake that becomes clear when the mud settles to the bottom. The potential for clarity is there in the lake, but the sediment is stirred up. All you need to do is allow everything to settle (Figure 5.4).

Sit quietly and try not to think about anything. Stay with each moment, without adding any thoughts. Inevitably, thoughts will crop up. As a thought occurs, notice it but let it go. Then return to thinking of nothing. Continue to notice any thoughts that come up, but try not to get involved in them. As soon as you can, return yourself to no thought. Eventually your thoughts will slow down, leaving you with a clear, calm consciousness.

Walking Meditation

Zen monks would traditionally intersperse their long day of meditation with walking meditation. Using the mindful meditation, stand up and begin walking slowly. Hold your hands together, palms touching. Walk slowly, with awareness on every step. Pay attention to how your foot meets the ground. Notice how your weight shifts from foot to foot. Keep your breathing and your body relaxed as you walk slowly. And maintain your mindful awareness of every step.

Fast Walking

When you are comfortable with the slow walking meditation, try fast walking. The monks used this meditation for exercise. Fast walking can be vigorous, stimulating, and challenging.

Allow your arms to hang at your sides and move freely as you walk. Take long strides and move quickly. Even though you are moving fast, maintain full awareness of every step. Be aware of weight shifts, how your foot meets the ground, how your body naturally coordinates with the movements. Stay fully focused on the moment-to-moment experience with a clear mind.

Searching for Your True Nature

This meditation is drawn directly from Zen Master Hakuin. Think carefully about this exchange. Clarify it for yourself. Hakuin advised people to keep thinking about it with single-minded devotion no matter what they were doing. So reflect upon these questions deeply, relying only on yourself. The answers can only be found within.

A student asked Hakuin, "What can I do to become awakened to my own mind?"

Hakuin answered with a series of questions: What is it that asks the question? Is it your mind? Is it your original nature? Is it some kind of spirit or demon? Is it inside you? Outside you? Is it somewhere in between? Is it blue, yellow, red, or white?

(Waddell, 1994, p. 61)

Koans

The idea is to unfold the Zen psychology in the mind of the uninitiated and to reproduce the state of consciousness of which these [koan] statements are the expression. That is to say, when the koans are understood, the master's state of mind is understood, which is satori and without which Zen is a sealed book.

(D. T. Suzuki, 1994, p. 81)

Koans are a unique teaching method that incorporate paradoxical stories and accounts from great Zen masters. The tradition, begun by Bodhidharma, was to be beyond words and letters (see Chapter 3), and so the use of words in Zen is used to provoke an experience beyond reason. Western thought typically proceeds through reason. We learn early in school to induce consequences from the idea of *either/or*, the Aristotelian logic of being versus nonbeing: either something is, or is not. Zen koans pose a different situation. A higher synthesis can be found, sparked by paradox, confusion, and not knowing. Milton Erickson incorporated similar interventions with his famous confusion technique that elicited a gap in perception, leading to change. With koans, the student struggles with a paradoxical problem that cannot be solved using logic. And in the struggle, the student is transformed.

We have chosen several classic and adapted koans that are most helpful for therapeutic change for you to try here. We offer others in the application chapters of this book. Take some time to contemplate each of these koans.

Ma-tzu's Stick

The stick of Chinese Zen Master Ma-tzu (709–788) is a famous koan that has been presented to students for many centuries. Ma-tzu held up a stick and then said, "If you call this a stick, I will hit you with it. If you don't call it a stick, I will hit you with it. Quickly, now, what is it?" The use of language in this koan creates the threat of punishment no matter how you answer. What should you say? You are faced with an insoluble problem, a double bind, what Gregory Bateson called "mutually contradictory commands being given by a person in authority with the threat of punishment if both commands were not carried out" (Low, 1995, p. 13). To the unenlightened, double binds are uncomfortable. They don't give meaning; they give confusion. But from a Zen master, the relationship between language use and its context in koans is a way to communicate the subtleties that facilitate enlightenment for the student.

A relationship is necessary for the double bind to work. Nearly all communications occur on two levels because of the context of meaning. The two levels of communication involve the class and the member of the class. The context is the background that gives meaning. A koan remains a double bind if we are stuck within the usual use of language and its context. But koans invite us to consider a new perspective, a new meaning for the word *stick,* lest we be (symbolically) struck.

Think About Nothing

One of our favorite koans is a modern adaptation that we have asked people of all ages. It engages an active search process. Once you let yourself get started, you may be surprised at how your thinking processes evolve.

Think about nothing but don't think anything about it.

Here are a few typical responses we have heard that might get you started: "How can I think about nothing without thinking something about it? Isn't nothing something?" "As soon as I think about nothing, I'm thinking about something: nothing! But that doesn't make sense."

Now, what do you think?

Practicing a Zen Art

When Westerners were first introduced to Zen, they were often encouraged to use the learning of a Zen art as a doorway into the experience. Eugen Herrigel, one of the first Westerners (1884–1955) to formally learn Zen in Japan, was told that he would only be taught Zen if he agreed to study a Zen art. He chose archery, and his wife, Gustie, picked flower arrangement, which they both expressed in books about their experiences (E. Herrigel, 1971; G. Herrigel, 1958). We have encouraged clients to engage in activity as a Zen art at times, such as our client Jennifer, who practiced gardening (Chapter 1); Andrew, who took up martial arts (Chapter 6); and Nancy, who found fulfillment in cooking (Chapter 9). When you enter into a Zen art, you not only learn artistic skills, but also develop your mind in the Zen Way. This is a viable pathway to experience enlightenment.

We offer instructions for creating haiku poetry, which can be easily integrated into treatment to offer clients a way to express themselves intuitively and nonrationally. Any form of art can be performed meditatively, so use the client's talents, either latent or expressed.

Haiku Specifics

Haiku has a simple, but very distinctive format: three lines, 17 syllables. Much like the other Zen arts, Haiku expresses certain values. With simplicity to the point of scarcity, this skeletal number of words points to an entire experience. Haiku is not romantic, lacking elaborate sentiments. Like Zen enlightenment, haiku is immediate, expressing the writer's direct experience and bringing the listener right there with him (or her) into the moment. The themes often center around nature, usually a small occurrence, thereby showing the significance of every moment, like this poem:

> Cool rain trickles down
> Quiet music soothes the street
> Peaceful emptiness
> (C. Alexander Simpkins)

Haiku Instructions

You can write your own haiku. Follow the simple rules for classical Japanese Haiku given earlier in which each poem has 17 syllables and three lines, with the form of five-seven-five. Modern haiku may deviate somewhat from the exact syllable count, although three lines is usual. The idea is to keep the poem short and express yourself with a minimum of words. There should be some reference to nature as it occurs now as a particular, concrete event or experience. Generalizations and abstractions are not considered Zen haiku. Keep the rules in mind as guidelines to help you get in touch with your poetic Zen spirit.

CONCLUSION

These methods are best learned and understood in their practice. As Dogen said, practice is enlightenment, which implies that you will not truly know these techniques without doing them yourself. And so, we encourage therapists to work with these techniques. Clients should be encouraged to work with these methods over time as well. Skills improve with practice, and so don't be discouraged if something seems difficult at first. Start small, with a few minutes of practice, and build from there. The positive results are well worth the effort!

III

Overcoming Clients' Suffering

From the root, we get the essence.

—(Zen Saying)

This old Zen saying gives us a new perspective on psychological problems. Our field has created helpful distinctions for discerning different disorders, carefully delineated in the *Diagnostic and Statistical Manual of Mental Disorders* (DSM-IV-R). However, many problems share common roots that, when addressed, can add intensity to your protocols. Each chapter in Part III deals with pivotal roots (emotions and affect, attention and sensation, impulse to action, and interpersonal relationships) as central features in a number of psychological problems. With examples from successful treatments and specific techniques to apply, you can help your clients tame the tiger of disturbance.

Chapter 6 provides a general protocol for integrating meditation into your treatments at every phase. Chapter 7 gives the latest models of emotion with the brain science behind them. You will learn why meditation is helpful with emotions, along with ways to apply it for problems such as depression and anger. Chapter 8 deals with anxiety and trauma, where attention and sensations are at the root of the problem. Chapter 9 addresses impulse control, including addiction and weight management. We are wired for loving relationships, and Chapter 10 shows how to facilitate these natural capacities for fulfilling attachments.

6

The Way of Zen Therapy: Following the Path for Treatment

In time's flowing moments problems seem
In truth's clear vision, they are only a dream
Beyond the horizon of all that we see
Problems disappear in totality.
                                        (C. Alexander Simpkins)

Psychological problems seem to take over, and the sufferer feels like the problem is everything. But we can all gain strength from the firm experiential realization, felt in Zen meditation, that we are more real than any problem, no matter how severe it may seem. Ultimately, Zen meditation brings us to face the fact that we are not just our problems. Sitting quietly and accepting both pleasant and unpleasant thoughts, feelings, and sensations, just as they are, we come to gain a certain inner strength and resilience.

The best way to add this source of strength for your client is to instill a clear, aware, and centered sense of being in the moment. Developing this realization begins where you are, in the midst of the problem itself. Not rational or conceptual, this felt sense is developed best using Zen meditation and mindfulness. You can make these meditation methods a viable part of the therapeutic approach you already practice. These meditation techniques fit seamlessly with most therapeutic protocols, adding an important dimension to treatment. This chapter presents an outline for a meditative therapeutic process that can be woven into the fabric of your treatments. Further details for using Zen meditations with specific problems are offered in Part III.

Zen Master Bankei was giving a talk for other Buddhist masters at a gathering, much like our modern conventions. As he was speaking, a monk stood up and said boldly, "The founder of *my* approach can really do something. Our method is far more powerful than yours. He can hold up a paintbrush on one side of a stream, while one of his disciples holds up paper on the other side. Then, our founder writes the name *Buddha* in the air and the name appears on the paper! I bet you can't do that!"

Bankei smiled and answered with a twinkle in his eye, "Magic tricks are one thing. But the true strength of what I am teaching is that when I feel hunger, I eat, and when I feel tired, I sleep."

Clients often hope that we can wave a magic wand to make their problems disappear. But the real magic they are seeking is to be able to get a good night's sleep, and do what they need and want in a day without hindrance from their problems. Zen offers this simple, yet profound capacity—open to anyone who is willing to enter on the meditative path.

BEYOND DIAGNOSIS

Myra came into the office looking visibly distraught. She was a homemaker in her 70s. Although she wore an expensive suit and had a stylish haircut, her face was pale and her makeup was slightly smudged. Her husband had died of cancer several years ago. She told us that she couldn't get past the overwhelming grief she continued to feel. She recognized that as time passed, she seemed to be getting worse, not better.

As she began to describe her feelings, tears flowed. "I miss him terribly. Life is empty without him." We listened carefully to what she said. But we also observed her as she spoke and noticed that her fists were clenched and her jaw set tight. While acknowledging her grief and how we could see the magnitude of her loss, we gently inquired as to what her fist might be trying to communicate. She paused in her weeping, and sat wordless for several minutes. Then, her face turned bright red and her eyes opened wide as she admitted with vehemence and surprise, "Why, that son of a gun! He up and left me! I'm furious with him!" Then her entire body relaxed and her tears stopped. We worked on helping her to recognize the full range of feelings that she had been ignoring, and over the course of several sessions, she learned to accept all of her feelings. Now unified in thought, feeling, and action, she found her sadness diminished as feelings of gratitude emerged, appreciating the wonderful years she had shared with her husband. After just three sessions, Myra began reengaging in the supportive relationships she had with her adult children, grandchildren, and long-time friends. By encountering Myra fully, with all that she brought into the first moment, we helped her to engage with the fullness of her deeper self. And in doing so, she made peace with death and returned to living.

Therapists are tasked with assessing what is the real problem. We have well laid out protocols to follow, with the different disorders clearly delineated. The DSM-IV provides ways to assess a client's symptoms and behaviors. And all of these tools are helpful for categorizing the problem into a known diagnosis of what is wrong. But we can do more. Once the diagnosis has been made, you can assess the client by opening your perception meditatively to gain a fuller perspective. Chapter 12 on therapeutic acumen offers you many ways to activate your own therapeutic sensitivities for better initial observations as well as sensitive attunement throughout the treatment protocol.

The philosopher Martin Heidegger (1889–1976) pointed out a way to understand why categories, though helpful, can be limiting. He asked, how can you truly know the *rockness* of a rock by categorizing it? Simply dividing it into smaller pieces, weighing it, and looking at its properties may tell you a great deal about what it is like, but what it is, its essence, its *rockness,* escapes such analysis (Heidegger, 2002). We can apply this idea similarly with our clients. We need to categorize the symptoms, noting which ones they have and how often the symptoms occur, but we should do so always with the idea that the true deeper nature of the client always transcends the diagnosis. We don't just treat the problem; we address the whole person, and in so doing, find creative solutions that draw on the unique resources and capacities arising from the client's innermost nature.

EARLY PHASE: GIVING THE CLIENT TOOLS

When clients enter therapy, they often lack the tools they need to succeed. We might ask them to tell us what they are thinking or feeling, but they have trouble deliberately directing their attention to inner experiencing. They are usually caught up in attitudes about what they think and feel, often blaming other people or outer situations. So, a portion of the early phase of ther- apy involves teaching preliminary tools. Skills involve training attention and balancing affect. You can use these exercises, and the focus meditations in Chapter 5, at the beginning or end of each session, encouraging clients to practice between sessions as homework. This chapter includes sample exer- cises to introduce the initial phase of therapy, but you will find many more training exercises as part of the application chapters.

Training Attention

Attention is an important capacity of the mind and brain, involving multiple behaviors and brain systems (Zillmer, Spires, & Culbertson, 2008). We use attention in meditation, and so these skills will help clients be able to learn meditation more easily. Clients may have deficits in one aspect of attention while remaining capable in others. You can offer clients different training exercises that can improve areas that are not working well and help build on the attentional strengths the client already has.

Different Kinds of Attention

The brain has a number of different pathways that correlate with different aspects of attention with many different models. One useful paradigm for therapists divides attention into three distinct brain systems. Each serves a different attentional function and can be trained.

The first kind of attention is deliberate and conscious. It involves attend- ing to word meanings and getting ready for action, such as planning, in- terpreting, and selecting what to do from a group of possibilities. It engages top-down control and is responsible for strategic placement of attention, both toward action. This form of attention correlates with activation of the front of the brain in frontal lobe, particularly engaging the anterior cingulate gyrus, and the prefrontal cortex. These areas form connections to the basal ganglia and the thalamus to help carry out the directing of attention. These areas are used in focus meditations (see Chapter 5 for focus meditation instructions).

Attention is activated, achieved, and maintained in an alert or vigilant state. Vigilance is sustained attention, that ability to maintain alertness and focus of attention for a prolonged period. Arousal is one of the key components that keeps us vigilant and is correlated with the subcortical brain regions of the reticular activating system. Higher brain areas are also activated when we are vigilant: The parietal lobe, the prefrontal cortex in the right hemisphere, and the superior temporal cortex in both hemispheres.

A posterior system includes a selective process of attention that happens bottom-up, for orienting automatically. This system is also involved when we disengage attention selectively from unimportant stimuli to focus on more relevant or new stimuli. Visual orienting is activated in the parietal lobe, responsible for focusing on a specific relevant location in space. The system engages visual, motor, and auditory pathways to direct our attention by moving the body and the eyes toward the object of attention. The superior colliculus, located in the midbrain, is involved with eye movements. The thalamus, as the relay station for the senses, plays an important role in picking out salient features in the environment. For more details on the neuroscience of attention, see our book, *The Dao of Neuroscience* (C. A. Simpkins & Simpkins, 2010a).

Training Deliberate Attention

Concentration is one of the tools of deliberate attention. When people do not concentrate well, they often have a degraded ability to recognize what they are experiencing as well as a poor reality sense. Such attention deficits can lead to psychological problems involving deluded thinking and rumination. People with ADHD often have difficulty concentrating, and as a result, their learning ability suffers. Other psychological problems such as depression, bipolarity, and anxiety also interfere with concentration of attention as well.

Through exercises that concentrate the attention on specific objects, you can bring deliberate attention under control, developing it more fully for use with meditation and in therapy. Similar to how exercise builds fitness, these exercises build attentional fitness.

Deliberate Observation

Observation is an important component of attention. People are often looking at one thing but thinking about something else. Learning to attend to what you observe will improve attention measurably. And experience will lead to the development of skills helpful for meditation.

One natural way to train the attention can be drawn from your everyday life. Observe the things presented to your senses. For example, go for a walk outdoors in nature—in the woods, a park, the desert, or the seashore. Time yourself, beginning with just a few minutes to make it manageable. As you walk, look at all the colors you can. Notice the spectrum, with its hues and tones. Then, making note of the time, look at the shapes of things as you walk along. Next, take a few minutes to notice textures. Pick one quality at a time and observe it carefully. You may choose to focus on a sense other than the visual—on sounds, for example, or smells. To end this exercise, spend a few minutes observing what you see—including colors, shapes, textures, and anything else that you notice. You will probably find that with practice, you notice more than you did when you began.

Testing Observation to Improve It

Walk into a room, look around for 1 minute, and then leave. Now attempt to describe everything in the room: the objects, the room itself, the atmosphere, the lighting. If you are doing this alone, you may find it helpful to jot down on paper what you remember. Return and compare the actual experience to your remembered one. Again, now, observe carefully. Spend a bit more time: 5 minutes. Observe carefully. Then leave and describe the room and its contents. Return. How many things do you notice this time? How detailed is your description?

Enhance Posterior Attention Through Relaxed Seeing

Seeing is an important component of automatic, bottom-up attention processing, but our eyes are often exhausted. We make great demands on our eyes in both work and play. Many jobs require long hours looking at a computer screen. We strain to read small print sometimes in poor light conditions. And then for leisure, many spend hours staring at the small glittering screen of a television. Rarely do we think about our eyes unless they become a problem to us. Eyes, however, just like other parts of the body, can be relaxed and freed from rigid patterns. Viable methods for training and improving vision were developed and used in Yoga and were later rediscovered in other systems. We include here some exercises that will help you to become more relaxed in your eyes, which will help with attention skills.

Eye Swings

Stand comfortably, weight balanced evenly between your two feet with hands at your sides. Begin to gently swing your arms around from one side of your body to the other. Allow your body to twist with your arms, pivoting your feet as well. Let your head turn while keeping it level and straight, along with your body. As you make each swing, keep your eyes relaxed and directed straight ahead, so that your field of vision moves with you as you move. Your surroundings may seem to rush past you. Do not stop your head from flowing with the movement. After several minutes of pivots, back and forth, your eyes will feel looser.

Palming

The eyes can become very tired, and this tension carries through your whole body. Palming can relieve and relax your eyes. Sit or lie down comfortably. Close your eyes. Place your palms very lightly over your eyelids. Your fingertips can rest on the top of your forehead. Do not press. Rest for several minutes. Allow your eyes to relax beneath your palms. Let go of any unnecessary tension you might notice in your face.

Training Vigilance

All of us have experienced the effort needed to stay awake or focused on a boring class or work assignment. This is an example of the use of vigilance. Vigilance is developed, in part, through the discipline of deliberately attending to something over time. With practice, it becomes easier to stay focused.

Begin by circling your arms, moving your legs a bit to raising your energy level so that you feel alert. Stretch your muscles a bit, as if warming up for exercise. Let your breathing be comfortable and open. Then, sit down and look at this classic Zen image of the fundamental shapes, circle, square, and triangle (Figure 6.1). Let your attention focus on this picture and only this picture. If your attention wanders, gently bring it back to focus on the picture as soon as you notice. Sustain your attention for one minute. Keep trying until you can keep it focused without wandering for one full minute. When you succeed with this amount of time, extend the time to two minutes. If you feel that you are becoming less alert, take a break, move your body a bit, and take a deep breath. Then try again. You will find that your attention span improves with practice.

Figure 6.1   Circle, Square, Triangle

Balancing Affect

Skills in affect regulation can begin by working with physiological response. From this perspective, the body can become a means to regulate emotions. Every cell is alive and active, with a kind of intelligence. All the parts work together in vibrant harmony. The nervous system allows us to interface from body to brain, to thoughts and feelings, setting in motion a healing process.

Emotion is processed in two ways: through a short path that goes directly from the stimulus through the thalamus to the amygdala, and a long path that is intercepted by higher order processing from the cortex. Both the short and long paths can be enlisted to help regulate affect, using specific techniques for working with each.

The automatic, unconscious, short pathway of emotions can be influenced by body methods that use the organism's built-in ability to balance itself instinctively. The long path deliberately enlists higher level cortical processing to have sensations deliberately bring about a corrective experience by, for example, becoming calmer or more vitalized.

Short Path Affect Regulation

Begin by lying prone on a wooden floor, mat, rug, or the grass outdoors. Rest your hands by your side on the floor, palms up. Close your eyes. Pay attention to the point of contact between you and the floor and feel any sensation you might notice. Do your arms and legs rest gently on the floor or are you holding them up or pushing them down? Allow the surface to fully support you by letting your body to sink down into the surface. Using your attention, notice sensations, starting with your feet and moving up through all parts of your body. Don't change anything, simply notice and allow any natural relaxation that occurs. If you practice this exercise when feeling emotionally stirred, you may find that the reaction settles naturally.

Long Path Affect Regulation by Easing Tensions

Lying prone, start at your head by paying attention to your face. If you discovered tension in a particular area such as in your eyes, forehead, or lips, turn your attention there. First, carefully trace out how you are holding these muscles, then, if possible, allow these muscles to relax. Letting go involves an opening, releasing feeling. Muscles will feel softer, lighter, larger, or smoother. Breathe comfortably and let the tension go with each exhalation of breath. Then direct attention down toward your shoulders. Pay close attention to them. Notice whether you are holding the muscles tight, and let go, if possible. If you noticed that your shoulders were held away from the floor, can you let them sink down and take support from the surface? Continue down through your body, first paying close attention and then trying to relax any extra tension. You may be surprised to notice areas that are held tight, but don't need to be. If attention wanders away from to outer concerns, bring it back. Do not force yourself to relax. Simply notice where you can or cannot relax, and gently keep trying to let go of unnecessary tension.

DEVELOPING MINDFUL AWARENESS

With some training of attention and better skills with affect regulation, we encourage introducing mindfulness training. Some clients can learn mindfulness training right away, but others will do better if they ease into it with the earlier training. Clients can practice between sessions, and will find that if you make the training clear, they will bring in interesting experiences to work through in therapy.

Nonjudgmental Awareness

Introduce mindfulness by explaining nonjudgmental awareness. This opens the way for clients to begin to observe themselves in a nonthreatening way. It builds a logical bridge to mindfulness meditation. Feelings, thoughts, and behaviors are to be observed and accepted as they are, and in doing so, become easier to handle. A process of self-acceptance is set in motion from the beginning.

Sharon, a woman in her mid-thirties, had suffered from anxiety attacks for years. She experienced an unusual childhood, growing up in a commune, moving from place to place in her early years. She told us that she had poor eyesight as a child, but that it wasn't diagnosed until she attended her first regular school in eighth grade. She felt unsure whether she had been sexually abused as a young child. All of the erratic experiences she had as a child left her with a feeling that something was wrong with her. She and her siblings all continued to have an uneasy and vaguely threatened experience of the world. To cope with this discomfort, she had become a highly motivated and successful professional. She had a take-charge personality, strong, highly rational, and organized. She had an excellent intellect, although she admitted, that she overused it. But despite all of her efforts to be in control, she still suffered from intense anxiety. Her thoughts raced in a continually disturbing monologue of all the things that could go wrong while also planning and arranging circumstances so they wouldn't. We could see early on that although she was bright and highly capable, she had lost touch with her deeper, true nature.

In the opening phase of therapy, we introduced the idea of the nonjudgmental attitude to begin a process of getting in touch mindfully of where she was and what she was experiencing, moment by moment. We asked her to carefully observe what she noticed during the week, but with a difference from her usual critical assessments. Instead, she was to set her judgments about these experiences aside and simply notice all the details, like a scientist collecting data. As she began to observe, she told us that things were shifting. She said, "As I observe, I felt something is loosening up—I'm not sure what." She began to see that she was very adept with the front of her mind but didn't know much about the back of her mind. She came to recognize that anxiety had a bigger grip on her daily life than she had thought.

We used hypnosis with her to help her let go and call forth her unconscious processing, allowing her natural, wordless, intuitive sense of things to emerge. Over time she learned to trust her intuition and was able to make decisions not just from her head but also from her heart. By starting with nonjudgmental awareness, she was able to tolerate some of the things she observed, and instead of feeling threatened by them, learned from them. Her anxiety subsided over time, as she began to make meaningful changes. She set a priority on improving her relationship with her husband, improving her relationships with her extended family, and having a child, which she intuitively knew that she truly wanted. Through these changes, she found herself living in the kind of comfortable and safe world that she had always dreamed of finding.

Bringing Mindfulness into Treatment

The section on mindfulness in Chapter 5 gives instructions for introducing the nonjudgmental attitude and performing mindfulness meditations. You can practice these meditations as part of the session until clients feel able to sustain the practice on their own. Encourage them to set aside several different times in the week to meditate. And encourage them to be mindful as they go through their day. They will bring in helpful material to work through, discovered from what they observe using the methods. Keep returning to mindfulness to help develop an aware, centered adjustment. We often devote a portion of each session to meditation or hypnosis. This gives clients a moment of calm, centered time that they come to rely on for relief. They gradually get to experience their deeper nature, unfettered by the obstructions of their conflicts. This healthy part of them grows stronger over time, making it easier to overcome the obstructions that stand in the way.

Raising Expectancies for Change: Impermanence

Clients come to therapy hoping to change, but they often feel like they can't. Early psychotherapy research found hope to be a powerful force for healing and hopelessness a primary aspect of mental disorders. When therapy is effective, it raises expectancies that change is possible (J. D. Frank & Frank, 1991).

Impermanence is the idea that things are always changing. According to Buddhism, nothing endures (see Chapter 4 and C. A. Simpkins & Simpkins, 2000). This concept can be good news for those with long-standing problems, and raises the hope that change is not only possible, but inevitable. If change is the true nature of the universe, then even a person with stubborn problems can change. It offers a ray of hope that their suffering can't last forever. By teaching clients about the impermanence of thoughts and the fleeting nature of feelings, they start a process of transformation. For those who want to go deeper, they can grapple with the Buddhist idea that all things in the universe are impermanent. Impermanence becomes a source for hope with clients who are stuck in an uncomfortable environment or a difficult situation.

Andrew was a juvenile delinquent with a long criminal record. He came to therapy because of an event that occurred just before his 18th birthday. He was driving on a quiet road behind another car when suddenly the car slowed down. Andrew grew impatient and started honking. But the car continued to crawl along the road. Andrew was steaming. He followed the car to a fast food restaurant and pulled into the parking lot closely behind the other driver. Then he grabbed his nunchaku (a weapon made of two hard sticks connected by a metal chain), from the backseat of his car and jumped out, ready to take out his rage on the unsuspecting driver. Fortunately, an off-duty policewoman was also in the parking lot, and quickly intervened before Andrew could take action. Andrew was arrested and sent to jail for the night. Since nothing had quite happened, he was offered a second chance if he would undergo 10 weeks of psychotherapy. Reluctantly, he agreed to do so, with the understanding that on turning 18, his record would be sealed shut and he could start his adult life with a clean slate.

When he came into our office, he told us right away that he was there because he had to be. He said that he really didn't think too much of therapy and planned to just mark his time until it was over. We acknowledged his skepticism and told him we would just talk a little bit and could teach him some meditation if he was interested. He said, "Meditation's dope (meaning very good)." But he also added, "So, we can do this, but it's really a waste of time."

We asked him about himself. He told us that he had a tough life and had to engage in petty crime to make ends meet. He had learned from his father, who was currently serving a long jail sentence for armed robbery, that work was for the weak. Crime paid better. His father's only problem was that he wasn't as smart as Andrew, proven by the fact that his father got caught and he hadn't been. He described himself: "I'm a punk looking for a fight." As we talked with Andrew, we could clearly see that he was convinced that the world was a jungle, and it was never going to change. He just had to do the best he could to survive.

We began by teaching him mindful breathing. We pointed out how each breath was different, and he was able to experience each breath anew.

We talked about the Buddhist idea of impermanence, but he scoffed at us. "Nothing changes in this #@& world." His language was always heavily laced with expletives. We challenged him to observe between sessions. "We bet you will see that life is filled with impermanence. Things are always changing. It's just that you aren't really looking."

He prided himself on being a savvy observer, so he said, "You're on," Then he shook hands to seal the bet.

The next week, he returned with a hint of eagerness showing through his cool-man attitude. He admitted that at first he thought it was bull. But he decided to humor us and observe the people at the bar where he hung out. He knew that the same people went there every night and nothing ever changed, so he figured he would easily prove us wrong. But each night he noticed more change than he had ever registered before. True, the same people were there, but things were different. For example, the first night his friend was bragging about how tough he was, but then the very next night this friend returned with a black eye and arm in a sling, having engaged in a big fight after he left the bar the night before. By the end of the week, Andrew had to admit that things really did change, much more than he had ever expected.

After this insight, we could offer some hope for Andrew to take charge of changes in his own life. Previously, he had never considered doing anything except crime; but as he continued to practice mindfulness in the sessions, he started thinking about what he might do. The only thing he enjoyed was fighting, so we suggested, why not get involved in martial arts? He had always thought karate was stupid, but he had never actually looked into it. Since we are both martial artists, we were able to have a detailed discussion about its merits as a Zen art that not only could give him something positive to do, but could also transform him.

By the time the 10 sessions were completed, Andrew had joined a martial arts school and was truly enjoying it. Also, he showed talent, since he was a good fighter. He continued to practice his meditation, and dropped by for a session from time to time. Several years later, after being awarded his black belt, he told us that he was earning money as a teacher at the dojo (karate school). He liked helping others to learn. And he enjoyed developing skills in fighting as an art and a sport. He had finally found meaning for his life, which all became possible when he recognized that life is filled with impermanence and so, from a positive perspective, things really could change.

Working With Resistance

People resist change for many reasons, some rational, some irrational. Our learned limitations hold us back, our beliefs about what we can and cannot do. One way to overcome such limitations is accomplished through reframing, offering a new perspective. But more often, rational approaches fall short. Using nonrational methods that appeal to the unconscious can bypass resistance, so that people just find themselves able to do what they could not accomplish before.

Koans offer one way to bypass the conscious mind, since the answer to a koan requires giving up conscious thought. We have used koans to help people break out of limited ways of thinking, to draw on different options. With clients who suffer from what the existential philosophers called hardening of the categories, offer a koan to consider. Here are a few possibilities to help people to break out of rigid thought patterns:

> Put your left hand behind your back. Now tell me, which hand is left?
> What is the sound of one hand clapping?
> When the wind blows, does the flag move, does the wind move, or does your mind move?

WORKING THROUGH: ENTERING THE VOID

> The mind that stops or is moved by something and sent into confusion—this is the affliction of the abiding place, and that is the common man. To be called, to respond without interval, is the wisdom of all Buddhas.
>
> (Takuan, 1986, p. 29)

Through mindfulness and acceptance of experiencing just as it is, clients come to a point of impasse. They have worked on conflicts, come to understand a great deal about how they got where they are, what binds them, and how these conflicted patterns prevent them from being happy or fulfilled. They wake up to an awareness of how they have been stuck. They observe that what they did before is no longer satisfying. And yet, what lies ahead is unknown. Now the client stands in the midst of nothingness—emptiness—the void. This is the point of pure process, *no-thingness,* an experience that is fundamental for deep and lasting change.

Most Westerners are brought up to fear the void. We spend much of our lives keeping busy since we certainly wouldn't want to do just nothing. But meditation teaches us in a real, experiential way, that emptiness is the foundation for all that is. When we enter the quiet, empty moment, we find that the void is not something to fear. Instead, emptiness is the creative moment when anything becomes possible. Nothing is there to stand in the way and so, growth, release, and transcendence can happen. New potential emerges, a miniature enlightenment, with an opportunity to move into new territory.

At this empty impasse, the void point in therapy, we introduce Zen meditation. Zen is that open, empty moment of allowing experience to be just as it is, the nonstopping mind of Takuan, the positive unconscious, open and without any object of focus. Zen meditation helps people to stay in the void, to experience it deeply and fully. Therein, the clients discover their path. Please revisit the instructions in Chapter 5 for Zen meditations, and find other ways to access emptiness in the application chapters.

When we can allow Zen emptiness to emerge, illusions are dispelled and conflicts dissolve. We become One with our own inner nature, without a problem. Perceptions become clearer, mind more concentrated and focused, and the energy of life is collected and gathered. What needs to be done can be done. The mind, cleared by meditation, can recognize the new direction it wants to follow. From the deepest, true nature, what is truly meaningful arises. Like the client who discovers a real interest to pursue, or uncovers a hidden talent, or has the courage to follow up on a longtime dream, the path to follow becomes clear. In the final phase of therapy, the meditating client embraces emptiness, through direct pointing to her true nature. As Mumon, also known as Ekai (1183-1260), wrote in the famous koan collection the *Mumonkon*:

> The great path has no gates,
> Thousands of roads enter it.
> When one passes through this gateless gate
> He walks freely between heaven and earth.
>
> (Reps, 1980, p. 114)

CONCLUSION

This chapter has presented a paradigm to draw upon, a framework for integrating meditation into therapy. You can begin the process by training attention meditatively. Mindful awareness in the moment can bring attention to deeper issues that emerge, now available to awareness for working through. By accepting what is noticed without judgment, a calm, clear nature emerges to be experienced. Problems dissolve and so people can let go of past difficulties as they experience the present moment, empty and open. We invite you to make these methods your own with creative individualizing, as all good therapists do.

7

Regulating Affect for Anger and Depression

When the mind is clear of illusion, we are enlightened, but when illusions are there, the mind is in agony. Humans create illusions, and by continuing to create illusions, we remain miserable. Enlightened beings stop using illusion to create more illusions. And by no longer using illusions to create more illusions, we live with peace of mind.
—(Paraphrased from Bodhidharma's Wake-Up Sermon)

MODERATING ANGER

We revisit the dialogue with Zen Master Bankei to learn how to reexperience situations for calmness. The monk said, "I know I should do something about it, but I was born this way and there's nothing I can do to stop it."

Bankei asked him, "Well then, show me your anger now."

The monk replied, "Oh, I'm not angry now. My temper just pops out at unexpected times, when someone provokes me. It's just the way I am!"

Bankei said, "Well, if you aren't angry now and it comes and goes when someone else provokes you, you couldn't have been born with it. The only thing you really inherited from your parents was your original nature. Everything else you have created yourself."

The monk was very surprised and felt hopeful that maybe he could change his outbursts. Bankei went on to explain that the source of his feeling was his opinions, tastes, and insistence that things had to be a certain way. When other people viewed matters differently, he felt enraged. He encouraged the monk to let go of these arbitrary definitions and be open to new possibilities.

Emotions are closest to us, and yet, often seem to be the furthest from our control. They pervade all aspects of living, helping to add color and texture to everything we think and do. Intuitively, we know how vital emotions are to us, and neuroscience research may have some explanations as to why. With emotions as a central feature of awareness itself, we can see why problems with emotions are at the core of many psychological disorders. This chapter explores the core quality of psychological disturbance: working with emotions and regulating affect to find a healthy, happy balance. We begin by delving into the nature of emotions themselves with new theories that reveal how emotions are part of our mind, brain, and body. We offer meditative treatments to balance affect, calm anger, and overcome depression.

THEORIES OF EMOTION AND AFFECT

One of the early theories of emotions was proposed by a founding father of modern psychology, William James. Emotion begins as a response to a situation with physiological sensations, such as muscle tension, increased heart rate, and perspiration. The feelings we have are the perception of this response to bodily changes. For example, seeing a snake on the ground brings a physiological response of rapid heart rate and a feeling of fear for many people, along with a strong impulse to move away. As another example, anger is a feeling in response to certain sensations experienced when participating in a situation we perceive to be annoying. James believed that emotions become habitual as we engage in them regularly. Thus, repeatedly venting anger, rather than relieving it, leads to having a temper, with a low tolerance for frustration and annoyance. But if positive behaviors are engaged in regularly instead, the tendency to be less easily frustrated and annoyed becomes more likely. This became a foundation for using role-playing and learning theories for therapeutic change.

Neurobiology of Emotion

James's theory has now been expanded to include the brain (Damasio, 2000). The insula plays a role in mapping the physiological states that are involved in our experience of emotions, a somatic marker, which then elicits our conscious feeling. The sensory information that we receive about our body's physiological responses is mapped in the insula, where it becomes accessible to conscious awareness. This mapping of bodily states in the brain leads to conscious awareness of these bodily experiences. The awareness of bodily experiences has been developed into a theory known as interoception (Craig, 2002).

Thus, the insula contributes to our conscious sense of emotions. In fact, functional magnetic resonance imaging (fMRI) studies have shown combined activation in the anterior insular cortex and the anterior cingulate cortex whenever people were experiencing emotions. Extensive studies (Singer, Critchley, & Preuschoff, 2009) reveal that the insula, especially in the anterior part (AI), is highly involved in a wide variety of emotional and intuitive experiences. For example, when people are emotionally aroused from touch, hunger, taste, craving, or pain, the AI is activated. The AI also responds to the intensity of these emotional experiences. It plays a part in decision making and empathy as well, as Chapters 9 and 10 describe. Researchers found activation when subjects felt any of the negative feelings, such as anger, fear, sadness, disgust, aversion, unfairness, and indignation. They also had activation of these two areas when people felt positive emotions, such as maternal and romantic love, sexual arousal, trust, and even an ecstatic union with God.

The insula is a large organ that is located deep in one of the folds of the cortex between the temporal and frontal lobes. It is widely interconnected to other brain regions. It is highly linked to the limbic system, a group of organs involved in the processing of emotions that are found throughout different parts of the brain. Key limbic areas are the amygdala and hippocampus for remembering emotions; the thalamus as a gateway for sensory information; the hypothalamus for regulating autonomic functions, biological rhythms, and stress; the pituitary gland for regulating hormones; the nucleus accumbens for producing rewards; the cingulate gyrus for monitoring conflicting emotions; and the orbitofrontal cortex for understanding and thinking about emotions. With so many varied brain structures involved, we can see why emotions play such an important role in every aspect of living.

Emotions as a Foundation for Awareness

A new discovery is that emotions are also fundamental to awareness itself. We have a uniquely human ability to be aware. Our awareness occurs through time as an emotional experience in the body. All that we experience is represented by feelings, experienced as internal body states. Self-awareness can be correlated with a certain part of the brain, the anterior insula, where these representations of emotions are mapped. "The AIC [anterior insular cortex] contains the anatomical substrate for the evolved capacity of humans to be aware of themselves, others, and the environment" (Craig, 2009, p. 66). Thus, self-awareness is based on felt experience in the body, mapped in the insula. The process repeats through time, and so we get our awareness of a continuous self over time. Similar to the Zen idea that each moment is new, our sense of continuity is just these moments in succession. For therapy, the implication is that we can make a change at any moment.

Cognitive Component in Emotion

Feeling our body sensations and reacting to them is part of emotional experiencing. But a labeling process occurs as well. The two-factor theory of Stanley Schachter and Jerome Singer described emotion as involving two components: physical arousal and cognitive labeling of the arousal. Cognitions are the way people give meaning to the physiological reactions to the outside world. Thus, the first step is to experience physiological arousal. Then, comes the explanation of the feeling by observing what we are experiencing. Emotion comes after the inchoate, ambiguous sensation of physiological arousal is interpreted. Physiological arousal leads to different emotions, depending on how the arousal is interpreted. The psychotherapeutic implication is that interpretation can lead to very different emotions, opening the door for cognitive therapies.

The power of cognition was emphasized by Richard Lazarus's cognitive appraisal theory of emotion. Cognitive appraisal or interpretation of a situation is the primary source of emotion. Our interpretation or appraisal of an experience, object, or situation comes first. Then, the appropriate emotion follows. For example, a remark by someone is experienced and interpreted or appraised as annoying, followed by the emotion of anger in response. By reinterpreting the situation or object through strategic cognitive appraisal, the emotional response transforms. Then the reaction to the situation can change. Strategic therapy and other active approaches to psychotherapy draw from this as a rationale for the therapeutic value of reinterpretation.

The Affect Model: A Manifold of Emotions

Wilhelm Wundt proposed a different approach to emotion from James, which has also been included in modern neurobiological models of emotion and incorporated into contemporary psychotherapy approaches. Wundt believed that emotion is a manifold of feelings along three distinct dimensions: pleasure-displeasure, arousing-subduing, and strain-relaxation (Wundt, 1897, p. 35). Wundt also believed that physiological correlates for each of these affect dimensions could be measured, but in his historical period, the technology did not exist for making these measurements, so this view was not followed. But recently, thanks to neuroimaging technologies, we know that distinct brain areas are involved in each dimension. The collection of these three dimensions of emotion is known as affect. Affect can be regulated, giving people better control over their emotions. Affect regulation is an important component of therapy.

The American Psychological Association defines affect as the experience of emotion or feeling (VandenBos, 2006, p. 26). Affect is associated with action: Our emotional feeling influences how we behave. Many of the contemporary neurobiological approaches to psychotherapy think of emotion in terms of affect because it offers a more inclusive perspective that can incorporate feelings, emotions, and moods in terms of how they are experienced and acted upon. The emphasis has shifted to regulation of affect as meaning that we can do something about lowering the intensity of a troubling emotion, or turn a feeling that seems negative into something positive. Altering the physiological arousal, lowering the intensity of the felt experience, and changing the valence (from negative to positive) are real and measurable dimensions within our control. Meditation has been shown to influence all three dimensions.

We have a sense of emotions as being embodied experiences with certain intensity, a level of arousal of our mind-brain-body system, and an experience of it being either positive or negative. Exploring this response as it occurs through time gives us some clues for how to work with emotional affect most effectively.

Two Emotion Networks: The Short Path and the Long Path

Two neural networks of emotion have been found: one short and the other long. Thus, emotional response can be quick or slow. Some emotional response travels through a short path, occurring quickly, without thought, as a reflexive response. Other responses take the long path. They are conscious, developing more slowly, and have a cognitive component as we think about the body sensations we feel. The long path is an executive control network that flows through the prefrontal cortex and the parietal lobes. The short path is an emotional salience network that involves anterior insula cortex, the anterior cingulate gyrus, the amygdala, and the hypothalamus (Seeley, 2007).

Using our earlier example, if you see something in the road that looks like a poisonous snake, a fear response occurs quickly, processed through a short path moving through the subcortical regions of the brain. You feel a sudden stab of fear as your heart rate increases, your palms become sweaty, and your face flushes, along with an immediate impulse to move away. You are alert and ready to run from danger.

But then, as you look more closely, you can think about what you are seeing and realize that what seemed like a snake is really just a twig. Then the fear goes away. This response involves a longer brain-pathway that travels up through the cortex as your higher-level cognitive processes get involved. First was the immediate, instinctive short path response, then the slower long path, with your thoughtful recognition that there was no danger. Different brain areas are involved in the two pathways, helping to explain how the experiences are so different.

Emotions may travel the short or the long path. If the emotional response travels the short route directly, it receives an input from the sensory pathways (for example, you see a truck barreling toward you as you step into the road to cross), setting off the amygdala, signaling the fear response of imminent danger. This triggers the hypothalamus to release hormones and neurotransmitters, which then set the autonomic nervous system to respond with an increased heart rate, sweating, and an urge to move quickly. The reaction arises before interpretation and is unconscious, outside of deliberate conscious control, often known as bottom-up processing. If instead we think about the response, realizing the truck is approaching a red light and is now slowing to stop, the emotion is consciously recognized and is processed top-down through the prefrontal cortex. These two paths of emotional response help to account for the quick reactions clients often have, usually occurring unconsciously, versus the slower responses with a conscious element involved. People sometimes switch to a different path when necessary. For example, when our quick, first reaction is reevaluated consciously, thereby changing the emotional response. Sometimes getting back in touch at the unconscious, sensory level brings calming, without the need for conscious intervention. Both top-down (long path) and bottom-up (short path) interventions for working with emotions are helpful. Therapy can offer methods for working with either the long path or short path to facilitate change.

Different Types of Emotions

We can all agree that emotions are not the same. Emotions can seem to be positive or negative. We know that negative emotions such as fear, anger, sadness, and disgust involve a facial expression, a motor action, along with physiological reactions. These emotions tend to be generated from the right side of the brain, and tend to involve the expending of energy through the activation of the sympathetic nervous system, accompanied by arousal, leading to withdrawal behavior that enlists survival emotions. These emotions are our natural response to an experienced threat, and are adaptive in the sense that they mobilize us to take some action through activation of the fear-stress, fight-or-flight pathway. (See the appendix for a description of the stress pathway.) These emotions first travel the short pathway, traveling up the lower brain areas through the limbic system without input from higher-level processing in the cortex (Craig, 2005). Even though these emotions are uncomfortable and often difficult to bear, they serve an important and at times, a life-saving role. And so, in the meditative sense, we should not judge them as negative in their essence, but rather in how they are experienced.

Emotions that are experienced as positive are not driven by the fight-or-flight response. In fact, they often serve to balance negative emotional reactions by calming the autonomic nervous system. They are associated with parasympathetic activity, energy nourishment, relaxation, approach behavior, and emotions involving others (Craig, 2005). They can also help to elicit our natural drive for pleasure by seeking loving attachments, food, sleep, and enjoyment, which activate the reward system and help to keep us alive and healthy. (See the appendix for a description of the reward system.) Also, positive emotions tend to help us broaden our perspectives and be more flexible (Rosen & Levenson, 2010).

Emotions combined with cognitive appraisal involve culture and social norms. Feelings like embarrassment, shame, guilt, and pride are examples. Since these emotions involve a cognitive assessment, they tend to take the long path and show deficits when people have damage to the prefrontal cortex where higher-level processing occurs (Damasio et al., 2000; Rosen & Levenson, 2010).

How We Regulate Emotions

We adjust our emotions all the time. We are always altering the magnitude, duration, and types of emotional responses we have to meet the demands of ever-changing situations. In fact, rarely do we have emotions that are not regulated in some way. The process begins with the focusing of attention on something. Next comes appraisal, followed by an adjustment that either suppresses or amplifies our response in our face, voice, movement, or autonomic nervous system. Not surprising to more clinicians, suppressing an emotion has a much larger physiological response than expressing it (Gross & Levenson, 1993). As Levenson said, "You are holding back a powerful charging horse trying to get out of the corral. That takes effort!" (Levenson, 2011).

ALTERING THE EMOTIONAL NETWORK

Georgios had just turned 40. He was over 6 feet tall, large boned, with a strong build that reflected his physically demanding job as a dockworker. His appearance was hearty and even gruff, so his mild, quiet voice seemed incongruous. His wife brought him to couples therapy because he had been violent, striking her several times when he got angry. He didn't want to do it, he said, but deep down he believed she was driving him to it. He told us that he was an even-tempered guy. But sometimes things got out of hand, and he couldn't do anything about it.

Since Georgios was out of touch and not taking responsibility for his emotions, therapy began at a concrete level. We taught him to become aware of his sensations. He practiced focus meditation to learn how to notice his breathing, his heartbeat, and the temperature of his skin. He learned to recognize the sensations he experienced when he got angry: heat, beating heart, and quick, short breaths. He practiced mindfulness, following his sensations moment by moment. With practice, he began to recognize the sensations as they occurred. In time, he was able to notice when he was starting to feel angry. Rather than engage in violence, we encouraged him to leave the room or take a walk, which he did. His wife agreed to allow him to take some time to gather himself. He would practice calming meditations as he walked. Through the course of therapy, Georgios and his wife were able to each take responsibility for their actions and reactions. They worked through the emotions that fueled their angry arguments. By addressing the sensation component of his emotional experience, Georgios was able to regulate his emotional reactions. He curbed his violence and she regained her confidence in him. He also gained the self-confidence to face his deeper problems and work them through in couples therapy.

An Integrative Theory for Working With Emotions

We can think of emotions as a complex network of interactions between the cognitive processes and the physiological body sensations eliciting patterns of brain activations and deactivations, always in response to our ongoing personal life with other people in our environment. All the conditions come together in a certain way for things to feel the way they do. The elements are interconnected. So, emotions are embodied and always in a social context as well. These interactions of body, brain, and environment are continually coming together in every moment with a certain intensity, level of arousal, and valence. Some elements are more heavily weighted than others, depending on the situation and the person. There is a network of cause-and-effect interrelationships among these different components. Beyond this momentary coming together, emotions don't really have a substantive existence. And yet, when they take form in the patterned network of interactions, they feel very real indeed.

Neurotic problems tend to be redundant, and people feel like they are stuck in intractable emotions, but actually, they are feeling a *relative* constancy. The emotional network always has the potential to change. Helping loosen the threads in the tightly woven fabric of the neurotic emotional network brings clients back to a more realistic and flexible position, with the ability to respond realistically to each moment as it occurs.

This view of emotions is analogous to Buddha's insight about the fabric of reality and to the modern neural network model of how the many neurons of the brain interact together. Buddhist literature includes a profound work known as the *Avatamsaka Sutra, The Flower Garland Sutra,* (Cleary, 1993). It presents an image that is a helpful way to represent the emotion network described here: We invite you to picture an extraordinary net, hung all across the heavens, the home of the great God, Indra. The net stretches infinitely in every direction, with a single glittering jewel at each juncture of the net. Because the net is infinite in its dimensions, there are infinite numbers of jewels. Each finely polished jewel glitters as brightly as a star. It reflects all the other jewels, and all the jewels are reflecting all the other jewels, infinitely shining and reflecting together. As you visualize this image, you can see how any change in one jewel changes all the others. Similarly, any intervention made to any of the components of emotion will have an effect on the entire network, thereby changing the emotional experience. The next part will provide methods to bring about changes to each of these components, using our meditative methods.

Working on any of its component parts can alter the network. Similar to the nodes of Indra's net, where each reflects all the others, making a change in one component will influence all the others. This chapter guides in methods for working with each of these components. Meditation works through either the short path or the long path, or a combination. We offer ways to regulate emotions through the short path and the long path. These methods will help people suffering from mood disorder, including bipolar disorder and depression. The chapter also addresses problems with anger and violence.

REGULATING AFFECT

The brain seeks equilibrium, the point of balance in the interaction between activity and rest, activation and deactivation. Self-regulation, the ability to keep emotions and energy levels in balance, is essential for a healthy life. Both conscious and unconscious awareness, working through the short path and long path, are the means to elicit direction from inner wisdom toward self-regulation.

Psychotherapy typically involves working on cognitions that influence emotions. This work is effective and often essential for real change. In addition, change can occur unconsciously, at a sensory, instinctual level. Working through the short path, we can often bypass resistances and learned limitations. Zen meditation goes to the root to find the essence, and if we nourish the roots of health, we discover the essence of cure. Sometimes the roots of health are buried underneath layers of negative habits and resistant attitudes. *Natura sanat,* nature heals, and meditation can release the bonds that prevent healing from happening. Meditation is a nonrational, experiential activity, which stimulates bottom-up processes for a naturally balanced mind-brain-body system. At the same time, it also fosters acute awareness and sensitive attunement, thus fostering top-down processing as well. The dual processes of both relaxation and alertness described in Chapters 1 and 2 are evidence that several levels of brain activations occur simultaneously. Meditations in this chapter will give you ways to activate all these positive built-in capacities that are already there, just waiting to be set free.

Altering Arousal for Affect Regulation

Arousal is one of the dimensions of affect. When people are having emotional problems, especially with anger and anxiety, their stress levels remain higher than normal. A new allostatic balance is formed at a chronically elevated level. Lowering the level of general arousal will definitely help people feel some relief. By lowering the stress levels back to more normal levels, people will be less volatile and tend to respond more calmly and rationally.

When clients are depressed, their arousal level is blunted, even though strong feelings may be seething beneath the surface. The meditations in this section can be used to help clients attune to their arousal level. As awareness develops, they will be able to address what is needed to return to balance.

Regulating arousal begins by sensitizing. Often, when there are problems, people either lack awareness of their arousal level or they may have a false conception of it. Georgios was completely out of touch with his level of arousal. He only knew he was angry when he found himself violently hitting his wife. On the other extreme was Patty (described later in this chapter), who feared that she was enraged when her voice was slightly raised. Both of these clients were out of touch with their emotional arousal and felt out of control of their emotions. You can help people gain emotional control by opening their perception to this important dimension of affect.

Focus on Arousal Meditation

You can elicit emotional arousal using the imagination and then think of a time when you felt your strong emotion. Wait for a moment to allow your emotion to build and your body to respond. Now turn your attention to the sensations, as you did in the previous series of exercises. Notice your heartbeat, your body temperature, your breathing, and general body sense. Get to know the network of sensations as they are occurring. Link the sensations you are experiencing to your emotional arousal. Just as you know other things about yourself, can you begin to learn that when you are having these experiences you are probably feeling strong emotional arousal?

Calming Emotional Arousal

Calming overaroused systems can allow strong emotions to ease down and give people better control over strong moods and emotions. Practicing these meditations builds skills over time. Be patient and persistent in practice.

The brain has many different pathways for performing similar functions. Different pathways can be elicited to bring about relaxation and calm. One way is through deliberate, conscious methods using top-down processing. Unconscious methods elicit relaxation indirectly, as a natural response. Both methods evoke responses that can be enlarged upon with sensitive and repetitive practice. People will vary as to which methods work better for them. Experiment, taking note of responsiveness to help guide the choice of methods.

Lowering Generalized Arousal Through Gentle Muscle Relaxation

People often carry chronic tension. This may add to emotional arousal and generalized stress. If your nervous system has become adapted to being stressed, a small stimulus can elicit a stronger-than-warranted reaction.

Using the skills that you have begun to develop with awareness of interoception (see Chapter 9), scan through your body. Begin at your head by paying attention to your face. If you discover tension in a particular area, such as in your eyes, forehead, or lips, turn your attention there. First, carefully trace out how you are holding the muscles as you did before, then, if possible, allow these muscles to relax. Letting go involves an opening, releasing feeling.

Muscles will feel softer, lighter, larger, or smoother. Breathe comfortably and let the tension go with each exhalation of your breath.

Then direct attention down toward your shoulders. Pay close attention to them. Notice whether you are holding the muscles tight and let go if possible. If you noticed that your shoulders were held away from the floor, can you let them sink down and take support from the surface? Continue down through your body, first paying close attention followed by trying to relax any extra tension. You may be surprised to notice areas that are tightly tensed, but don't need to be. If attention wanders away to outer concerns, bring it back. Do not force yourself to relax. Simply notice where you can or cannot relax, and gently keep trying to let go of unnecessary tension.

Calming Generalized Arousal Indirectly Through the Ideomotor Effect

Calm can be achieved indirectly by activating the mind-body's natural ideomotor link. The thoughts we have naturally elicit a body response. William James originally described this link as the ideomotor phenomenon (James, 1896). For example, vividly imagine eating a tart lemon. As you imagine tasting the lemon, does your mouth automatically begin to salivate? This is the natural response, from an idea to a body response. You can use this natural responsiveness to elicit calming.

Imagine a time when you felt completely relaxed. It could be a time when you were with someone you care about, out in nature, or curled up in bed. Picture the experience as vividly as possible, recalling sensory and emotional details as well as what you were doing and thinking. Be there for several minutes and wait for your natural relaxation response to occur.

Activating When Underaroused

Affect regulation is a neutral term that allows for lowering or raising arousal levels as needed. Sometimes people are underaroused and unresponsive. Those suffering from depression feel lowered energy and a lack of interest in their world. The next exercise can help to activate arousal levels to help return balance to the system.

This exercise can be performed standing up. Slow, regular movement combined with meditation can gently raise energy and help the autonomic nervous system to rebalance at a more comfortable level. Begin by slowly raising your arms out from your sides and around, upward to a position overhead, with fingertips extended while inhaling. Then slowly lower your arms around back down to your sides as you exhale. Continue to inhale as you raise your arms overhead and exhale as you lower your arms. Breathe softly and move slowly and smoothly, coordinating breathing and movement together for several minutes. When you feel finished, close your eyes and notice your sensations. You may feel a tingling sensation in your fingertips, hands, and arms. Allow the sensation to spread through your body. Practice gentle, slow movements at regular intervals through the day and you will begin to feel your vitality rise.

Regulating Emotional Intensity

Intensity of emotions is another quality of affect. We can regulate the intensity of emotions to help people cope better. Then new options emerge for a different adjustment that will lead to a change in feelings. The work can be done through short path bottom-up and long path top-down processes. These meditations offer options for calming overly intense emotions.

Calming Emotional Intensity Directly

Next time you are feeling a strong, undesired emotion, deliberately try to relax your muscles. Use the instructions in the previous sections on muscle relaxation and mindful sensory experiencing. You probably noticed that some of your muscles are chronically tight when feeling a strong emotion, and that the tension occurs in certain areas of your body with specific sensations. For example, anger typically involves warmth in the face or stomach area or both, a racing heart, and short, quick breaths. All of these natural responses are clues to the network of interactions involved in your emotional response. Get to know how you respond by turning your attention mindfully to what you are experiencing moment by moment while you are feeling the emotion. Once you are aware of the sensations, try to let go of any tensions that you can. Gently bring your breathing to a more relaxed rhythm. Let your heart rate settle. In time, the intensity diminishes a bit as your emotional response eases.

Calming Emotional Intensity Indirectly

Now you can use the ideomotor effect to lower the intensity of your emotion. When you are feeling an uncomfortable, strong emotion, recall and visualize yourself at a time when you were not feeling this emotion, perhaps imaginatively going to a place or situation in which you felt relaxed and calm. Wait for your response and allow your arousal level to gently lower.

Altering Valence

We often think of anger, fear, disgust, and sadness as negative emotions. But considered from a larger, realistic perspective, these emotions can be helpful. Fear can mobilize us to get away from danger. Anger might mobilize us to take a firm stand against an injustice. Disgust can prevent us from ingesting a poison, and grief helps us to work through a loss of a loved one. A first step is to ask yourself, are you judging your feeling as bad? Often, the secondary judgments we make about our reactions can magnify the discomfort enormously.

Think about your assessment of your troubling feeling. Do you sometimes say, "I hate feeling this way"? What is your aversion based on? As you explore, you will eventually come back to your ideas about yourself. "I don't deserve to suffer," or "it isn't fair" are common thoughts that people have about enduring discomfort. But in the meditative sense, emotions are not good or bad; they just are. And perhaps by holding on to these negative appraisals, you are perpetuating the discomfort and not allowing it to ease naturally, as emotions inevitably do. You add your judgment to the situation, but your fundamental nature is an ongoing experience with the potential for a different reaction that can lead to a more comfortable feeling at any moment. Meditate, allowing your mind to clear. Your reaction will become less uncomfortable as you let go of these interpretations.

Next time you feel yourself becoming upset, try to notice what you are feeling, just as it is, without adding a negative judgment. Change may take time, but if you can set aside the negative interpretations you are telling yourself about the emotions, and simply allow experiencing to be as it is, you begin a process of transformation.

When you can let go of your judging ego with its strong personal preferences, you will find that strong emotional reactions can't be induced inappropriately by others. You gain more self control. Along with the reduction of your uncomfortable emotional reactions, you will cope with more restraint and compassion. Then you can find more harmonious ways to cope. And your mature response can encourage less upsetting actions from others, which will improve matters.

Mindful Exploration of Thoughts

What we think can influence how we feel, as cognitive therapies have so aptly pointed out (Ellis & Ellis, 2011). We can use mindfulness meditation to help become aware of ruminations that fuel emotional reactions to deepen depression and anger problems. Through the simple exercise of awareness that observes and accepts, the power of thinking over emotions is eased.

Sit quietly and turn attention to your thoughts. Follow each thought as it occurs, but with a difference. Don't allow yourself to become lost in any one thought. Simply observe that you are thinking it. Like sitting on the bank of a river and watching the leaves and twigs float by, notice each leaf and twig as they flow by. Let go of the thought after you think it, and then observe the next thought.

Don't assess whether it is a good thought or bad thought, happy or sad. Instead, just as you wouldn't judge a twig or leaf as good or bad, simply observe each one. In time, the flow of ruminating thoughts slows down and you begin to feel calmer and more comfortable.

Radical Self-Acceptance of Emotions

Japanese swordsman Tesshu gave a Zen perspective on our human emotional nature:

> When there is happiness, be happy. When there is anger, be angry. When there is sorrow, be sad. When there is pleasure, rejoice in it. This is acting accordingly free of hindrance.
>
> (Stevens, 1989, p. 144)

This statement was made by the Japanese Zen master and swordsman, Tesshu (1836–1888). We find it easier to experience the pleasant feelings. Anger, sadness, and frustration are feelings that people often do not want to have. But in the attempt to avoid discomfort, we may miss something important. The beautiful lotus flower blooms even in muddy swamps. Emotions become meaningful signposts for therapeutic understanding when accepted and felt through. Learning to tolerate, accept, and even embrace the range of emotions brings greater control and a more fulfilling engagement with the world.

Patty was a tall, willowy, attractive, young 21-year-old woman who seemed timid and spoke very little, but when she did say something, her voice was thin and quiet. She had a sweet disposition and was a pleasant person to be around. She was working as a waitress while she attended college, had a boyfriend, and felt relatively satisfied with her life. She told us that she came to therapy because she just had one problem. She was suffering from recurring, disturbing nightmares of being chased by frightening creatures.

As she began to practice mindfulness meditation, she became aware of angry feelings she never knew she had. The more she paid attention, the angrier she felt. This revelation disturbed her. She said, "I don't believe in getting angry. I'm a nice person. I hate angry people! And I don't think I could get angry even if I wanted to."

We discussed the idea of accepting all her feelings, how each emotion had its importance. We encouraged her to keep meditating, noticing each feeling as it occurred. We also told her that it might be connected to the nightmares, and so she continued. During her mindfulness meditation, she noticed associated memories of when she was a young child. She had been close to both parents, but especially to her father who spent quality time with her. Her mother had a short temper and bitterly argued with her father. They eventually divorced. Patty felt intense sadness over the loss of her father's company. She now vividly remembered a long forgotten promise she had made to herself: Never be angry! She believed her mother's angry temper had driven her father away. She decided to never let herself be like that!

She had lived without getting angry until recently, when she and her boyfriend had some disagreements. As she became more able to accept her feelings, she realized that she did feel anger about some of the things he did, but had not been able to express it. We talked about how her anger was part of her ability to assert herself. She wanted to work things out with her boyfriend and began to recognize the value of accepting all her feelings. She gradually learned to express angry feelings. She experienced these feelings as being overly strong, but in witnessing her anger, we could see that she had a mild and moderate way of expressing herself when angry. Her boyfriend actually felt grateful, she told us, because he was frustrated that she had never been willing to discuss things before. Now they could work out their differences. And her nightmares disappeared. The creatures had been her own repressed anger, trying to get her attention!

Begin With an Inward Glance

Noticing what you are feeling is an important component of getting in touch with your deeper emotional being. As you go through your day, take an inward glance at what you are feeling with meditation.

Next time you are feeling somewhat frustrated, annoyed, or unhappy, and before you reach the point of just reacting, stop for a moment and experiment with meditation. As you become more skilled, it will be easier to apply it when you are having much stronger intensity of emotion. Allow yourself to feel what you are feeling in the moment. Remember not to judge it, but simply sense what is there. Describe it to yourself, beginning with, now I feel this, now I feel that. Breathe comfortably as you sit. When you have a little more time, try the next exercise.

Accepting Emotions Meditation

As you begin to be able to sense what you are feeling, stay with the feeling, including the sensations and thoughts. Every emotion is a gateway to your deeper nature. Whether the feeling seems good or bad, pleasant or unpleasant, accept it as part of a larger whole, revealing to you clues about your deeper nature. Let yourself feel, noticing whatever is there. Your feeling will begin to alter, usually opening a window to your deeper emotional understanding in that moment. Stay with your feeling and perception, accepting all as your attunement to the world, and thus valuable in and of itself.

Don't stubbornly try to hold on to the original situation or the original feeling. We learn from meditation not to make something rigid or fixed of our experience. For example, perhaps you started off feeling grief from loss of a loved one, but as you pay attention, the emotion changes to a deeper sense of aloneness. Probing further, perhaps you can sense the ultimate emptiness in all things, leading you to deeper sense of peace. Start from where you are and meditate. Any moment is a good place to begin.

Try to meditate whenever you are having a strong emotional response, especially if the reaction is related to something you are working on in therapy. Keep attending to these emotional responses meditatively, and eventually, you will sense beyond the superficial feeling to make a connection with your true nature—what Zen calls *mind*. Try to allow yourself to feel fully. Accept yourself, all of your reactions and experiences, and you will find harmony.

> Sailing for the stars,
> Leave the muddy past behind.
> Boldly create tomorrow's destiny,
> With a tranquil and positive mind.
> (C. Alexander Simpkins)

Letting Go

Sometimes you may need to let go of your feeling. This skill is especially helpful when clients have worked through and resolved a conflict, and yet they continue to feel disturbed even though their rational mind tells them

Figure 7.1   Zen Mountain

not to feel that way. Sometimes, the habitual emotional response is slow to leave. This meditation can be helpful for clearing the way for something new. Combined with repeated cognitive working-through, regular meditation will bring a profound and lasting change, when the client will no longer feel the old emotions, even when exposed to similar situations.

When you are experiencing the return of an old reaction, sit down to meditate. First, notice what you are feeling. Then, relax your body and clear your mind of thoughts. Whenever a disturbing thought or sensation appears, just notice it, accept it, and let it go. As soon as possible, return to no-thought. Keep working at it until the reaction alters. You will gradually feel yourself calming down, thoughts clearing, and emotions settling. In time, you will share in the wisdom of the Zen masters, moments of complete peace, happy and at ease on the mountaintop of meditation (Figure 7.1).

Letting Go Using Koans

Some clients have difficulty letting go, experiencing the empty moment. This classic koan from the koan collection, *Mumonkon,* is used to open an emptiness known as *Joshu's Mu* (Sekida, 1997).

The koan states: A monk asked Joshu, "Has a dog the Buddha nature? Joshu answered, "Mu" (Sekida, 1997, p. 27). The koan itself is followed by a section of the author's comment. Mumon explains that Mu is the main gate of Zen and that if you pass through it, you will see Joshu face to face. It is not nothing, nor is it relative. He urges the reader to concentrate on Mu with every ounce of energy. If you do this, you will be enlightened.

We experience our taken-for-granted, everyday world, and believe that what we experience is real. But sometimes it is most helpful to suspend belief and seek understanding through an experience beyond thought in the empty moment. We do not have to assume reality is constant and unchanging. Nor should we assume it is not. Start with how things seem, how we experience, and then proceed from there. This search for the experienced ground of reality is like the search for meaning in a koan. Wonder what it means and strive to understand. Then, in the darkness, may come the flash realization as the client breaks out of patterns to discover something new.

CONCLUSION

Emotions are central to most aspects of functioning. They engage large portions of our brain and are experienced by the mind and body together.

Meditation can help regulate emotions when they are out of balance in depression, anger, and violence. Through regular meditation, we learn to notice what we are feeling and thinking about our emotions. We can accept what we feel. Then, as the roots of the emotional problems have been observed, accepted, and understood, the troubling emotion or mood can be let go of and released. Free of encumbrances in the present moment, people discover the resource within for optimal emotional functioning.

8

Dissolving Anxiety and Trauma

Your true nature is completely empty, calm, quiet, and clear; Wonderful and mystifying, it brings peace and contentment, with no room for anything else. Allow yourself to experience it by opening yourself fully to it.
—(Paraphrased from Zen Master Huang-Po [d. 850])

Long ago, a small village was being terrorized by a hungry pack of wolves. Every night, the wolves prowled through the town, attacking anyone who ventured outside. They killed livestock and destroyed crops. The whole town felt afraid and anxious. They could barely sleep at night, awakened by the frightening howls. They felt helpless to do anything. As the months passed, the town adjusted to living in fear. They never went outdoors after sunset, stopped having any celebrations, and spent their days trying to clean up after the ravage of the wolves the night before. The smallest howl-like sound set off intense anxiety.

The local Zen master could see that the entire town was traumatized. He felt concern and decided to help them. He had been telling them that meditators should be able to keep a calm, peaceful mind even in the face of danger, but nobody was listening. He decided to demonstrate the power of meditation himself to help them face their fear and overcome it.

Despite protests from everyone, the next night, just as the sun began to set, the Zen master went out alone into the middle of the town, sat down, and began to meditate. He developed a peaceful mind, sitting calmly and quietly alone in the pitch darkness. The wolves ran wildly through the streets, as they did each night, howling and foraging. When they came upon the Zen master, they saw him sitting still, unwaveringly calm and unafraid. Curious, the wolves ventured close to him, sniffing at his neck and ears. The master continued to meditate deeply without moving. The wolves watched and circled, but they left him alone. A few of them even curled up beside him and went to sleep.

The next day, the master explained that the real opponent is not the outer circumstances but what lies within us. As he said, "Deluded thoughts are indeed more terrifying than wolves and tigers."

The next night three of the bravest men and women went out with the Zen master and sat quietly meditating. The night after that, another six people joined in. Within a week, the whole town was sitting quietly outside in meditation, with wolves snuggled up around them. As the townspeople felt more comfortable, they began leaving food out for the wolves. In time, the wolves stopped damaging the town, and even provided protection against other wild beasts.

This story illustrates the capability of a clear meditative center for overcoming even the most terrifying situations, threatening fears, and prolonged anxieties. When people have suffered from anxiety or trauma for an extended period, they come to think of themselves as anxious, much like the townspeople, who had adjusted to living in fear. We have had clients define themselves by their problem as they told us, "Oh, I'm an anxious person," or "I'm high strung," or "I'm off kilter." They have forgotten that their original nature is neither afraid nor not afraid, anxious nor not anxious. Other times, people feel the opposite, that they find themselves off course since the trauma—"I'm not myself since this awful thing happened," we have often heard them say. They have lost the flexibility built into human wiring to respond to threat with a healthy fear, to be anxiously wary of dangerous situations and then to be able to let it go and return to calm balance when the threat has passed. The fact that they continue to react in a constantly alerted state is a primary source of the problem. Zen meditation is well suited for helping people to relearn how to respond moment to moment to what is actually present, not to react to fears and dangers that are long past. Flexible attunement in the moment, as life's situations unfold, is a source for inner strength and resilience that can help people overcome traumas, let go of fear, and live comfortably without anxiety. This chapter provides meditative methods for overcoming problems of anxiety, fear, and trauma.

NEUROBIOLOGY OF FEAR AND STRESS

Fear is a natural response built into the mind-brain-body fight-or-flight system to respond to danger and threat. When the sense of danger is sustained over time, it becomes stress. Anxiety, fear, and PTSD all have a strong stress component that sustains the reaction.

We have an unconscious system that helps us to detect a threat to our safety, a brain-body response at the level of the nervous system known as neuroception (Porges, 2011). Several brain systems with a link to cognitions and emotions are involved. When facing a perceived threat, the amygdala sends messages to the endocrine system as part of a pathway that links the hypothalamus, pituitary, and adrenal glands together, known as the hypothalamic-pituitary-adrenal (HPA) pathway. The hippocampus, where memories are stored, is closely linked to the amygdala for the processing of emotional memories. Thus, the HPA pathway is not only activated by an immediate threat, but also from remembering a threat from the past.

The hypothalamus receives the input and releases hormones and neurotransmitters that are routed quickly to the circulatory system, giving us that immediate alerted reaction to danger that makes it possible to respond fast. Several hormones are produced and released to activate the fight-or-flight response to danger and when under a sustained stress. Corticotrophin-releasing hormone (CRH) from the hypothalamus, adrenocorticotropic hormone (ACTH) from the pituitary, and cortisol from the adrenal glands trigger the heart to race, palms to sweat, and breathing to become shallow. Cortisol helps release the stored sugar in the body, glucose, giving a burst of energy we need to take action.

The normal system has a balancing set of hormones and neurotransmitters to slow down the stress reaction when the danger has passed. Production and release of glucocorticoids is fed back into the brain and pituitary to slow down the synthesis of CRH and ACTH.

This circular process of activation and deactivation is usually kept in balance. So, our system is well equipped to respond rapidly to a traumatic, frightening, or dangerous event with a large increase in activity along the HPA pathway (see Figure A.10 in the appendix). And it is equally well equipped to calm down as soon as the threat has passed and return to balance.

When people suffer from a long-standing or severe trauma, such as abuse, illnesses, war, natural disasters, or even from mental disorders, the HPA pathway remains continuously activated. The mind-brain-body system eventually forms a balance at this higher level, giving the experience of feeling stressed, anxious, or fearful.

Thus, people who have been through a trauma or suffer from fears and anxiety are under increased stress. They have learned to have an exaggerated fear response, mediated by the amygdala. In essence, the brain can't shut off the fear reaction. Like keeping a car revving, they maintain their nervous system balance at heightened arousal.

Because of neuroplasticity, some changes occur in the brain when the system stays on high alert. Decreased anterior cingulate activity, a crucial area for conflict resolution and decision making, perpetuates the problem by making it harder to resolve conflicts or formulate good decisions. Stress has been shown to inhibit the growth of new neurons in the hippocampus (Gould, Beylin, Tanapat, Reeves, & Shors, 1999) and has a generalized inhibitory effect on neurogenesis. Adults who suffer from extensive stress have a smaller hippocampus than those who aren't under stress (F. Gage, Kempermann, & Hongjun, 2008). A smaller hippocampus makes learning more difficult.

The good news is that these processes are dynamic. Although the brain patterns become entrenched, they are reversible. Neuroplasticity works both ways, so with the right experiences, an underactive, smaller hippocampus can be activated to grow. For example, cab drivers tend to be continually engaged in spatial orientation tasks, a function of the hippocampus. They had a larger hippocampus than those of the same age who are not cab drivers (McGuire et al., 2000). This research indicates that learning experiences that foster hippocampus activity led to an increase in its size. Neurogenesis can occur in the hippocampus at any age. Even elderly patients who were dying from cancer showed growth in their hippocampus (F. H. Gage, Erikkson, Perfilieva, & Bjork-Erikkson, 1998).

Most people are not born with an overactivated stress response. And, in general, the body wants to return to a normal balance. The fight-or-flight pathway is always changing in response to situations, and so a process moving toward a lower activation can be started at any point. Even though the fight-or-flight response occurs quickly, it can be influenced in varying ways. Thoughts and memories, processed in the prefrontal cortex, can help to calm the system down or keep it revving through a long path of neural processing. Our thoughts, emotions, and sensations are always functioning together in a highly interactive network. We can calm an overaroused nervous system through the long brain pathway by altering cognitions. We can also intervene directly through a short path by changing breathing, relaxing muscles, or altering sensations. From either path, long or short, a more comfortable balance can be found. The generalized, overall rebalancing of the brain's stress reaction can be a powerful force for alleviating anxiety and fears.

CALMING

Anyone suffering from anxiety or trauma will benefit from the regular practice of calming. The meditations in this section can help to rebalance the autonomic nervous system at a lower activation. You can also use any of the relaxation and calming meditations found in Chapter 5, for mindful relaxation, Chapter 7 for calming affect, and Chapter 9 for calm breathing. Take frequent short breaks to meditate. Sometimes even a brief moment of calm can help to ease discomfort just enough to encourage the brain-body pathways to return to balance. Research shows that skilled meditators can create a peaceful moment no matter what mood the subjects had before meditating (Kohr, 1977), and so you can encourage more inner calm even when feeling uncomfortable. Evoke the moment of relief using any of the meditations included here. Increase the time spent as you are able. Meditate intermittently during the day and every day for a stronger effect.

Calming in the Present Moment

Meditation is a moment to sit quietly in the present moment. Anxiety often involves leaving the present moment, either to relive an uncomfortable past or to anticipate a feared future. The ability to stay in the present moment, quietly and calmly, is a skill that can be gained with practice. Begin this meditation for a brief time, even as short as a few minutes. Then, as you are able, increase the time.

Sit quietly and comfortably. Practice mindfulness by noticing what you are experiencing now, in the present moment. Begin by grounding yourself in the present by turning your attention briefly to your body awareness, noticing your sitting position, how you meet the surface you are sitting on, and the temperature of your skin. Pay attention to your breathing, noticing how each breath, in and out, is new. Once you feel fairly in touch with your sitting right now, turn to your thoughts. Notice what you are thinking and whether your thoughts wander to something about the past or the future. If you start thinking about something past or future, gently bring your thoughts back to the present moment. This takes a deliberate effort at first, and you may find that you get lost in thoughts about the past or future. But as soon as you notice, come back to here and now. Reassure yourself that now you are here in the present moment, just thinking about sitting quietly now, and that later, you can attend to these future or past thoughts if needed. Keep returning to the present moment. As you improve in this skill, you will find it easier to sustain thoughts that stay centered in the present moment.

Inviting Relaxation

We use our conscious mind through the long path of the brain when we tell ourselves to relax, direct ourselves to tighten muscles and relax them, or consciously think of a relaxing place. Meditation can evoke an unconscious response subtly and indirectly that activates the short path. This kind of automatic, unconscious relaxation begins with the genuine wish and intention that sets a process in motion and then steps back to allow it to happen.

Sit comfortably and invite yourself to relax. Wonder about how your body will go about it. Will your arms relax first or your legs? Will you feel a comfortable warmth or coolness? Will your mind evoke specific imagery that relaxes you? Wait for your response with open curiosity. You don't know just what form the relaxation will take, but trust that when you are ready, you can allow your capacity for relaxation to take place naturally and effortlessly.

Relaxation in Motion

People who suffer from anxiety may find that sitting quietly is difficult, and may even bring on more anxiety. Relaxation can be performed while moving.

Meditative walking is a classic Zen tradition. It can be a 5- or 10-minute walk outdoors or even around the house.

Walk slowly, aware of each step, focused on the sensation of your foot as it meets the floor, your arms as they swing by the sides, while breathing in tune with each step. Keep your attention focused only on walking. If your mind wanders, gently bring it back to your walking as soon as you notice. Continue walking, be comfortably aware, and in time you will feel your tension levels diminish.

Letting Go of Tension

Tension often becomes an unconscious habit that adds to generalized discomfort. People tense up and don't even know they are doing so. Mindfulness meditation can help notice when you are tensing and then give you an opportunity to let it go.

As you are going about your day, take a moment to turn your attention to notice your tensions. Observe whether you are holding some part of your body unnecessarily tight, for example tensing your neck or raising your shoulders as you sit. Can you let go of this tension a bit? Notice whether you are tensing whenever you think of it. Breathe comfortably and let your thoughts go. Be aware of yourself without judging. Simply invite yourself to be more relaxed. Take time out during your day to allow yourself to relax. Sometimes, just a few minutes scattered throughout the day can help bring about a change. You will eventually turn the tides of a tense adjustment to lower the general levels of discomfort in your life. You may be surprised that your calm center can emerge by itself.

WORKING WITH ANXIETY

Buddha tied a knot in a silk handkerchief and asked his disciple, Ananda, "What is this?"

Ananda answered, "A knot."

Then Buddha tied another knot and asked, "What is this?" Ananda answered, "Another knot."

He continued to tie knots and asked Ananda, "What is this?" until he had six knots. Each time Ananda answered the same way. Buddha said, "When I showed you the first knot you called it a knot, and when I showed you the second, and third, and so on, you still insisted they were all knots."

Ananda was confused and asked, "Why do you imply I am wrong to call these knots?"

Buddha answered, "The handkerchief is one whole, one piece of woven silk. By my tying knots nothing has changed except its appearance. It is still a handkerchief" (paraphrased from the *Surangama Sutra* in Yutang, 1942).

Buddha's point was that our senses, our ideas, our thoughts are all simply part of the flow of consciousness. Even though things fill our consciousness, our original mind is always clear and calm. Sometimes, we identify ourselves more with our problems (like the knots) than with our clear mind (the handkerchief), and this identification brings discomfort. We feel trapped, experiencing ourselves tied up in problems instead of recognizing that the problems are only a quality of our being, not our being itself. Anxiety can be overcome as clients begin to recognize how they are creating it by mistaking the knots for the handkerchief.

Untying the Mental Knots of Anxiety Meditation

When you begin to feel an anxiety reaction, notice what you are telling yourself. Are you worrying that something is fundamentally wrong with you? Do you interpret your uncomfortable sensations as meaning that you are unhealthy? Then, do you pass judgment on this experience and tell yourself it's awful?

Pay mindful attention to what you are saying to yourself. Notice that these thoughts are abstractions from the experience along with assessments, not the experience itself.

Meditating on Just What It Is

Now get in touch with what you are actually experiencing. Begin with the emotions—perhaps fear or worry. How do you sense the emotion? Do you have certain sensations that give you cues, such as tightness in your chest or churning in your stomach? Recognize each element as it is, without putting it all together as our client did who added all the elements up to mean: pending heart attack.

Observe each concrete experience such as your heart rate or breathing. As you separate it from your interpretation, let the sensation or emotion be. So, if your breathing is labored, notice it and let it be as it is. Notice how each breath in and out is a new breath. Even though they are similar, every breath is slightly different. Stay with your breathing for a few minutes. Without interjecting any interpretive thoughts, your body will gradually find its natural balance. Do this with any other prominent sensations or feelings. Gradually, most people will find that the reaction begins to settle and they feel more at ease.

Letting Go of the Knots

Now that you are aware of what you are experiencing, allow yourself to relax just a bit if possible. So, if your breathing is labored and tight, ask yourself, "Can I let my breathing be just a little slower and calmer?" If your stomach is churning and tight, can you let go of any unnecessary tension there? Scan through your body and invite more relaxation wherever possible. As you do so, you may notice an easing of emotions as well. If you find yourself passing negative judgments, notice that you are making a negative judgment and set it aside as such. In time, you will begin to feel more comfortable and help the anxiety pass away naturally.

Closing the Gap Between Now and Later

Often, when people feel anxious, they have created a gap between now and later. The future is always experienced from the present moment, cultivating a firm foundation in the *now*. From now as the base, there is no gap for anxiety to fill. This meditation exercise will help people to recognize how and when they lose touch with the present.

Verbalize what you are experiencing by saying, "Now I notice this. Now I notice that. Here I am sitting. Here I am noticing what I experience. Now I notice that I am thinking about the future." Deliberately tie each statement to the present moment. Even though you are thinking about the past or the future, tie it to the now as you are doing so. In time, a transformation takes place as you begin to truly experience yourself, here and now, in this moment.

Discerning the Handkerchief Through the Knots Meditation 1

As the problems are worked through in therapy, practice experiencing your original, clear mind in meditation to facilitate the recovery process. Here is one method that draws upon recalling a past experience. You can also use the emptiness meditations given in other chapters of this book.

When you have some time without any demands, sit quietly in meditation, and think back to a time when you felt comfortable and happy, just being yourself. You may have been on vacation, doing something you like, or enjoying the company of someone you care about. Vividly recall this positive experience. Recall how you felt an effortless calm without having to do anything to bring it about. You just felt good. Now allow yourself to have that experience as you sit here now, without anything to get in the way.

Discerning the Handkerchief Through the Knots Meditation 2

Now, as you have accessed a memory of feeling relaxed and comfortable, allow yourself to experience your deeper calm nature here and now. You are that calm and comfortable person from the past, and can be free of anxiety now for a moment in meditation. Allow the sensations to spread as you enjoy this calm moment. Breathe, relax, and just be present now. Begin with a short period and extend the time spent in meditation, as you are able.

Prevention: Reading the Signs Ahead of Time

As you have been able to become aware of the different elements in your reaction pattern, you have the tools you need to change future anxiety attacks. Try to be mindful of the signs when the sensations, thoughts, and feelings are just beginning. Separate the elements as you did in the previous exercises, pay attention, and allow the reaction to ease down. Empty your mind using Zazen meditation, staying with each moment, and return to emptiness as soon as you can. You may find, with practice, that the reaction does not take hold at all.

TRAUMA

People who have experienced trauma have undergone a shock to the nervous system, which takes time to abate. As they continue to think about it later, which is the natural thing to do, the nervous system remains in an alerted state. More worry and emotional disturbance follows, to reinforce a negative cycle. You can intervene in this process with meditation to provide a means to calm the nervous system. Meditation will also give people a source of inner strength and a strong sense of security. The meditations in this section, along with the calming meditations provided earlier in the chapter, can be used as part of psychotherapy to facilitate healing at every stage of treatment.

About Trauma Disorders

Traumatic events can involve a threat of death or serious injury to oneself or to another. A trauma is usually experienced personally, but it can also occur when witnessing someone else suffering. The sufferer experiences intense fear and horror, along with an overwhelming sense of helplessness. Anyone who undergoes such an extreme situation will suffer an immediate, short-lived reaction, but symptoms often persist long after the event. In cases of abuse or prolonged wars or environmental disasters, trauma may be ongoing through a child's entire developmental process. Meditation can be extremely helpful in all trauma-related disorders.

Different Types

Those who have had a single traumatic event, such as an injury from a car crash or damaging storm, but have otherwise led a normal life are often diagnosed with acute stress disorder (ASD). ASD sufferers will tend to get over the problem in several months, especially with meditation and brief psychotherapy.

When trauma recurs, such as from a war, rape, or a more serious one-time trauma, the diagnosis will be posttraumatic stress disorder (PTSD), and recovery may take longer. The most extreme form of PTSD that derives from horrific events, such as active-duty soldiers in battle, multiple rapes, or exposure to repeated trauma, usually requires longer-term treatment.

Developmental trauma disorder (DTD) occurs when someone has been raised with continual abuse, lacking a supportive environment, or growing up in a war-torn area. Such individuals require a long-term therapy with a strong therapeutic relationship. They also need guidance in developing healthy psychological and physical habits, which they never received growing up.

The Symptoms

The symptoms of ASD, PTSD, and DTD include repeated, automatic remembering of the trauma in dreams, images, thoughts, flashbacks, and hallucinations. These troubling experiences are often triggered by minimal cues that would have little or no effect normally. People avoid anything that reminds them of the event, which leads to restricting how they interact and express their emotions. They remain persistently hyperaroused, so that they are easily startled, have trouble sleeping, and find difficulty concentrating. In the most severe cases, everyday life is altered. People have trouble carrying out their everyday responsibilities and find little joy or satisfaction from work, friends, and family.

Treating Trauma Disorders

Meditation can be integrated into regular treatment. These methods work seamlessly with cognitive-behavioral, dynamic, and humanistic methods. The meditations included here provide a sanctuary from suffering, a felt sense of self-support, and help to establish healthy psychological habits.

The Wisdom of Insecurity

When people have suffered trauma, they carry a sense of danger with them. They see the world as an unsafe place, finding threats lurking everywhere. One client who was raised in a cult told us that before therapy, she always felt unsafe. A war veteran found even a moderately loud sound made him feel as if he were stepping on a land mine. Meditation develops a calm center, a sense of being safe and secure from within. Not dependent on anything outside of your own resources, meditation can bring that refuge that trauma sufferers so desperately seek.

Ultimately, life is always changing. According to Buddhist philosophy, there is no enduring security. But just as true is the fact that there is no lasting insecurity, either. Things just happen as they do, moment to moment. You can find your most profound sense of security as you recognize and accept the

Figure 8.1   Beach Sunset

ever-changing nature of the universe. The real source for secure grounding is your own clear mind. We offer two methods for developing a personal sense of security, drawing on the wellsprings within.

Visualizing Sanctuary

Use your own experiences from the past to visualize a safe place and go there imaginatively as a resource. Think of a time when you felt calm and comfortable. People usually think of a tranquil place in nature, but you might also have a memory of being in a room that you enjoyed. We offer a peaceful scene in Figure 8.1 of being near the ocean, but please feel free to visualize your own sanctuary.

You are sitting on the sand at a beach late in the afternoon. The sand feels warm as the sun shines with just a few fluffy white clouds. The sea breeze is cool and refreshing on your skin. You can smell the fresh salt air as you take a deep breath in and relax. The waves are coming in regular, perfectly formed sets. You can hear the wave break along the shore, a soothing sound that fills your consciousness with nature's wonder. Some time passes as you feel completely relaxed, and the sun begins to set over the ocean. Gradually, rich red and orange streaks stretch across the sky. As the sun lowers, the colors intensify and deepen. The bright yellow-orange sun sinks behind the horizon, and as it finally goes, you see a green flash. Now the sky turns purple-red, and you feel awed by the majestic beauty all around you. Every sunset is unique, and you can always return to this place and enjoy the calm beauty of the ocean.

Discovering Sanctuary Through Ritual: The Tea Ceremony

One of the great Zen traditions, the tea ceremony, Cha-no-yu, is a long-lived tradition that invites centering in a tranquil moment that puts the mind at ease. A sanctuary from anxiety and stress, the tea ceremony brings you into the present moment, and brings a feeling of calm-centered awareness (see Figure 8.2).

Zen tea embodies certain virtues: reverence, harmony, purity, and tranquility. Performing a simple tea ceremony can elicit all these virtues along with a relaxation response, like a breath of fresh air, a moment's repose in the midst of difficulties. Fully immerse yourself in what you are doing, and your thoughts become unified with your action. In this way, you become present. The quality of awareness that you develop will stay with you as a resource.

Here are the simple instructions for a tea ceremony we have performed with many people over the years. Even a child can do it, and yet these few

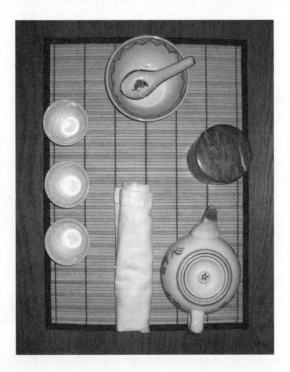

Figure 8.2 Tea Ceremony

moments immersed in this simple ritual can provide a profound experience. You can perform it alone or with family, friends, or clients.

1. What you need:
   a. Utensils: A mat, a teapot, a bowl, a spoon, a pot to hold the hot water, and a teacup for each person.
   b. Tea: We perform this ceremony using peppermint tea because of its pleasant aroma and delicious taste. But please use any tea that you like. If you cannot obtain the tea as loose tea leaves, open the teabags and empty several into the bowl.
2. Preheat the water and then bring it to the tea area.
3. Set out your utensils out as pictured and give everyone a teacup, set down in front of them. We often perform tea sitting in a circle on the floor, but you can also do it sitting at a low table or even sitting around a dining table.
4. If sharing tea with others, begin by briefly explaining the ceremony. There is no talking once the ceremony begins. Each person will be quietly aware and experience everything deeply. Once the tea is poured, everyone turns his cup before drinking (Instruction 8).
5. Meditate for several minutes to settle quietly before you begin.
6. Scoop up a spoonful of tea leaves and place them in the pot. Lightly tap the spoon against the teapot three times. Repeat spooning, placing, and tapping several times until all the tea is in the pot. Listen carefully to the sound of the tapping.
7. Pour in the hot water, listening carefully to the sound of the water as it enters the pot and smelling the aroma of the tea as it begins to brew. Make your movements slow and precise without tension. Place the cover on the pot and then rotate the pot three times in a clockwise direction, then three times in a counterclockwise direction.
8. Pick up the teapot and pour the tea into each teacup, one by one, and then pour a cup for yourself last.
9. Once all the teacups have been filled, everyone rotates his cup three times clockwise and three times counterclockwise.
10. Lift the cup slowly, smell the aroma of the tea, look at the color and patterns in the cup, then slowly sip the tea, letting the flavor sit on the tongue for a moment. Keep your mind clear, focused on your actions and sensations. Listen to the sounds, smell the aromas, savor the taste

of the tea, and let yourself relax. Refrain from talking. At the end, take a moment for meditation to savor the experience. Paradoxically, as you fill yourself with the experience, you experience emptiness.

Finding Sanctuary in Your Own Clear Mind

Meditation can give you sanctuary in your own here and now moment of mindful presence, empty of thought. You can carry peace of mind with you always and anywhere.

Sit quietly in meditation. Let all your sensations settle. Breathe comfortably, in and out, allowing your breathing rate to be relaxed and calm. Now let your mind clear of all thought. As soon as a new thought appears, let it go and return to meditating without thought. Keep working on letting your stream of consciousness be clear of thought. In that moment of no-thought, there is no worry or stress. Everything is serene and peaceful. Here is true sanctuary, always available if you simply make the effort to recognize that it is there.

Working Through Traumatic Memories

Our memory has two main systems, one explicit and conscious, and the other implicit and unconscious. Explicit memory includes the memorizing of ideas as well as episodic memory for events we have experienced. It works through the higher-level prefrontal cortex and the hippocampus. The implicit memory system is involved when we learn a skill, such as driving a car. Once you have mastered the skills, you always remember how to make a left turn without having to think about it. Memory of a trauma is influenced by the release of stress hormones during the traumatic experience. The explicit memory system is blocked by the rush of hormones, which helps explain why people often have a conscious amnesia for the event itself. And yet, the stress response activates the short path through the emotional parts of the brain, the limbic system involved in implicit memory. Thus, we remember the feeling vividly without any rational input from the long path to help us put it into perspective.

Shifting from the short path to the long path of memory processing can alter traumatic memory. Meditative awareness is key. Freud advised where id was, there ego shall be, and traumatic memory offers an opportunity to use our rational faculties to quell the strong implicit experiences that are disturbing. You may recall earlier when we described the short and long path of fear. If someone sees a snake in her path and feels afraid but then looks more closely and realizes that it is just a stick, the fear evaporates. Here the long path helps to mitigate the strong, immediate fear response from the short path. You can now reconsider the traumatic event by activating the long path. Cognitive therapy can be used to help work through negative judgments and reactions that interfere with recovery.

Are you telling yourself how awful it was, how unfair it is, how disturbed you feel? In a Zen sense, each experience is just what it is and should be accepted as such. The judgments you make add to the suffering. No matter how terrible, you have survived. You have felt your feelings and recognized the horror of what you experienced. But now it has passed. You are starting a healing process. By letting go of your judgments and simply accepting what you experienced as now in the past, you are free of trauma now in this new moment.

Meditate now and consider what you tend to tell yourselves about the trauma. Notice how you might be revving your reactions by telling yourself how bad it was and how terrible you feel. Can you let these thoughts go, recognizing that although there may be much truth in the fact that the event was terrible, your assessments now are detrimental to your healing. Bring yourself to the present moment now, aware in each moment. Keep working on questioning these negative thoughts. Albert Ellis, one of the founding fathers of cognitive therapy, often said that the world is not fair, but this can be handled gracefully. When you can accept this fact, you open the way for your nervous system to ease down as you start to feel better.

Nurturing Self-Support

The experience you have while meditating brings a sense of how you are the master of your life. You may not be able to control contingency, but you can control how you interpret it. You can grow to be at peace, even when you have experienced a traumatic event by cultivating acceptance meditatively.

Meditate on breathing for a few minutes, noticing each breath, in and out. Recognize how your breathing finds its own natural rhythm without your having to do anything except allow it to happen. Contemplate how many things are like this. When you have the flu, you can drink extra water and get sufficient rest, but ultimately, nature takes its course and your body eventually heals. Similarly with trauma, if you take care of your physical and psychological health, your brain-mind-body system will find its natural balance again. Nature will take its course. Think of other examples of how the mind-brain-body system can restore balance to itself. As you sit in meditation now, allow yourself to accept yourself as you are now and to trust that you can return to normal when the time is right. Allow your recovery process to take the time it needs. Our brains are capable of neuroplasticity and neurogenesis, to grow and develop as needed. Have confidence in the process.

CONCLUSION

Meditation is an invaluable tool for overcoming anxiety and trauma. We apply mindful attention to sensations and experience them as just what they are, but nothing more. We can intervene in the short-path fear response by enlisting unbiased attention and awareness. And we can develop a strong faith in our own capacities to be relaxed and calm, even when circumstances challenge our limits. Meditate regularly to enhance the power of meditation's dual effect, to keep us calm and alert, for optimal handling of all that we experience.

9

Taming Impulse for Addiction and Weight Management

When you undergo painful anguish and torment of hell, you see only burning fires whereas those who are enlightened experience an everlasting place of gentle light. Now tell me, what are you seeing?
                                    —*(Paraphrased from Zen Master Hakuin)*

THE GATES OF HEAVEN AND THE GATES OF HELL

Once long ago there was an accomplished swordsman. The king heard about his great skill and summoned him to teach his army what he knew. In those days, you did not refuse an invitation from the king, and so the swordsman made the trip to the palace. When he finally arrived, the king gathered all his top guards to join in on the lesson. The swordsman said, "I can beat anyone with only two techniques. No one can stop me."

Angered by the swordsman's seeming arrogance, the king impulsively ordered his best soldier to step into the ring with the swordsman and commanded, "Cut him down!

The swordsman seemed unaffected and said calmly, "So be it."

The king's guard lifted his sword over the swordsman's head threateningly.

The swordsman knelt down, ready to receive the deathblow, and said, "Here open the gates of hell."

Suddenly, in that dramatic moment, the king thought, and realized that he was being taught. With a humbled voice he said, "Wait, spare him," at which point the guard stepped back and returned his sword to its sheath.

The swordsman rose, gestured widely, and said, "Here open the gates of heaven."

The king bowed to the swordsman and said, "Please accept me as your student." The king learned the swordsman's subtle art, and with the wisdom he gained, ruled with restraint and compassion.

■ ■ ■

Impulsive behavior is like opening the gates of hell and all the negative consequences that follow. And yet, the gates of heaven are always there too, waiting as potential to be opened. Why do some people consistently make the wrong choices, while others, seeming to have similar backgrounds and circumstances, make the right ones? The answer is found in the way people handle impulses and make decisions about how to act upon them. Impulse and decision making are the common roots that can be found in many problems like substance abuse, violence, criminal behavior, and eating disorders. By understanding the root, we find an important essence that will help guide treatments.

Meditation has been shown to trigger positive responses that interrupt an impulse and shift the nervous system out of impulsive behavior patterns. The meditative treatments included here will give you vital tools for developing a calm center that will allow your clients to open the gates of heaven.

IMPULSE AND URGE IN DECISION MAKING

According to Socratic theory, people always make their decisions based on what they think is best for their happiness at that time. Obviously, people often make unhealthy, self-destructive, and unwise decisions, and so this statement seems puzzling. But what turns out to be a poor decision may have seemed the best decision in that moment. For example, when someone eats a rich dessert, she has decided that the enjoyment she feels today is worth the weight she gains tomorrow. We have recent evidence that refines the Socratic view, based on new findings about the brain.

People act either on reflection that activates the long pathway in the brain (the dieter puts off the pleasure of that rich dessert for her continuing weight loss) or simply respond directly to the impulse through the short pathway (she decides to eat the dessert now). An impulse is a feeling state that has a strong motivational push to want to do something right now. The impulse has both a body component, experienced as a strong physical urge, and an emotional component. These different brain pathways have been found to respond to impulse differently, resulting in divergent types of decisions.

The Two Brain Systems for Handling Impulse and Decision Making

The reflective system is a long path that works slowly and involves thinking about decisions, based on a rational, reasoning process. The brain processes this information in the prefrontal cortex. There are many factors involved in how people come to these decisions. We look at our options and assign values that help us decide what actions to take. We also weigh out the risks and rewards. And we balance out the anticipated gain or loss in relation to time delays (Rolls, McCabe, & Redoute, 2008). Cognitive therapy works with these kinds of decision-making processes.

Another system is also involved: a short path. This fast-acting system responds to physiological urges. The body signals the urge and, based on these signals, the limbic system makes an adjustment directly to return the system to homeostasis (Figure 9.1).

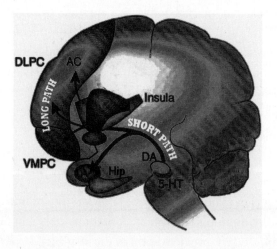

Figure 9.1   Impulse Systems in the Brain

How Interoception Links the Two Systems

These long and short paths work together through interoception, engaging an insula circuit that is connected to both. In a sense, the insula guides toward pushing the accelerator to drive an impulse or pressing the brakes to stop it. Recall that the insula has a map of internal body sensations, functioning somewhat like the motor map in the motor cortex and the sensory map in the parietal cortex. According to the somatic marker hypothesis, (also discussed in Chapter 7), the insula and posterior cingulate system receive sensory stimuli, which the prefrontal cortex and memory systems in the amygdala and hippocampus interpret as either a positive or negative experience. This interpretation influences the release of neurotransmitters.

All of the factors, such as value, risk, time, and effort, are dependent on our internal body state. Interoception provides constant input to the brain from multimodal afferents that carry signals to the brain. Inputs such as temperature, pain, sensual touch, and even sensing of internal organs in actions such as breathing, gastrointestinal activity, and the cardiovascular system are continuously coming in. This system is intimately integrated with emotions (Craig, 2009), as we described in Chapter 7. Interoception helps the organism keep in balance even under differing conditions. And researchers are finding this interaction at many levels. For example, research has found that people assign value to their options and make their decisions based on the assigned value in conjunction, not competition, with visceral sensations (Monterosso & Lou, 2010).

The core idea is that internal body states are more involved in what we feel and do than we might think. What we experience on the outside depends to a large degree on what we feel on the inside. Inner and outer are interrelated, and the interaction goes both ways. Just as inner experience influences outer behavior, so, too, repeated stimuli from the external world can lead to changes in our internal states. Thus, psychotherapy changes brain responses as healing effects take place.

Problems in Interoception

When interoception malfunctions, people make risky or impulsive decisions (Paulus, Rogalsky, Simmons, Feinstein, & Stein, 2003; Preuschoff, Quartz, & Bossaerts, 2008). In fact, overactivation of the insula has been correlated with higher neuroticism in general (Paulus & Stein, 2006). People suffering from depression and anxiety tend to appraise interoceptive events more negatively. Anxiety increases the response to potential risk, thus leading to the avoidant behavior often seen with anxiety (see Chapter 8).

Damage to any part of the system affects decision making. For example, when people have prefrontal cortex dysfunction from brain injury, drug addiction, or impulse control disorders, they tend to make impulsive decisions, driven by short-path sensations rather than long-path thought.

DEVELOPING INTEROCEPTION AWARENESS

As we have seen, interoception connects how we think and feel with what we do, so developing interoceptive awareness is a good place to begin a change process that will reach out to affect many psychological problems. Meditation works directly with interoception, providing the sensitivities and clarity that are needed to help people develop healthy responses. These exercises will guide clients in becoming more aware of their inner experiencing.

Enhancing Interoception Using Sensory Mindfulness

When clients feel strong, troublesome impulses, they have accompanying sensory experiences that contribute to their experience. Interoception is automatic, but we can enhance awareness of the somatic level. Paying mindful attention to sensations can have a moderating effect on the impulse. Attuning to the sensory level can be developed through practice of mindfulness meditations.

Begin With General Body Awareness

Try this exercise and the series of sensory exercises that follow when you are feeling relatively comfortable. Once you have built the skills, apply the same exercise when immersed in an emotional reaction. As you do all the exercises in the series, try to perceive without judgment. Each sensation is a quality to experience, but don't assess whether it is good or bad. Accept each sensation as just that—a sensory experience. So whether you notice a painful sensation or a pleasant sensation, just try to carefully follow each sensation as it is and set aside your opinions or assessments.

Sit in a chair or lie down comfortably on your back on a couch or bed. Close your eyes and turn your attention to your body. Allow your attention to scan, beginning at your feet and moving up through your body to your head, and notice whatever occurs to you. How long is it from your feet to your waist? How far does it feel from shoulder to shoulder? Sense how long your arms feel. Now pay attention to how your body meets the surface you are sitting or lying on. Do you take support from the chair or bed or do you feel like you are pushing down on it? Take a few moments now to allow awareness of your body as it occurs to you.

Now turn your attention to your muscles as you scan through your body again. Are some muscles tight and others loose? Move through your body, noticing sensations in each muscle group: legs, arms, back, front, and neck to head. Don't change anything; simply notice what you perceive. You may find that as you attend to your muscles, some will want to relax naturally. Allow this to occur but don't force anything. Now sit or lie quietly for several minutes and allow your body to settle. When you feel ready, stretch and stand up.

Awareness of Temperature

Now, pay attention to your body temperature. Notice the air in the room. Is it cool or warm? Turn your attention to your skin and pay attention to how warm or cool it feels. You may notice variations, such as warmth in your midsection or face, and coolness in your hands or feet. Pay attention to body temperature and notice if it changes over time.

Awareness of Heartbeat

Turn your attention to your heartbeat. Begin by putting a hand lightly on your pulse at the wrist. Notice the rate as you breathe comfortably and relax. Now, place your hand lightly on your chest at your heart, and turn your attention there to notice your heartbeat. You may need to allow this to develop over time. If you have trouble feeling your heartbeat, get up and walk around for a few minutes. Then sit down again and return your hand to your heart. You may find it easier now to feel your heartbeat. Next, move your attention deeper within. Can you sense the beating of your heart and perhaps the circulation of your blood through areas of your body? You might feel pulsing somewhere, or sense the pumping itself.

Awareness of Breathing

Pay attention to your breathing. Begin by noticing the air that goes in through your nose. Is it cool or warm? Notice the sensation as the air travels down through your breathing passages and into your lungs. Allow your ribcage to expand as it fills with air. Then softly allow the air to flow out as you exhale. Try to keep your breathing relaxed and normal, without breathing differently as you pay attention. People sometimes try to breathe deeper or make longer breaths, but in this exercise, you are simply trying to be aware of how you breathe naturally. If your breathing naturally wants to relax or slow down as you become aware, allow that to happen as it will. Stay with attention to breathing for several minutes.

MODERATING IMPULSE IN ADDICTION

Meditation works directly with key brain areas to help restore a more normal balance and better adjustment. And Zen provides helpful ways to reframe the suffering that people feel as they withdraw from long-time substance use. But it does so in a different way from traditional therapies and without the potentially harmful side effects of pharmacological treatments.

Users believe they are gaining great pleasure from indulging in their habit. And as Socrates would predict, they make the bad choice to use their substance because they believe it will bring them pleasure. But the pleasure is always transitory; soon they need more, and the pleasure even diminishes. Habituation inevitably makes the drug less satisfying as the brain adjusts to the use over time. Fear of pain from withdrawal can develop, with behavior that avoids the pain by continuing to choose the substance. Abusers are on a pleasure and pain cycle that keeps repeating. Typically, cognitive approaches to therapy try to extinguish a craving by challenging false assumptions to lessen discomfort. Meditation offers an alternative to add to these treatments: to address the issue of pleasure and pain itself.

Shelly had started using heroin as a troubled teenager. She came from a seemingly good family in an upper-middle-class home. But turmoil and argument was the norm in her household. With a high-strung mother and a passive-aggressive father, she found solace with her friends, spending as much time as possible away from home. Her younger sister made a different adjustment, involving herself in school activities and excelling academically. Her sister's success added to Shelly's discomfort, since she was often chided by her parents, who asked her, "Why can't you be more like your sister? What's wrong with you?"

Shelly found heroin did far more than relieve her tensions. It also gave her a strong sense of self. She could handle everything calmly and coolly. She thought of herself as being above it all, and heroin use made it possible for her to stay that way no matter how much the family yelled and screamed.

She was referred for therapy after she nearly died from an overdose. She told us she wanted to stop using heroin but just didn't think she could live without it. She told us, "I am a user, and that's it." She liked her fellow user friends and didn't know or like anyone who didn't use drugs.

We taught her the meditation series in this chapter. She had some moments of being completely calm and began to experience herself that way without the drug producing her calmness. She gradually discovered that the ability to be calm under pressure was actually her own capacity. She experienced firsthand, through meditation, that drugs didn't make her that way—she did. As she was able to acknowledge her inner strength that had always been there, she could let go of her belief that she needed heroin to provide it for her.

She volunteered to undergo withdrawal. She had careful medical monitoring and succeeded in going through the process. Being mindful of herself in her home situation, she understood what she could and could not control. Her parents were not willing to change, and so as soon as she turned 18, she got her own apartment. She worked part-time to support herself until she was ready to return to school. She pursued her education at a junior college and grew stronger and centered, requesting an occasional supportive session when she felt the need, until she no longer felt that the sessions were necessary. We saw her in passing some years later. She had not returned to drugs, and she continued to turn to her personal meditation as a resource.

Mindfulness Series for Addiction

This series applies mindfulness meditation specifically for people who are being treated for substance abuse. The series can be begun even when the client is still using the substance and carried through to help with the discomfort of withdrawal.

Begin With Observation

The first step is to simply observe, without judgment or change, when feeling comfortable and relaxed. Practice is easier when tensions are lower. Then, as the skills develop, mindfulness becomes a resource that can be called upon when needed. Begin to develop mindfulness skills by focusing attention during the therapy session. Be mindful of sensations, feelings, thoughts, and objects of thoughts.

Keep thinking on a concrete level of simply noticing the momentary experience as it occurs. If an evaluation of whether this experience is good or bad, liked or disliked, is added, notice that too. After the ability to sustain mindfulness improves and some confidence is felt, apply it to the problem.

Foster a Calmer General Adjustment Through Breathing

Relaxing and calming may help in overcoming substance abuse. Part of what drives people is the discomfort they feel in their lives. Developing calm will offer some relief of tensions as well as adding the confidence needed to stay with the process.

Extensive drug use throws the nervous system out of balance. According to the polyvagal theory (see Chapter 10), breathing is a fundamental link to the heart and brain. Meditative breathing is one way that is often used to ease a disturbed nervous system and bring it back to a calmer balance. Use any of the breathing meditations in other chapters along with this meditation to breathe with the whole body. Shift between relaxing for a brief period and then returning to nonattachment.

Lie down and let your body relax. With each breath in, imagine that the air spreads through your entire body, all the way down to your toes. With each breath out, imagine that tensions flow out. For a variation, you may imagine that the air coming in is light colored and bright and the air going out is murky and dark. Allow your muscles to relax and tensions to ease.

Practice Nonattachment

The ability to be nonattached when needed is helpful for facing discomfort. It begins when we stop seeking pleasure and avoiding pain. Paradoxically, when we free ourselves from loving pleasure and hating pain, we gain more self-control and internal balance.

Nonattachment can be practiced, at first, on small likes and dislikes, such as eating a food that you feel neutral about. When chewing, pay close attention to the taste, texture, and aroma. Note the qualities of the taste, without like or dislike. Simply be aware of the sensations and accept them as they are. Repeat the experiment with a food that you slightly dislike. Instead of thinking about how much you dislike this food, simply notice the taste. Is it salty or sweet, bitter or sour? What is the texture like: crunchy or smooth, crispy or soft? And does it have an aroma that you notice? Do the same experiment with a favorite food. The development of an accepting but disengaged attitude takes practice.

Extend the range of objects for this meditation to bring about a less strong reaction to pleasure or discomfort. A middle way of personal satisfaction develops, which leads to a more accommodating feeling about everyday preferences.

Disengaging the Craving Impulse Mindfully

When craving occurs, sit down and focus your attention on it. Observe the sensations with each passing moment. If you start to label them as negative, notice that. Keep returning to the fullness of the experience without being drawn away from the moment-to-moment experiencing. Practice your nonattachment by not liking or disliking the sensations of craving.

Let your muscles relax while sitting quietly. Shift your attention to breathing, observe your rhythm, and then let your breathing settle into a relaxed pattern as well. Allow any unnecessary tensions to ease. If your thoughts move away from the moment, gently bring them back. Continue to breathe as comfortably as possible while observing. Notice any changes as they occur. After a time, your sensations will alter in various ways. Usually the steady craving feeling will ease or diminish in patterns, often in waves, of less and at times, of more.

Meditative awareness of this difference allows for movement toward less craving, once these patterns of feeling have been recognized and the possibility for comfortable lessening has been accepted as real.

Differentiating the Features of Cravings

Closely observing the general craving experience mindfully, you may notice that the craving is not just one overwhelming experience: It has various contributing parts. Try to distinguish the parts by observing your ongoing sensations. Do you feel the sensations in one part of your body as much as in another part? For example, is your stomach hurting? Or perhaps you feel tension in your neck? What is the quality of your breathing? Are your breaths long or short? Do you feel any emotions right now? If so, notice what they are. Refine your perception of each feeling, such as, "Now I feel sadness, and I also feel tired." And what are the types of thoughts? Maintain your meditative awareness, calm and steady.

Extend your practice of mindfulness into other settings. Sometimes drug use is triggered by the circumstances you are in (state dependent). Notice the places where your craving is stimulated. Are certain people associated with it, too? Do you have personal behaviors and thoughts that go with that place or those people? This will require that you stop to observe mindfully at times through the day and evening. Then, when you recognize some of these triggers, notice how they are interconnected in the momentary experiencing. For example, do you start thinking about someone and the craving increases? Or perhaps you have a memory of a place where you used drugs and then you felt the craving. Notice any cues that signal and elicit your desire for the drug, whether the cues come from persons, places, or things. At first, withdrawal from them may be essential to freedom from the habit.

Use the skills developed from practicing nonattachment in the earlier exercise with any feelings of pleasure and pain that might emerge. Remember, "my craving" is just a group of sensations, not actually fundamental to who you are. Pleasure and pain are transitory, so seek the middle way between them, calm and centered in meditation.

Choosing Renunciation

As skills in awareness and detachment develop, clients gain more insight into what they are doing and how the involvement in the substance or impulse is actually affecting life in adverse ways. They may begin to feel motivated to give up the harmful substance or behavior that is having a destructive effect. When someone is going to undergo withdrawal, always take the precaution that they get medical care to monitor the process. The therapist can guide in choosing a hospital or medical facility that will ensure a safe and healthy withdrawal.

Dependency may seem entrenched. But meditation can help clients gain courage to make a healthy decision. The dependence was created by the mind/body interactions and because it has been created, it can be dismantled.

When ready to take the steps, enter the appropriate place for you to forgo taking the substance. Notice the tensions and other feelings mindfully. Mindfulness and nonattachment help to face the discomfort and accept it is as it occurs, and then calm down anyway.

Notice any doubts or worries, but don't let them distract from what is occurring in this moment. For example, if thinking a thought such as, "I might not ever get over this problem," or "I've always had troubles," consider it just part of the flow in this moment, as you are fully aware. Accept all thoughts as part of the mindful flow. Whatever you feel about the past or the future, or even what you are feeling right now, can all be viewed as mindful moments now. The next moment is not determined by the previous moment. Your future is open and filled with potential.

Return to the Primary Point, Original Mind

We build our sense of self from what we do, think, and feel. But we are always evolving and changing through time. The self that we are today is not the self we were 10 years ago, and yet, something endures. This traditional Zen story helps to illustrate.

Before I started to study Zen, mountains were mountains and rivers were rivers. But as I began to study Zen and learn about the transitory moment-by-moment change and how all things are thus impermanent and empty, mountains were no longer mountains and rivers were no longer rivers. But now after much meditation and a deeper understanding, mountains are once again mountains and rivers are once again rivers (Figure 9.2).

This story can be expanded to include our sense of self. If asked, most would say that they know who they are and have a firm sense of self. But, as we come to recognize that the self we are today is far different from the self we were 10 years ago, we might question whether we have a lasting self. The idea that we have an unchanging self seems to be an illusion according to Buddhist theory. This idea can be helpful to those who are trying to overcome compulsions and cravings. Often the sense of self is overly linked to the substance. The user feels identified with the substance and all that that use entails and may have difficulty letting go of their self-concept as a user. But

Figure 9.2 Mountains Are Mountains (ink on rice paper hanging scroll, 20th century China)

Source: Simpkins private collection

without the anchor of a lasting self, some might feel adrift and lost. Meditation can help clients reclaim their original nature, to come back to a deeper sense of self that is free of substance use and centered in living a healthy and happy life.

When clients come to therapy for substance abuse, especially those who have relapsed, they are often still emotionally identified with the substance, even if they say that they want to quit. Part of the problem is in their enduring sense of themselves as a user. The therapist can help people to recognize what they think they gain from drug use, and then recognize that they possess the capacities they crave without the drug. Meditation can give a different experience, of a deeper nature that is not at all involved in drugs.

Deconstructing the Fixed Sense of Self

Begin with a familiar mindful meditation on breathing to notice how each breath is new, a different breath. Sense how the surrounding circumstances change with each passing moment. Perhaps there is a breeze now, and then it stops. Or maybe there is a sound of a passing car, then silence. Gradually shift the focus of meditation to include the sense of yourself right now. Notice how you might be thinking about yourself in this moment while sitting on this seat now. Pay close attention to whatever is noticed. Perform this meditation again at a later time or on a different day. You might have new thoughts or feelings about yourself. Become aware of all the ways that each moment is a unique combination of thoughts, feelings, and sensations, including the personal sense of self. Recognize that beyond all these moment-to-moment thoughts and feelings, you are always you, calmly sitting in these moments, calm, quiet, and in tune.

Meditation on Deeper Nature

How do you understand your true self? What are you? Do you know? If you don't know, only go straight—don't know. Then this don't-know mind cuts off all thinking, and your only-me situation, only-me consideration, and only-me opinion disappear. Then your correct situation, correct condition, and correct opinion appear—very simple.

(Seung, 1992, p. 12)

Meditate quietly beyond thought. Simply sit quietly. Let all your thoughts settle and keep returning to the quiet moment. As you sustain this quiet meditation for a few minutes, you will begin to feel a sense of self emerge that relies on nothing outside of yourself. You are simply here and now, breathing, sitting, and being quietly present in each passing moment. Although thoughts, worries, and fears might interfere at times, moments of peace can also occur. The peaceful moments grow longer and your sense of peace grows stronger as you practice. Even a fleeting moment of a quiet, unperturbed mind begins the process. Keep practicing and allowing your strong sense of self, based in the experience of calm clarity in meditation, to develop.

WORKING WITH THE URGE TO EAT IN WEIGHT MANAGEMENT

When students today fail to make progress, where's the fault? The fault lies in the fact that they don't have faith in themselves! If you don't have faith in yourself, then you'll be forever in a hurry trying to keep up with everything around you, and you'll be twisted and turned by whatever environment you're in and never move freely. But if you can just stop this mind that goes rushing around moment by moment, looking for something, then you'll be no different from the patriarchs and the buddhas.

(Zen Master Lin Chi quoted in Watson, 1993, p. 23)

Eating is an activity that everyone engages in, but it often takes on many qualities that have nothing to do with eating's real purpose of taking in life sustaining nourishment. Those who struggle with weight management are often looking for something outside of themselves to make them feel good, or completely fulfilled. Their weight becomes an expression of something they feel they lack. Zen therapy gets people to get in tune with their deeper nature through meditation. Its practice allows the important issues to emerge and be worked on. Using meditation, people can renew their faith in themselves and find true fulfillment.

A middle-aged woman came in for therapy to lose weight. Nancy was 25 pounds overweight. She worked at a store as a salesperson. She was married with two sons, who were both in high school. She had tried to lose weight countless times and had gone up and down in her weight for years. She told us that she felt constantly stressed, that life was difficult, and that she was always tired. But she tried to make the best of it and just keep going. She thought she would try meditation therapy, since someone had told her that it "worked for losing weight."

Nancy learned meditation and practiced between sessions. As she became more aware, she realized that she was always rushing. She said, "I never noticed that from the moment I get up, I'm racing. I shower, wash and dry my hair, hurry to get dressed, make a quick breakfast for the family, pack the kids' lunches, and then run off to work."

With this new awareness, we asked her to think about whether there was any small change she could make to give herself more time. Her immediate response was that she couldn't possibly wake up any earlier because she needed every possible minute of sleep she could get. We said that might not be the only solution, and asked her to think about it.

Nancy came back the next week with a new hairdo. She explained that she had given it a great deal of thought and finally decided to have her hair permed. Now she could just wash it when she showered and let it air dry. With the extra 10 minutes she had been spending drying her hair, her whole life transformed. Like a domino effect, she felt like she had plenty of time to accomplish everything without hurrying.

Now functioning at what felt like a slower pace, she could take the time to be aware through the day. She practiced mindful eating and found that she truly enjoyed the preparation and taste of gourmet food. She was surprised to discover that she had an interest in cooking. She began by preparing gourmet meals for her family. Now that her children were in high school, she decided to take some cooking classes offered at a local store. As she improved the quality of the food she served and ate, she found herself more satisfied with less quantity. She delved deeper into cooking as a Zen art, preparing the food mindfully. Coming from a clear mind as she worked, her meals were not only delicious but also beautiful. Nancy found deep satisfaction in the experience of creation. Gradually, she lost the weight while also finding fulfillment in what she did as she did it.

Mindful Eating

A good place to begin working on an eating disorder is to begin where you are, by turning attention to eating mindfully. Start with one simple food and do this meditation for an interesting experience. In the moment of eating, you plant the seeds for healing.

Pick a piece of fresh fruit that you like to eat. Hold it in your hand and look at it. Notice the colors. Feel its weight. Is it warm or cool? Peel it slowly (if it has a skin to be removed, such as an orange or tangerine). Smell the sweet aroma. Then take a bite. Notice as the juice sprays into your mouth. Bite slowly, tasting attentively. For this moment, eating this piece of fruit is the only activity in your life. There is no goal; just contemplate your experience of eating.

Mindful Mealtime

Many Zen monasteries make eating meals a moment that embodies the Zen experience. Everyone sits together, facing each other in two lines. All have their own bowl and chopsticks. One monk serves the food into each bowl until the individual indicates to stop. People learn to take only the amount of food they can eat. There is no wasting. Everyone eats together in silence. You can hear the clicking of chopsticks and feel a calm atmosphere. All food is completely consumed. When everyone is finished, water is poured into each bowl. The members swish it around to clean the bowl, and then must drink the water, followed by wiping the bowl and chopsticks with a clean cloth. Thus, eating and cleaning are all done as one process.

If you want to discover healthier eating habits, Zen discourages people from analyzing their feelings or thoughts about food. Instead, just practice. As you engage in meditative eating, you will make discoveries that start a change process.

Meditative Meal

Choose a meal for meditation. If you are preparing the food, do so mindfully, paying close attention as you open cans and packages, cut fresh foods, and cook them. Listen to the sounds and notice the aromas. Set the table and place everything in an exact pattern, attentively noticing as each utensil and plate meets the table. Ask your family or friends to participate in meditating during the meal, or if you are alone, have complete silence through the meal. Sit down at the table, notice your sitting position, and take a moment to clear your thoughts before you begin. As you begin to eat, notice the aroma, the texture, and temperature of the food. Taste each bite. Chew the food all the way down to liquid. Don't hurry. Eat only as much as needed to satisfy hunger and no more. Keep attention focused on eating. Maintain a meditative quality of mind through out the meal. Clean the dishes when finished, maintaining your quiet, meditative awareness.

Working Through Meditative Meals

As you meditate while you eat, thoughts, feelings, and impulses might emerge. People sometimes feel impatient with eating slowly. They might start to think of other things, or maybe find it hard to keep focused on eating itself. Notice what you experience during the meal, perhaps even noting it down in a journal right after the meal and cleanup are completed. What you discover are valuable clues to deeper understanding about your eating problems. Practice your meditative eating regularly. Use the interoception exercises in the beginning of this chapter to work on impulsive eating behavior, to recognize and regulate the impulses. You may find that some of your difficulties dissolve. Persistent disturbance can be discussed in therapy.

Self-Acceptance

As Zen Master Lin Chi taught in the quote at the beginning of the weight management section, we find enlightenment when we can wholeheartedly accept ourselves, just as we are. He often told his students that nothing is missing. We have everything we need to be happy. But when people want to lose weight, they are often passing judgment on themselves, believing that something is fundamentally wrong with them. Learning to accept yourself in each moment can bring a transformation that will naturally lead to taking care of your body in a nurturing and healthy way.

Sit quietly in meditation and notice what you are experiencing. Don't think of it as good or bad, right or wrong. Stop any judging that you may be doing. Don't wish for something beyond this moment or regret something that has passed. Keep returning to the present moment of experiencing, accepting what is, just as it is. Just be as you are right now, sitting quietly noticing your experiencing. Practice this meditation regularly, accepting yourself just as you are.

CONCLUSION

Impulse problems can be improved by working with different brain pathways. You can develop sensory awareness to enhance interoception, so that the sensations driving impulses through the short path, bottom-up processing can be recognized and dealt with differently. You can also develop mindful awareness, not simply to get in touch with impulsive behavior but also to learn from it. Problems with addiction and weight management ultimately involve facing yourself and absolutely accepting that you can be healthy and happy from within. Your true nature is complete, and you can become attuned to it by the regular practice of meditation.

10

Fostering Loving Relationships

Events cast shadows, flickers on a wall
But we're captured in chains and enthralled.
Wondering at all we think we see,
Spellbound by shadows of reality.
If we light the lamp of wisdom's vision
Meditation will free us from our prison.
(C. Alexander Simpkins & Annellen M. Simpkins)

IF YOU LOVE, LOVE OPENLY

A group of monks and one nun were practicing meditation together. The nun was beautiful even though she dressed in simple nun's robes. The monks all loved her, and one of them secretly slipped her a love note, asking to meet after the meditation session. The master spoke to the group and then, just when all were about to leave, the nun stood up and said, "If you truly love me, come and hug me right now!" The monk then bowed for the teaching.

Relationships can become embroiled in hidden agendas and miscommunications. False ideas interfere with direct perception of each other, person to person. Learning how to clear away the misconceptions and misunderstandings allows the natural capacities for love and compassion to emerge. This

Figure 10.1   Meditating Together (acrylic on paper)
Source: Carmen Z. Simpkins, American artist, 1980

chapter offers a meditative approach that guides in overcoming the barriers to intimacy while also planting the seeds that will allow a natural tendency toward healthy relationships to grow (Figure 10.1).

According to Zen, we are all interconnected. The separations between people are artificial. Our experience tells us that we are social beings who devote much of our energy to seeking loving relationships. Research shows that our neurobiology is wired for relationships. Thus, when there are problems preventing interpersonal closeness, we feel disturbed.

Meditation can facilitate a process that leads us back to our natural capacity for intimacy. It can heal wounds from the past and help reach out in the present moment, to rediscover the loving relationships that are our birthright.

THE NEUROBIOLOGY OF SOCIAL INTERACTIONS

We all know that interpersonal relationships are important to us, but recently researchers have come to recognize the ways that we are hardwired to be social. Darwin (1872) first recognized that our emotional state is an interaction between facial expressions of others with our own nervous system. A new branch of science has evolved, known as affective neuroscience, that investigates how our mind-brain-body system interacts with other people. The assumption is that we are embodied beings, and so our feelings, thoughts, and actions with other people are always in an intimate interaction with our brain-body reactions. We take a step away from Descartes' separation of mind and body, and view ourselves as the philosopher Martin Heidegger (1962) envisioned, as "being-in-the-world." The modern neuroscience view correlates with the ancient wisdom of Zen, that we are always one with others—there is no real distinction to be made. We offer three modern theories that help to explain how we are embodied beings-in-the-world, always in relationship with others: the polyvagal theory, attachment theory, and mirror neurons.

The Polyvagal Theory of Social Interactions

A recent method for determining stress is to measure the activity of the tenth cranial nerve, the vagus nerve. The vagus nerve has both sensory and motor attachments, with a complex neural network of connections and feedback mechanisms. The measure, called vagal tone, monitors how well the individual is reacting to stress and how vulnerable the person is to stress. Thus, vagal tone can be used as an index of homeostasis (Porges, 1992).

The polyvagal theory (Porges, 2011), based in the vagus nerve system, is a comprehensive model of how our mind-brain-body system functions in a continual feedback–feed-forward interaction with others and with the environment. Mammals are polevagal, with each vagus playing a different role in regulation. Thus, when orienting, there might be an increase in vagal tone to breathing with a lessening of vagal tone to the heart. Thus, the concept of vagal tone is better understood as a complex of interactions that help us to react and respond. The polyvagal system includes many dimensions that involve the heart, the speech centers, the breathing passages, and the movement of the face and head. Thus, these vagal systems connect our brain, heart, and breathing with emotions and social feelings.

Social interaction is mediated through the muscles of the face. We receive and send social cues through facial expressions, eye gaze, vocalizing from the speech centers, and head positioning. It is through these facial and verbal centers that our social communications take place, and thus vagal tone has a fundamental influence on how we interact with others. As a direct result of signals from the vagal system, we are motivated to come closer to others or to move away. The polyvagal theory of social behavior predicts that people suffering from psychiatric disorders will have specific deficits in these vagal systems.

As clinicians, we often notice that many patients have poor eye gaze, a lack of affect, or difficulties with their verbal communications. These observations can signal to us a malfunction at the neurobiological level. The meditation methods provided can help to alter these malfunctions in these key nervous system pathways, giving people more choice and the ability to address and change at the psychological level. The implications of the polyvagal theory open new treatment potentials that address problems at a neurobiological level. Methods such as meditation and hypnosis can alter the systems, opening the way for better receptivity for cognitive therapy methods.

Attachment Theory and Our Instinct for Loving Relationships

Many behaviors, emotions, and functions occur instinctually, without deliberate awareness. One instinctual pattern is the reflex response of the parasympathetic nervous system to freeze when feeling afraid. An additional instinctive reflex is to fight or flee, occurring automatically from the sympathetic nervous system. And another wired-in response comes from the reward system which motivates us to seek the pleasures of food and sex that keep us healthy and reproducing. All of these systems can function outside of awareness, driving what we think, feel, and do.

According to attachment theory, love is also instinctual, as fundamental as sex and food. We are all prewired for love. People know when they are in love, and they seek it throughout life (Johnson, 2008). Another bit of evidence for love as crucial for healthy living is that love engages many regions on both sides of the brain to activate or deactivate. We find increased bilateral activity in the insula and anterior cingulate and in parts of the basal ganglia: the caudate and putamen. Reduced activity is also seen in the posterior cingulate and in the amygdala as well as the right prefrontal cortex (Bartels & Zeki, 2000).

Our ability to find and maintain loving relationships is influenced by our early primary relationship with our mother or caregiver, called an attachment relationship. Attachment styles of how we relate interpersonally, all through life, develop based on the quality of this formative relationship with our early primary caregiver. Attachment styles lead to affect styles. Our typical style of affect is repeated in relationships throughout life.

Three attachment styles were derived from John Bowlby's original attachment theory (Bowlby, 1983, 2005). How well people regulate their affect is described as self-regulation (Schore, 2003). The quality of the attachment formed during the first few years of life has a significant impact on the individual's future ability to regulate affect.

One of the core principles of attachment theories is that human beings rely on their primary attachment relationships for safety. From the base of a secure attachment, a child will have the confidence to explore his social and emotional world. But the exploration is always in balance between relying on the parent and relying on her own abilities. Secure attachment develops naturally, when the parent is available, sensitive, and responsive. Parents can teach their children how to regulate their emotions even during stressful situations. They can also foster positive experiences and facilitate the ability to reflect on oneself. So, through this interpersonal interaction, we learn how to solve conflicts, handle emotions, and cope well with stress. Attachment relationships are important throughout life, even into old age.

The developmental process of learning to self-regulate occurs without direct awareness. The right hemisphere is thought to be dominant during the first two years of life (Badenoch, 2008), so many of the functions that are controlled by the right brain, such as emotion, body experience, and autonomic processes, develop naturally through the secure attachment. In fact, the sense of attachment develops from the mother's right brain to the child's right brain in an unconscious manner. The emotional processing that arises from early right-brain attachment experiences continues to have an unconscious influence on later experiencing.

Unfortunately, not all mother-infant attachments are secure. Poor parenting can result in an insecure/avoidant attachment, or an insecure/anxious/ambivalent attachment (Ainsworth, Blehat, Waters, & Wall, 1978). When people form secure attachments, they find the satisfactions of love and enduring relationships (Johnson, 2008). But when they have formed avoidant or anxious ways of attaching because of problems in early developmental experiences, difficulties may develop later in life. Psychotherapy can correct this, by giving the client a secure attachment experience through the therapeutic relationship. Meditation can help correct the disregulated, often unconscious autonomic nervous system responses. In addition, it can provide a means for nonattachment that clears the way for healthy attachment, described later in this chapter.

Social Understanding at the Neuronal Level: Mirror Neurons

The brain contains a system of neurons that respond directly to the intentional actions and emotions of others. The mirror neuron system makes it possible for us to understand the actions of others as we do our own actions. The sense of another person resonates within as a primitive, felt sense. Our sense of others begins with our own brain response. Through the activation of the mirror neuron system, we have the capacity to infer what and how others think, feel, and experience. In this sense, our social understanding is based an empathic experience beginning at the neuronal level. As the discoverer of mirror neurons explained:

> Most of the time, we have a direct access to the world of others. Direct understanding does not require explanation. This particular dimension of social cognition is embodied in that it mediates between the multimodal experiential knowledge of our own lived body and the way we experience others.
>
> (Gallese, 2009, p. 166)

Certain neurons in the premotor cortex have mirror qualities. We would expect to find a motor area activated, since mirroring involves observing or participating in a movement. The second mirror area is located in the inferior parietal lobe (IPL). The parietal lobe is involved in sensory processing, and thus it is activated during hand grasping, specifically in two subareas of the inferior parietal cortex, PF and PFG. Many of the first mirror neuron studies involved grasping of an object, and so the activation of this area is not surprising. A third area is also activated, found in two sections located close together: the middle temporal gyrus and the superior temporal sulcus (STS). These areas take part in motion perception and vision. Thus, mirror neurons are found in the frontal, parietal, and temporal lobes. In a broad sense, mirror neurons are involved in seeing, sensing, and motion with a purpose.

Generally, what distinguishes mirror neurons from other neurons is that mirror neurons fire both when executing a movement oneself and when observing that motion in another. They don't fire to just any motion, such as watching a waterfall, but only fire to motion with an intention, purpose, or meaning (Cochin, Barthelemy, Roux, & Martineau, 1999).

These neural systems create a bridge of emotional empathy between one person and another. We literally feel for and with others through our brain activations. Zen meditation resonates with others in this direct way, where we are responding directly in our own brain at a very fundamental level.

Additional Research Findings

These new theories just described, combined with the findings from other relationship research, offer us clear indications of what distinguishes happily married couples from those who end up in divorce. With these understandings, we can tailor our treatments to foster healthy bonds and repair unhealthy ones. Much of the research agrees on key issues, so we combine and summarize here where there is consensus.

When people are having trouble in their relationships, they are in a perpetual state of emotional arousal. This triggers a stress response that leads to being quick to anger and having poor affect regulation (Solomon & Tatkin, 2011). They also show impaired judgment, since the prefrontal cortex is deactivated when under stress. Unhappy couples have much more negativity than positivity in their relationships. The ratio of positive to negative when discussing their conflicts has been predictive of whether the couple would later divorce (Gottman & Levenson, 1992). Not all negativity is found to be harmful to relationships. Some anger is inevitable, but when it fuels blame, it tends to be destructive (Gottman, 2011). These findings remind us that the full range of emotions is part of relationships—even anger. But keeping optimism as a central component, even during conflict, is key.

Arguments are inevitable, but how couples handle their conflicts is important. Different attachment styles and personality needs require that the couple make adjustments to ensure that both partners feel secure and cared for (Johnson, 2008). There is no one way that works for all couples, nor is any situation without its inevitable problems. Successful relationships have developed ways to meet situations well together. They know how to work problems out as they occur and repair damage when one or the other partner has betrayed the trust (Gottman, 2011).

Successful couples think in terms of *we* rather than *me*. Each individual portrays his or her life in terms of the shared relationship. Troubled couples tend to be more concerned about their personal interest than about the shared relationship. They attribute blame to their partner and minimize their own errors, a common human tendency (Heider, 1958). Learning to share a vision together and promote each other is key to mutual happiness and fulfillment (Gottman, 2011).

MEDITATION FOR RELATIONSHIPS

Meditation can be used to help couples create a relationship that is successful and satisfying. These methods can be used alone or integrated into typical couples therapy methods to facilitate positive change.

Meditation might seem to be a solitary experience, and yet the process of becoming inwardly attuned will automatically elicit awareness of others. Since our nervous systems are tuned for relating, improving inner awareness meditatively will naturally lead to better attunement to others. Research has found that when people meditate, they become more compassionate than nonmeditators (Lutz, Brefczynski-Lewis, Johnstone, & Davidson, 2008). Teaching couples and families to meditate can enhance the level of caring, an important factor in developing a mutually respectful and supportive attunement, which leads to a better relationship.

Relationship therapy can help from two directions: to overcome the negative and to enhance the positive. Troubled relationships are rife with conflict, and therapy can give people ways to repair the damage that comes from hostile encounters. Relationships are also, in their essence, the source for happiness and fulfillment. Thus, facilitating the positive qualities that relationships offer is essential. Meditation can help with both sides of relationships.

Recognizing Conflict Styles

Attachment theory explains how people develop different relationship styles, based on the quality of their original attachment to the caregiver/mother, as either secure, avoidant, or anxious. We see these styles emerge in everyday relating and exaggerated during conflict. Often couples develop conflict because of their different relationship styles.

Alessia and Albert seemed to have much in common, but they had very different conflict styles. They were both in their late thirties. They had been married for 10 years and had three children. They thought of themselves as happily married, but in recent years they had argued constantly. When a problem emerged, Alessia felt a need to talk about it right away, but Albert put her off. The more he avoided talking, the more assertive she became. As she pushed harder to be heard, he withdrew more. Finally, Albert would say, "I can't take this anymore!" Then he would stomp out, slamming the door and leaving her feeling frantic. She would call him every 15 minutes, leaving messages about how worried she was about him. And he refused to answer her calls, feeling like he needed more time to unwind. They repeated this pattern frequently, never resolving what started the argument—usually a small thing.

Both Alessia and Albert felt threatened when they argued, and their hyperaroused nervous systems triggered a stress reaction. They remained highly aroused for hours after, since they had not worked anything out. Clearly, Alessia's style was to anxiously confront, whereas Albert's was to flee. Each had resorted to the characteristic way to handle threat that they had used since childhood. Instead of supporting and helping each other, they were hurting each other.

Working with meditation, we began treatment by intervening in the pattern. We introduced the idea of different conflict styles in their therapy sessions. They explored the personal meaning of their conflict style, discovering how it evolved from early experiences. Albert recalled that as a child he had witnessed his divorced mother arguing with her boyfriends. He found comfort in escaping off to himself, away from the turmoil. Alessia's parents were always working. She found that the only time she was heard was when she was aggressive and assertive.

They learned mindfulness meditations and began taking a moment to notice, breathe, and calm down just enough to slow down. Alessia learned to moderate her anxiety, and Albert was able to tolerate talking about things. As they became more aware, they could recognize that their relationship did not have to repeat the patterns from their early parental bonds. They felt free to explore other options.

They practiced empathy exercises, imagining the other's point of view. Alessia learned to grant Albert the space he needed to gather himself. Her acceptance made him want to try talking about the issues. They felt compassion for each other, recognizing that they had both suffered from the fights. They each took responsibility for the part they played in the pattern. By sharing in the responsibility, they felt a common bond, a place to begin building something new.

One of the early steps in couples therapy is to help both people become aware of the way they approach conflict. In mismatched conflict styles, one person wants to avoid conflict, while the other pushes hard to confront. But even matched conflict styles can cause problems. If both confront, the arguments escalate quickly. Another typical pattern is when neither person wants to deal with problems. Hostilities simmer under the surface, making both people stressed and hyperaroused.

Learning to accept each person's style and make room for it brings a paradoxical effect. When Alessia consented to give Albert some time to gather himself, Albert felt motivated to cooperate. Eventually he didn't need to leave the house at all. He could take a short meditative moment to calm down and then be ready to talk things through. In seeing that Albert was willing to talk things out, Alessia found herself feeling less anxious and desperate. Meditation can help couples to become aware of their conflict styles. It can encourage each to accept how they are and find ways to accommodate each other's needs.

Think back on a time you were engaged in an argument that mattered, with someone you cared about. Did you feel like getting away in order to calm down, or did you feel a tense, urgent need to address the problem immediately? Did the other have similar tendencies? Observe and consider these qualities about yourself and your partner. Sometimes conflicts are prolonged because two people have different natural tendencies for timing. You may learn from recalling other instances with other people, with whom to compare for a sense of personal style. Once you have recognized the form of the conflict, can you extend tolerance and compassion for the other's style of arguing as you do for your own? Allow compassion to develop.

Mindful Meditations for Couples

Given that we are in such close interrelationship with others, we can expect to learn more about ourselves through relating mindfully. As the renowned meditation teacher J. Krishnamurti said in one of his speeches, "Self-knowledge lies in the unfolding of relationship" (Krishnamurti, 1949). Thus, when partners turn mindfully to experiencing together, they will awaken deeper understanding within themselves. This series of meditations will help couples attune and become more aware on many levels.

Darwin first pointed out (and the polyvagal theory developed further) that we send and receive social cues through facial expressions, head positioning, eye gaze, and vocalizations. Thus, being mindfully aware of these qualities will enhance social awareness. Couples who come to therapy have often become out of touch with each other. As the argument escalates, they might seem to be looking, but they don't really see. They make a pretense of listening, but they have stopped hearing. Reawakening the ability for both people to truly look and listen can make a tremendous difference.

Mindful Looking, Speaking, and Listening

Begin by deliberately having a mindful conversation, either during a therapy session or at home between sessions. Sit facing your partner and look at each other, without judgment—simply look. Notice the facial expression and how your partner is sitting. Then, as you begin to have a conversation, listen to what you say as you speak. If you have ever listened to yourself on a recording, you were probably somewhat surprised by how you sounded and what you said. Observe and listen to what you say, and you can begin to know yourself.

Become aware of the tone of what you are saying. Give your partner the same mindful attention as you listen to what she or he is saying. Do you and your partner speak with malice, sarcasm, sadness, or anger? Are you expressing your emotions directly or are you letting them out indirectly, as subtle digs or innuendos? Continue to be aware of what each of you says in every moment, listening to the sound of your voices, the meanings you are communicating, and the emotions you express. As you begin to be more aware in each moment, you will find yourselves communicating in harmony with your true nature.

Nonjudgmental Listening

Continue listening to yourself and to your partner as you engage in a conversation, but with one difference: Practice nonjudgmental awareness. So, if the other says something that you usually think is annoying, stupid, and so on, set that judgment aside temporarily and return to just listening. As you both practice listening without judgment, you may be surprised to learn something new about what you are both trying to communicate.

Experiential Sensing of Another's Movements

Sensing without thought can help in attuning to each other. This exercise draws upon an ancient meditative tradition known as Qi-sao practiced in martial arts. It can enhance the mirror neuron system, since it focuses on intentional movement, thereby enhancing a bottom-up processing for empathy. The exercise is performed as a couple and provides an opportunity to attune nonverbally.

Let one of you be the guide, and the other be the follower. Stand a few feet apart, facing each other. Begin by emptying your mind of all thought as completely as possible and center yourself in the present moment. Touch your right hands together lightly at your wrists and close your eyes. Both people should remain as relaxed as possible. The guide moves her arm around slowly in a relaxed way, extending back and forth, up and down. The follower keeps his eyes closed, and maintains light contact as he follows along without adding any force. After several minutes, switch roles. Repeat the exercise with the other hand as well.

Mindful Qi-Sao

You can extend Qi-sao as a meditative way to sensitively follow your partner's communications much like attuning to the other's movements. Listen carefully to what your partner is saying as in the earlier listening exercises. Be mindful of her logic, thoughts, and feelings. Follow along with her point of view as you mindfully pay attention, without judging or adding anything to it. Often when the other is truly heard, she will be more open as well. Communication can flow back and forth in harmony. Differences may resolve naturally by working together to restore balance for both. Change roles now to give yourself an opportunity to be heard and accepted fully.

Fostering Trust

Trust in the relationship is an essential element for a lasting, loving bond. High levels of trust increase resilience of the relationship. The presence of trust makes all interacting easier and less complicated. Researchers have found that even when there is little information, complex problems, or unexpected catastrophes, trust makes it possible for couples to weather the storms together.

Research on the neurobiology of trust has shown that the hormones oxytocin and vasopressin are involved when we are having positive social interactions. These hormones also counter the effects of stress and make it easier to handle challenges (Carter, Grippo, Pournajafi-Nazarloo, Ruscio, & Porges, 2008). According to Gottman (2011), oxytocin and vasopressin can be thought of as the hormones of trust. In fact, one research group found that oxytocin increases trust (Kosfeld, Heinrichs, Zak, Fischbacher, & Fehr, 2005).

Meditating together may enhance oxytocin release that correlates with feelings of trust and well-being (Uvnas-Moberg, 1998). Thus, there is evidence that regular practice of meditation can enhance the quality of social interactions. People often pay a great deal of attention to problems and conflicts, but rarely devote much effort to cultivating trust. The meditations that follow will enhance feelings of oneness. And a moment of shared peace and harmony builds trust.

Trust Meditation

Sit either facing each other or side by side. Be quiet and still, together. You can start with as little as a 2-minute session and increase the time as skills improve. Close your eyes if you like. Allow breathing to be natural and regular, and try to keep muscles comfortably relaxed. Meditate together regularly, increasing the time to at least 10 minutes, sitting together in calm stillness. This can be a very nice experience to share. Other variations are possible, but the most important criterion is that both partners engage in it sincerely. Keep the meditation time simple and positive. The effects of sharing meditative experiences can begin to build trust again even when it has been lost.

Repairing Broken Trust After Betrayal

Often what brings couples to therapy is a betrayal of trust that cannot be ignored or simply smoothed over. Real pain and suffering have occurred, leaving a sense of irreparable damage. Therapy must address these situations in order to move forward.

Opening the Potential for Repair

The first step for repairing trust is to believe that healing is possible. People often despair, especially when traumatic events have occurred. Without any hope, the couple is stuck. When both parties are willing to work on the issues, change has a good chance. This story of the legendary King Asoka of India provides evidence that redemption is possible.

King Asoka (ruled 274–236 B.C.) began his career as a military leader of India. After conquering Magadha, he was crowned king. His six brothers were each given their own cities to rule. But Asoka brutally killed all six of his brothers and continued his murderous rampage until the entire territory was his. Many legends tell of Asoka's cruelty. He built a sacrificial house where executions were performed, and he ordered that anyone who entered the house be killed. Thousands of innocent people died in this house of horror.

One day Samudra, a young Buddhist monk, wandered into the sacrificial house by mistake. Raising his sword, the executioner approached the monk and said, "Now that you have entered, I am ordered to kill you."

Samudra said, "I will accept my fate, but leave me here for seven days. I will not move from this spot." The executioner agreed and left. The monk sat down amid all the blood and began to meditate. On the seventh day, the executioner returned to kill the monk. He placed Samudra in a cauldron of burning oil for a whole day, but the enlightened monk was impervious to harm. Hearing about this strange event, the king strode into the house to see for himself. The executioner looked visibly upset. "Sire! You have entered the house, and now by your own order, I must kill you!"

The monk interrupted, saying, "I have miraculously been able to endure this burning oil because of my meditation!" In a persuasive speech about the benefits of meditation, he urged the king to repent of his sins. Deeply moved, the king underwent a complete transformation. He destroyed his slaughterhouse and put all his efforts into learning. He urged his citizens to become moral, act justly, and live lives filled with love and compassion. Not only did he build Buddhist temples and monasteries all around India, but he also established hospitals for both people and animals and planted gardens. He denounced war, asserting firmly that the only conquest left for him was the dharma, Buddhist teachings. Asoka's story can be an inspiration to anyone on the wrong path.

Meditation lore is filled with stories of people who had committed terrible acts of violence and betrayal and still were able to change. What is involved is a sincere and deep awakening to different possibilities.

Accepting Responsibility

The next steps involve repairing the damage. When one of the partners has betrayed the trust, with an affair or abuse, that person must begin by accepting responsibility. Sincerity can be deepened when the abuser faces his guilt in meditation. Alone with oneself in meditation, the gravity of the situation can be faced and felt through without any excuses.

Roger had been violent with his wife. He didn't know that he felt angry until he found himself standing over his crying and injured wife. He told us that he had no awareness while he struck her, although he recognized that he had done it after it happened.

He learned mindfulness meditation, to become aware of himself as he did things. He began by practicing on small tasks—washing his car or taking a bike ride. But gradually he was able to extend his skills to become aware of his anger as it occurred. In time, he learned how to recognize the signs of feeling angry and then calm down enough to express his emotion in words instead of in violent action.

But facing the anger was only the beginning. The more difficult part was facing his guilt. He loved his wife and felt deeply ashamed, saddened, and angry at himself. We encouraged him to extend a realistic nonjudgmental acceptance of himself. He lucidly faced the harm he had caused with his violent actions. The more he took responsibility, the more motivated he felt to make amends.

We required him to ask forgiveness from his wife and promise to change. The session was intensely moving, as they both cried. He kept his promise with real actions, fostering her career, helping in the house, and performing community service. In time, he transformed into the kind of person he wanted to be. He and his wife found fulfillment in having a supportive relationship. He helped her, and she forgave him and was able to extend her support of his needs for a mutually satisfying bond.

Changing Me *Concern* to Our *Concern*

In couples therapy, we often see one or both partners who are overly centered on their own needs and wants. This can lead to betrayal of relationship vows and agreements. The self-absorbed individual may not even be aware of it, but too much self-involvement interferes with mutuality and trust in the relationship. Meditation offers a selfless moment, in which people learn to let go of self-centered concerns as they simply experience. This letting go can generalize to the relationship.

Taking the Other's View Meditation

Next time you are embroiled in an argument, take a meditation break as a couple. Pause for a moment to gather yourself in meditation. If you are accustomed to meditation, you can do this very quickly. Feel your body, the tightness in your stomach, chest, or wherever you are experiencing. Can you let go a bit? Think about the difficulty or annoyance. Consider what the other person is feeling. Can you imagine how she feels from her own point of view? Your own view may differ, but can you accept the validity of the other's perspective? As you contemplate these things, think about the larger context of your relationship, the greater whole. Put the problematic moment into perspective as you consider some of the positive aspects. Breathe comfortably and try to relax your tension a little more. Seek your center. When you feel an overall sense of calm, open your eyes. You may find that you can begin to work out your differences now.

Opening to a Larger Context

Another component for overcoming self-absorption meditatively is to recognize a larger context beyond the confines of your personal likes and dislikes, private situation, and personal loss or gain. Sit down in a quiet place and allow your thoughts to settle. Feel your place in the room or where you are outdoors, the larger context within which you are sitting now. Let your sense of the grander stage emerge, your city, the country, our world, and how you are a part of it. Allow yourself to marvel at the grandeur of nature, in all its complexity unfolding without any effort from you as day turns to night and the planet revolves around the sun. If you have a spiritual feeling for a higher power, allow yourself to go to it now, sensing that there is a mysterious wonder in the universe.

If I Hurt You, I Hurt Me

In the Mysterious Oneness
Of the Universe
None is better, none is worse.
(C. Alexander Simpkins)

In troubled relationships, one person often feels at a disadvantage. The other seems to have an easier time, even to be given preferential treatment. Meditation can address this problem at its root by challenging the idea of hierarchies. People often think in terms of rankings: This one is higher than that one. But from a meditational perspective, hierarchies are ultimately invalid. There are no comparisons. At the core, no one thing or person is better than another. Lin Chi, founder of the famous Rinzai sect of Zen, spoke of the person of no rank as the truly enlightened one. He stated: "He is without form, without characteristics, without root, without source, without any dwelling place, yet is brisk and lively" (Lin Chi in Dumoulin, 1988, p. 193). True merit does not come from the praise of others, from prizes or promotions. The real source is from our enlightened actions. We all can make a positive difference in the universe, and none is better; none is worse.

The couple should perform this mindfulness meditation regularly. It takes practice to develop a nondiscriminating attitude. Start with what you are experiencing right now. As you sit, notice how your body meets the surface you are sitting on, but don't assess whether it feels good or bad, or whether you could be sitting straighter; just notice that you are sitting. Focus on breathing, and do the same thing—pay attention without deciding if your breathing is too short or too tight. Look now at your partner, just noticing him as he is sitting in meditation. Observe anything that you notice, but don't evaluate whether he looks better than he did yesterday, angry at you, or disapproving. Just notice the details of how he is sitting, his chest moving slightly as he breathes, the clothes he is wearing, or anything else that you notice here and now. Extend this meditation in other contexts. Keep working on staying with what you are aware of moment by moment right now. If you start judging, guessing, or drawing conclusions, notice that you are doing so, and then return to your present-moment experience.

Flexible Action

There may be no help but to do something twice, but do not try it a third time.

(Miyamoto Musashi in Musashi, 1974, p. 80)

Sometimes you may find that the conflict does not get resolved. The harder you try, the less you progress. When there seems to be no possible solution, you may have become entangled in an inflexible spirit. The follow-ing meditation, adapted from Miyamoto Musashi, the Japanese swordsman and philosopher of strategy, provides a technique for meditation to enhance flexibility.

Flexibility Meditation 1

Instead of continuing with the same approach, withdraw for a moment. Clear your mind of the difficulty. You can use any number of meditation exercises from the book. Change your spirit. For example, if you have been strongly insisting on a straight-on encounter, what would a more circular approach be like? Create a new alternative. When you feel that your spirit is changed, reengage your efforts, but from the new perspective.

Meditation can help you discover different alternatives. What is important is to resolve matters, not to stubbornly try to win some particular point.

Flexibility Meditation 2

As in the preceding exercise, first withdraw from your frustrated efforts by meditating. Then, instead of repeating the same thing over and over without success, consider doing the opposite. If you are seeking a solution by rea-soning things out, try your intuition. If you are passionately engaged, step back and calm down, and then try again. If calm, cool logic is not working, draw upon your emotions. If you are unable to advance, try retreating, letting things be. Then resolution takes place naturally. Even if the opposite is not exactly correct, new possibilities will occur to you.

Developing Compassion

All of the virtuous states of mind—compassion, tolerance, forgiveness, caring, and so on . . . cannot co-exist with ill feelings or negative states of mind.

(Dalai Lama & Cutler, 1998, pp. 308–309)

It is almost impossible to exaggerate the value of increased social feeling for mental well-being. Feelings of worth and value are enhanced, bringing self-confidence and an optimistic view. Unselfish actions and behavior can help eradicate or resolve tensions from imbalances, whether from within your own personality or from within the relationship. Acting, doing something, especially with regard to others, can help you break out of this circle. "Empathy and understanding are facts of social feeling, of harmony with the universe" (Adler & Deutsch, 1959, p. 41).

Overcoming Resistance to Compassion

Benevolence and compassion are part of the tradition of meditation. But sometimes people resist empathizing with others. They feel engulfed by their own needs to just get by. Clients often express feeling that they have nothing left to give to anyone else. But what they fail to recognize is that we are all interconnected. We have offered this koan to foster the sense of interconnection:

> When the cows of Eshu are well fed with grain, the horses of Ekishu have full stomachs.

Or you can substitute familiar geographic areas:

> When the cows of Ohio are well fed with grain, the horses of Montana have full stomachs.

Compassion Meditations

Regular practice of compassion meditation will bring positive feelings into the relationship, enhancing it at every level. You can learn to engage in situations in ways that are more complex than either-or, or black and white. The whole is greater than the sum of its parts. So, if you truly empathize with the other and you search benevolently for what you have in common, the big issues lead you to a wider perspective. That perspective includes both the other's point of view and yours, together as one. Find the dynamic balance point, beyond conflict. Together you will uncover the way out of conflict between you. You can train your mind to make it more receptive to this kind of conflict resolution. Meditating on positive mental states, you will realize your benevolence within and find it easier to recognize the positive nature in others.

Sit quietly. Then, think of your partner. Allow your feeling of love for that person to fill your thoughts. Extend that feeling out to people you know and like. Then reach further out, to people of your community, and then to all humanity. Let your feelings of loving-kindness directed outward to the world also reach inward through your whole being.

CONCLUSION

Meditation can help to foster better relationships. Encourage couples to keep meditating, even after the problems have been resolved. In the empty shared moment, nothing is there to interfere with intimacy and closeness. Couples will renew their connection as they enjoy the experience of sharing in meditation together.

IV

Facilitating Therapists

Ripples from our deeds
Glide over the pond of life
Till done
To influence others
In ways we cannot know
They become
Born on the winds of destiny
  (C. Alexander Simpkins)

Therapists are in a unique position to strongly influence the course of life for others. But our work puts unique stresses upon us and often, like the cobbler whose children are the last to get shoes, we put our client's welfare before our own. This section is for the care and enhancement of therapists. Meditation can bring tremendous relief from the everyday stresses and strains that are unique to our profession. In addition, as a refined set of tools that hones perception, sensation, emotions, and cognition, meditation is uniquely suited to enhance the skills we need to better help our clients.

Chapter 11 provides meditative ways to reduce stress and burnout. Chapter 12 gives you meditative training to increase your therapeutic sensitivities. The conclusion is a culmination, so that you can discover Zen in every moment. Together, these chapters give you practices that can open the way, not just to feel and do better, but to find enlightenment, fulfillment, and happiness for you and your clients.

11

Relieving Stress and Burnout

Alone, I sit, it seems
Searching in the cold night of dreams
Thinking of the path my life has taken
I return to center and then awaken.
(C. Alexander Simpkins &
Annellen M. Simpkins)

Hui-k'o (the Second Patriarch of Zen) said to Bodhidharma, "I have studied. I have learned everything I should know, and yet my mind is still not at peace. I beg you, Teacher, please give me peace."

Bodhidharma answered, "Bring your mind to me, and I will give it peace."

Hui-k'o answered, "I keep looking for my mind, but I cannot find it!"

Bodhidharma said, "Then I have given your mind peace."

With these words, Hui-k'o was enlightened.

■ ■ ■

As a therapist, you know a great deal about psychological disorders and how to treat them, and yet, by the end of a long day with clients, you may sometimes feel your own mind is not at peace. If so, you look for ways to put your mind

Figure 11.1   Hotei, the Happy Buddha (ink on rice paper hanging scroll, Japan 17th century)

Source: Simpkins private collection

at ease, and probably use methods to temporarily lessen your stress reaction. But then, after another long day, once again, you may find your mind is not at ease.

Though we may be guardians of mental health, we are not immune to becoming vulnerable to stress ourselves. In classical theory, stress is a universal human process we all suffer; it is just a matter of degree. We can only hope to reduce the intensity and negative effects. When temporary measures don't address the problem, you may need to make a fundamental change. Bodhidharma's conversation with Hui-k'o opens new potentials for altering how you deal with stress and its more extreme work-related form, burnout.

This chapter addresses therapists' stress and burnout from a Zen meditational perspective. Hui-k'o's encounter with Bodhidharma presents a koan to ponder. Zen masters have been guiding disciples on these issues for centuries using the koan method. Combined with what is now known about the mind and brain, you can apply mindfulness and Zen meditation to relieve stress and burnout. And as you discover your own answer to Bodhidharma, you will make a lasting change. Through meditation, you can discover your natural mind—a mind that is at peace in any situation, even in the midst of a stressful workload or difficult circumstances (Figure 11.1).

ABOUT STRESS AND BURNOUT

Stress is a natural reaction of the mind-brain-body system. It accompanies most mental dysfunction and is an important component to deal with when treating problems. Thus, you may want to adapt some of the methods presented in this chapter for working with clients.

Stress is a nonspecific reaction. It occurs automatically in the nervous system when we feel threatened, sending a message to the muscles to flee, fight, or freeze. Brain processes activate in a patterned way when facing danger, to help us take some immediate action. This response can be helpful and protective. But when it is prolonged by misperceiving a life situation as filled with threat or because of continued strain, this adaptive response turns into a problem, which we experience as stress and/or burnout.

How Stress Affects the Nervous System

The autonomic nervous system prepares the body for action by getting excited in some ways but also by calming at the same time. The autonomic nervous system has two parts that are intimately involved in our stress reactions: the sympathetic nervous system (SNS) to activate and the parasympathetic nervous system (PNS) to calm. The excitation in the sympathetic nervous system response directs the adrenal glands to secrete hormones that cause the heart to beat more rapidly, muscles to tense, and blood pressure to rise. Breathing rate increases and pupils dilate. Blood flow is directed to the brain and muscles, away from internal organs and skin. The parasympathetic system helps maintain an internal balance by calming the nonessential systems while keeping the normal maintenance systems going. These are all normal responses that ready the body to either confront or flee from an experienced threat. These responses occur quickly and automatically.

This generalized reaction can be a good thing when a real threat is present. We certainly would not want to have a mind-brain-body system that signals us to just sit down and wait for a hungry tiger to attack. But although it serves a purpose, sustained stress becomes a problem. Our system is well-suited to handle a short burst of energy to meet the demands of imminent danger, but like keeping a car revving in high gear, overactivation for extended periods of time is harmful to many body systems and takes a toll on health. Studies show that people who suffer from chronic stress and burnout are more prone to heart disease, type II diabetes, and other physical problems (Melamed, Shirom, Toker, Berliner, & Shapiro, 2006). In addition, long periods of stress lead to psychological symptoms such as irritability, substance abuse, depression, and anxiety.

The positive side is that the nervous system is dynamic, always changing and responding to circumstances, which means we can reverse this reaction by what we do, either to alleviate the stressors or at least cope well, so that we handle the stress better.

The Signs of Burnout

Sometimes, during sessions, we listen to heart-wrenching stories of abuse, disasters, deaths, wars, and violence. We share in the suffering, to help our clients navigate their dark stormy journeys. As sensitive and empathic listeners, we resonate with them at times, feeling painful emotions of our own within. This day-in, day-out exposure leads some therapists to experience what has become identified as burnout syndrome.

Burnout has been defined as "prolonged response to chronic emotional and interpersonal stressors on the job, determined by the dimensions of exhaustion, cynicism, and inefficacy" (Maslach, Schaufeli, & Leiter, 2001, p. 2). It has been traditionally associated with people in the health care fields, such as psychotherapy, social work, and nursing and has also been found among teachers. Burnout has three main components: feeling exhausted; experiencing a loss of enthusiasm for the work; and feeling overwhelmed, incompetent, and trapped.

The word *burnout* implies being used up and spent. In the final phases, mental and emotional exhaustion is difficult to recover from. But burning also implies a certain passion, and often those people who suffer from burnout are the very ones who were most excited and enthusiastic when they first started practicing psychotherapy (Korunka, Tement, Zdrehus, & Borza, 2010).

The symptoms of burnout can sneak up on people, often taking many years to develop. And since we all feel tired, have a cynical moment, or worry about not doing a good enough job from time to time, burnout may be difficult to recognize.

Here are some signs to help you identify if you have burnout. Emotional signals are depressed mood, tension, anxiety, and emotional exhaustion.

Crying may accompany these. Cognitive components are loss of meaning and hope, powerlessness, a sense of failure, low self-esteem, and even suicidal ideation. Physically, you might experience headaches, nausea, muscle pain, dizziness, and stomach problems, with an overall sense of physical exhaustion. Behaviors change, with more hyperactive and impulsive behaviors along with excessive use of coffee, smoking, alcohol, and/or drugs. Also, you might forgo exercise and make little to no time for recreation. Motivation is affected as well, signaled by feeling disappointed and cynical, with loss of the original idealism (Korunka et al., 2010).

Here is a simple checklist you can use if you suspect that you might be on the road to burnout:

1. Are you always exhausted and unable to be replenished, even after a good night's sleep or a weekend off?
2. Do you feel bored when sitting in sessions?
3. Are you consumed by your work, thinking about clients incessantly between sessions?
4. Do you feel like you can never get everything done or that you are always running behind?
5. Are you neglecting your health: missing sleep, not exercising, and eating poorly?
6. Do you tend to avoid seeing people except when you have to?
7. Do you feel frustrated or even annoyed by clients' problems?
8. Do you feel like you are incompetent or unable to handle your work?
9. Are you turning to escapes such as drugs or alcohol?

STARTING THE PROCESS: RETURNING TO BEGINNER MIND

A seasoned therapist had read about the new research on meditation and had heard that there was a renowned Zen master with unusual healing abilities living nearby, and so he decided to pay him a visit.

The master greeted him at the door and the therapist said, "You are famous for your powerful healing methods. Would you be willing to teach me? I know a lot about therapy. I have studied the classics—Freud, Jung, and Adler—and have added many modern methods as well. I am well versed in the latest therapies. I've studied EMDR, DBT, and ACT. You probably

Figure 11.2 Empty Cup (wood on wood, mahogany, walnut, and birch)
Source: Created by C. A. Simpkins and A. M. Simpkins, 2008

know that meditation is being integrated into therapy and there's a great deal of research to support it. I am greatly experienced in all the latest therapeutic approaches, but I am eager to learn your techniques."

The master smiled gently and answered quietly, "Ah yes, of course. Come in and have some tea!"

The therapist was pleased and said, "Well, thank you. I would enjoy a cup of tea." He followed the master into a sparsely furnished room. He barely noticed the worn wooden floor covered by several small straw mats. A single, perfect flower sat in an earthenware vase on a simple, hand-hewn wood shelf. As they walked, the therapist continued his running commentary. "I know a lot about tea. I've sampled many kinds of tea: oolong tea, green tea, black tea, and fermented tea, but my favorite tea is peppermint tea because it doesn't have any caffeine and it's good for you. In fact, I like all kinds of herbal teas, like chamomile and rosehips; and then there are healing teas like goldenseal, burdock. . . ."

The therapist paused for a moment. Then he realized the master was already seated and had motioned him to sit down, too. The therapist sat down, and the master quietly began preparing the tea. As the master silently worked, the therapist glanced at the teacups and said, "Oh, that's nice pottery. What dynasty? I love pottery. Tang Dynasty pottery is elegant, but I also think that porcelain raku is very beautiful. Do you know that it is fired at a very high temperature, which makes it exceptionally hard? Korean Yi dynasty pottery is distinctive and individualized, but some of the new materials are interesting as well, and they don't break or wear out."

As the therapist continued talking, the master began to pour tea into the therapist's cup. The therapist kept a steady flow of conversation. "I wanted to ask you about your theories of therapy. What kind of meditation do you recommend? And do you think that clients are best treated individually or in groups? I have given these matters quite a bit of thought and believe. . . ." As he half-watched the tea fill the cup to the top and spill over the sides, he suddenly realized what was happening and shouted, "Master! Master! My cup is overflowing!"

"Yes," answered the Master softly. "As is your mind! First, empty your cup. Then it can be filled." (Figure 11.2)

After years of practice, we form beliefs about ourselves, theories of psychotherapy, and perspectives on clients that fill our consciousness. Many of these theories are helpful. But too much conceptualization can become a problem. If you are feeling stress or burnout in your practice, your mind may be overly filled from the years of experience, some of which have led you to feel bitter or disappointed. You may have lost the early enthusiasm you once had for your profession. One way to begin to recover from stress and burnout is to return to what in Zen is known as beginner mind.

Beginners have it easy, in a way. They do not have accumulations from their past to obscure their experience of the present moment. They are free of biases and preconceptions. They have no bad experiences to get over. Nor do they have a concept of their own past limitations with which to compare their present performance.

We all have experienced beginner mind, that exciting period of life when you feel enthusiastic, excited, and hopeful. All of these emotions are resources that are still with you as potentials from your past experiences. They can be accessed just as much as the negative experiences you are having now. You can bring back these positive resources by rediscovering your beginner mind.

Beginner Mind Meditation

Let your thoughts drift back to when you first began to be a therapist. Think about it for a moment: how you felt, and what you did in your first sessions. Now, think back to earlier, when you were still in graduate school. Recall the preparation you went through, the supervision, the papers you wrote, the research you did, the topics you studied, and how you felt when you were so intensely focused. Continue to think back, to earlier, remembering your undergraduate time, before you had begun your practical training. What did you think then, when you knew very little about psychotherapy? How did you feel? Try to vividly reexperience it, as you remember. Can you recall what it felt like, to not know anything? Allow yourself to feel the excitement and interest you had when you began. Stay with that memory and let it fill you now. Meditate deeply. Contemplate this question meditatively: What was your original nature? Allow all your resources and strengths that you may have left in the past to emerge now: your original nature, enthusiastic and committed. Your beginner mind is part of you. Allow its best qualities help you now.

LETTING GO OF STRESS WHEN YOU CAN

The first place to begin when dealing with a stress problem is to institute some moments of relaxation and calm. This sets a process in motion to begin easing your overactivated nervous system. When people experiment with these calming meditations, they don't always feel the results immediately and so may doubt that they are working. Keep in mind that the nervous system does not turn on and off in an instant. Signals take time to readjust, so you might not feel different until later. Without the direct feedback in the moment, the cues are subtle and may be easily missed. Be open to subtleties and patient about seeing results, and you will initiate a positive process.

Initiating the Process

This exercise helps you to create the circumstances that will allow you to clear away what obstructs being at ease now that you have a few minutes to sit quietly. As a metaphor, this exercise allows you to relax indirectly. The image can become an invitation for you to allow your natural response to happen effortlessly and automatically.

Sit quietly with your eyes closed. Imagine that you are sitting on the shore of a pond. The pond is alive with activity. Frogs croak; crickets sing; birds fly overhead; a fish jumps out of the water, feeding on insects, splashes back, and jumps again after a bit, in another spot. Wind whips over the water, stirring up the muddy bottom. All is movement. Then gradually as the day passes, the conditions begin to shift. The wind dies down. The frogs settle in for a nap, the crickets are silent, the birds perch in the trees, the fish stops jumping and waits. The pond is quiet. The murky rippled surface calms as the mud sinks to the bottom, and the water is crystal clear, reflecting the natural surroundings. All is stillness. Imagine this scene vividly for several minutes. Stay with the quiet, clear water, watching.

Discovering Your Clear Consciousness Meditation

Sit quietly and allow the flow of thoughts. Don't let yourself get carried away by any one thought. Just let thoughts flow by, like leaves moving along the current on a river. Stay in the moment, without thinking anything in particular, just letting thoughts go. In time, moments without thought will appear. Just allow this to develop naturally, as it will, as you sit quietly now. After some time with this meditation, like Hui-k'o, you may find that there is no disturbed mind to be found.

Drawing on the Calm of Nature

All natural objects make a kindred impression when the mind is open to their influence.

(Emerson, 1965, p. 181)

When you are trying to become calmer within, you may find that putting yourself into a calming outer situation may stimulate a conditioned response. We may go outdoors to work out or to get somewhere, but we are often too goal directed to allow nature's calming qualities to have their effects. Yet nature is always there, even if we aren't noticing. Just walk out into the park, sit in your garden, or even take a moment to look at a tree, and you can stir your instincts to feel soothed. By attuning to nature's calm, you awaken your own balance and harmony within.

Meditation in Nature

Go somewhere outdoors in nature, a local park, your own backyard, a beach, or a grassy area under a tree. If possible, sit down and let your thoughts settle. Listen to the sounds, feel the breeze, notice the temperature. Pay attention

Figure 11.3 Meditating One with Nature

to the air as you breathe it into your body and then back out into the environment. Can you experience the ongoing exchange between you and the world without thinking anything beyond the experience itself? If you find your mind wandering to other topics, gently bring it back to this moment now, in nature, experiencing. Take in the beauty you see and feel around you. Notice nature's perfect imperfection, how each blade of grass is different from the next, and yet sharing some common features. Sense the calm, quiet stability that is there in a tree, a bush, and a flower. Nature is just there, to be seen and sensed, asking nothing from you. Breathe, look, and enjoy the moment. Your nervous system responds of itself, as the stress reaction begins to fade a bit (Figure 11.3).

Oneness With Nature

> In the beautiful garden
> That nature provides
> Are patterns to relax with,
> Tension subsides
> With wind, clouds, and light's rays
> We melt into oneness
> And feel we're okay.
> (C. Alexander Simpkins &
Annellen M. Simpkins)

Enjoying nature's calming effects opens your senses for deeper attunement. As part of this teaching, Zen master Nansen (748–834) pointed to a flower and said, "People of these days see this flower as though they were in a dream" (Sekida, 1997, p. 255). Experiencing nature fully and directly is something we rarely do. The Zen Masters believed that if you do this, you will enter and walk on a path that we have often thought of only as a boundary between our sensations of the world and our concepts of it. In this moment when they come together as a path, we find no stress, only feelings of peace, and a mind at ease. Cognition unified with sensation in the present moment is beautiful.

Go out on a porch, into your backyard, or visit a park where there is grass. Lie down on your back and look up into the sky. Watch the clouds as they float by. Keep watching, forgetting your daily routines and responsibilities for a few minutes. While watching, allow yourself to become fully absorbed in the passing clouds and sky. Can you let go of learning and conditioning for a moment, and simply allow your sensory experience to unite with your cognition? Often we think of them as separate: first a sensation, then a thought about it. Sensory experiencing does not have to be separated from thinking. In this experiment, allow your sensory experiences of looking at the sky to interact so closely with your thinking about it that sense, thought, and nature become one in this moment of experiencing.

FINDING CALM IN THE STORM FOR HANDLING STRESS AND BURNOUT

Through meditation practice, you can wake up to the no-mind, beyond conceptual thought, where the mind is at ease. But what about when you are in the midst of a real stressor, something that must be handled and shouldn't or can't be avoided? You can find peace and put your mind at ease drawing upon several different meditative methods and traditions.

Creating a Strong Center

The unconscious means to have no-mind in all circumstances, that is to say, not to be determined by any conditions. . . To face all objective conditions, and yet to be eternally free from any form of stirring, this is the Unconscious."

(D. T. Suzuki, 1969, p. 62)

We are accustomed to being constantly engaged in thinking about our circumstances. And we should, since difficult problems require careful thought. When thinking helps solve problems and navigate stress better, the cognitive processing is positive. But more often, we also indulge in worries and doubts that only serve to add to the stress load. By overthinking problems, we stir the waters of the mind.

To carry less stress, there are times when we need to be able to let go of the unnecessary stirrings. In the quote above, D. T. Suzuki described what he called the Zen unconscious. Attunement of the mind to the situation will keep you close enough to the stressful situation to maneuver through it, while remaining in control and balanced. You can find your harmony with difficult situations in this way, utilizing what may be there to help you cope, while not getting thrown off from your center.

Korean Zen Master Seung Sahn explained the unconscious centering process as being like the zero point on a scale. The zero point on the scale is analogous to your primary point. If you add weight to the scale, the pointer registers the weight. When you remove weight from the scale, the pointer returns to zero, the primary point. A stressful situation may shift the scale, but when you come to know your primary point, you can always return there. Before you have discovered your primary point, it is as if you left some weight on the scale. If you add even more weight, the scale no longer measures accurately. And as more weights are heaped on, eventually, the scale will break. The key to handling even the heaviest burdens is to find your primary point and keep returning to it (Seung, 1992).

With the meditations in this chapter and throughout the book, you can develop your primary point, your center, drawing on the Zen unconscious. You can keep it strong, in continual responsiveness moment by moment, while simultaneously maintaining the engagement you need for coping well with whatever comes your way.

Centered in Your Environment

Zen does not choose one thing over another. If your mind is not at peace, even a quiet place in nature will seem disturbing, whereas if your mind is at ease, even a noisy city street corner can be peaceful. You can find your primary point anywhere, standing on a busy street corner or sitting in the midst of a traffic jam. Meditation teaches us to accept our circumstances, adapting and flowing effortlessly. You can explore your link to your environment, by taking the time to mindfully experience whatever is there. A sense of being at ease in *your* world, whatever it is, will emerge experientially, with a centering effect.

Find a place outdoors near where you live. Look carefully around at all that is there, noticing without judgment what you see: buildings, people, trees, or grass. Also, look at the colors, shapes, and textures. Notice the smells, and listen to the sounds. Relax for a few minutes. Let your breathing become comfortable and quiet. Notice how the ground supports you. If you are sitting on a bench or the ground, place your hands palm down on the surface and try to sense the mass under you. Whether you hear the sounds of traffic, people talking, or birds chirping, allow yourself to experience how you are part of this scene and in this sense, not separate from it. Experience openly and nonjudgmentally each sound, sensation, feeling, and thought that occurs, just as it is. When you feel ready, stop and notice how you feel. This exercise can also be done in your office before a client arrives, or at home to gather yourself before or after a busy day. Take the time to center regularly, and you will gradually develop a deep sense of feeling grounded in your environment.

Finding Your Center Now

True centering is independent of the surroundings while being intimately at one with them. This meditation can be practiced anywhere and anytime when you have a few moments.

Sit quietly and close your eyes. Begin by centering in your sitting position by gently shifting forward and backward until you feel the place between where you are aligned with gravity. Shift side to side, rocking gently. Find the center point between, and allow yourself to sit effortlessly, aligned with gravity. Now, follow your breathing and allow it to be calm and comfortable, not too slow and not too fast. Turn to your muscles and let them be relaxed but not flaccid, to hold you upright but not rigid. Can you now let your thoughts be effortlessly balanced in this moment, not thinking of anything before or later, just centered in the present moment, attending to experiencing as it unfolds now? Let your emotions settle, being calmly present in the moment. Sit quietly in balance here and now, letting go of any other focus of attention but this moment. You will begin to have a clear feeling of your primary point—balanced, clear, and aware of now.

Practicing Work Meditatively

From the early days of Zen, work was considered an essential part of practice. The Pai-Chang (720–824) is credited with setting up the routines for monastic life that are still followed today. He showed by his actions how working is intimately integrated into the Zen experience.

One day, when Pai-Chang was elderly and ill, his students thought they would ease his burden by hiding his gardening tool. But instead of being grateful, Pai-Chang told them emphatically, "A day without work is a day without food," and refused to eat. The students began to fear for his health, and so they finally returned his tools and let him labor in the garden. Daily life in Zen monasteries always includes daily work.

Work is a meaningful way to use your talents to contribute to the world and make a difference. Each person has his or her talents: Some people are naturally strong, others can intuitively grasp mechanical things, and others can comprehend abstract ideas, to name a few. Each person finds expression for these talents in work. So, doing your work fully can express your true nature, and is an important part of living a benevolent life. Earning a living and producing goods are acts of offering your talents to the world.

Overcoming Barriers

The things that are most difficult for us have the most to teach us.

(Whitmyer, 1994, p. 34)

Work challenges our limits, calling upon us do something in the world. But, how do you respond? These work-related challenges can also become opportunities for growth and awareness. Great Zen masters in history responded by putting themselves fully into the experience. Hakuin would strap himself up in a sitting position at night so that he could keep meditating without falling over. Dogen gave up every comfort to pursue his meditation. Meditation can help you dig down deep to discover hidden inner resources you may not have known were there.

If you find that work is difficult, perform it mindfully, without passing judgment. For example, if you tell yourself how hard you are working, your judgment about the difficulty of your work splits you away from your direct action. A secondary problem arises: your attitudes about hard work. Some people feel angry to have to work hard. Others feel overwhelmed. Many other reactions are possible. But all of these attitudes are added. The real situation is just the work itself. If you attend to it fully and alertly, work is neither hard nor easy. When working, just work.

People sometimes feel that their freedom is being restricted because work takes a lot of their time. They would rather be free to do whatever they please.

Similarly, some might find meditation instructions restrictive. You are told how to sit quietly and focus your attention in a particular way. In this sense, meditation directions structure your experience. Meditation uses structure and discipline to achieve meaningful freedom. You keep returning to the situation and face yourself there, doing what needs to be done. Whether you are a psychologist, a psychiatrist, a counselor, a nurse, or physical therapist, part of a large company or self-employed, you have your chance to do something with what you are in that role. Within this structure, your experience is in the moment. It doesn't matter if you are typing, reading, making a speech, or sitting in a meeting; you are free to be immersed in the moment. Nothing holds you back.

CONCLUSION

Going back to Bodhidharma's question, we ask you, where is the stress now? Many Zen masters teach that our original nature is at ease. Our mind-brain-body system finds a balance with what is needed. Even when great demands are placed on the system, we can draw on our original nature, as primary point, as a resource for calm and balance.

When feeling stressed, take a moment to ponder this teaching from Bodhidharma. Return to your balance point often. Take a few moments to be mindful as you sit with your clients. Bodhidharma challenges us to show him the problem here and now. The mind that suffers is our own creation. Ask yourself, is there a real and lasting stress now, after all the clients are gone and the office is empty, and you are sitting meditatively, centered in the moment? We may go through suffering with clients, but flowers bloom in the garden, and waves roll in and out at the beach. The enduring truth is that your true nature, outside of the daily vicissitudes of circumstance, is clear and wise. Meditation that returns you to that open moment is your pathway to setting your mind at peace.

12

Developing Acumen

I call Buddha Mind the Unborn. *This unborn mind is wonderful, with perfect wisdom. When you live according to the Unborn, you gain the ability to perceive others just as they are.*
—(Paraphrased from Zen Master Bankei [1622–1693])

Long ago, a young samurai trained hard and felt confident in his quick reflexes and powerful techniques. He would periodically challenge well-known fighters, and since he always won, his reputation grew. He heard of a renowned Zen swordsman who lived in a remote region and decided to go there to challenge him. When he finally arrived, he knocked loudly on the door. A diminutive servant answered the door and said in a thin voice, "Hello, may I help you?"

The samurai answered brashly, "I have come to challenge the master to a duel!"

The servant calmly bowed and said, "Just a moment, I will give him your message."

A few minutes later, the servant returned. "Sir, the master asks you to return in one hour."

Figure 12.1　Bursts of Insights (acrylic on paper)

Source: Carmen Z. Simpkins, American artist, 1985

The samurai wondered if this so-called master was really a coward, but decided to give him the hour to get up his courage. He swaggered outside to wait, swinging his sword confidently.

Meanwhile, the master instructed his servant to go out into the woods and cut one of the beautiful wild orchids that grew there (Figure 12.1). When he returned with the flower, the master placed it in a wooden stand. Then he stood in front of it, sword in the scabbard at his belt, and meditated deeply. Suddenly, in one graceful, sweeping motion, he drew his sword, raised it high overhead, swung down swiftly, and effortlessly returned the sword to its sheath. The flower fell to the ground, severed in two perfect halves, one on either side. The stand was left untouched. He picked up the two halves and carefully placed them, spaced as they had fallen, on a piece of rice paper, and folded the ends over to form an envelope. Then he composed the following note: "I don't think it would be appropriate for us to duel at this time."

When the samurai returned, the servant gave him the envelope. The samurai looked at the two perfectly cut parts of the flower. Recognizing the counterchallenge, he asked the servant to get him a flower just like the one the master had used. When the servant returned with the flower, he set it into the same stand the master had used, and took a step back. The samurai sneered, quickly drew his sword, and smashed down on the flower with all his might. The flower was cut into two jagged, torn halves, along with the stand. He placed his flower side by side with the master's flower and compared them. Clearly, he could see that his technique was no match for the master's. He would have been destroyed. He realized that the master had compassionately spared him.

"Tell me, servant, what did the master do to get such a perfect cut?"

The servant answered with a quiet smile, "The blade is sharp, but the mind is sharper!"

Realizing that he had much to learn, the samurai bowed and said, "Please ask the master to accept me as his student!" The master agreed. The samurai vowed to learn the ways of the mind, rather than just the technique of the sword. The samurai eventually became one of his best students, a proponent of the sword of no sword, the technique of no technique.

This story illustrates the importance of the mental attitude as the way to mastery. Zen Master Bankei called this mental attitude the Unborn or Buddha Mind. It is known by many different names: true nature, primary point, the unconscious, and Mind. Techniques and methods can go only so far. True mastery always involves quality of mind. Whether your therapeutic method is cognitive, hypnotic, dynamic, or humanistic, you can bring mastery to your practice by developing the quality of the consciousness you have for yourself and with others. We begin with methods that will help you stay balanced and calm, even in the midst of stress. This chapter offers mental training that has been shown experimentally to enhance different aspects of consciousness and as a result, will improve functioning.

We encourage you to practice these meditations regularly, even if only for a brief time. At first, the effects may be subtle, but over time, you will feel a transformation in the quality of your awareness and presence. And, from this change, you will find yourself at ease with your own experience as well as in synchrony with your clients' needs.

HONING YOUR THERAPEUTIC TOOLS

Every profession has its tools. As therapists, we use a subtle yet real set of primary tools: our senses, our attention, and our emotions. With these tools, we reach out to understand the client on multiple levels, and combined with our expertise about human psychology and therapeutic methods, we guide our clients through dark territory. Like any professional, we can always improve our tools. This section helps you hone your therapeutic tools meditatively. You can enhance your sensory awareness, sharpen and gain flexibility with attention, and regulate affect, in both intensity and quality.

Sensory Awareness Exercise

Awareness can begin at the sensory level. We need to be able to notice subtle cues, often overlooked and missed. By becoming aware of your own sensory experiencing, your sensitivity to the world and to others is heightened. This series of exercises will develop your sensory awareness using meditation methods. Thus, these approaches are experiential, so you will benefit most by doing each exercise, even if only briefly.

Recognizing Sensory Experiencing

Begin by lying flat on your back on a wooden floor, mat, rug, or on the grass outdoors. Rest your hands by your side on the floor, palms up. Close your eyes. Scan through your body with your attention. Notice sensations, starting with your feet and moving up through all parts of your body. Sense how long your legs are, how far it is between your shoulder blades. Do you notice any tightness in your muscles? How does your body meet the floor? Feel the temperature of your skin. Without changing anything deliberately, keep your attention focused on your body. Allow any little adjustments in breathing, muscle tone, and so forth that might occur automatically. Let go of any other thoughts and don't try to do anything except be aware. Continually bring your mind back to your body. When you are ready, open your eyes and stretch.

Following Breathing Experientially

Now turn your attention to breathing. Notice as the air goes in through your nose and down into your lungs, and then travels out through your nose again.

Observe your feelings and sensations. Do not alter anything. Do not force your breaths to be deeper or shallower. Simply follow your breathing mindfully. What do you sense? Can you notice how each breath is a unique experience, with its own sensations and experiences? Every moment is new, even when breathing. Stay with your breathing for five minutes, adding more time as you are able.

Sensing Touch

We can use any of the senses to enhance awareness. Here is an exercise for the sense of touch, by sensing an object, in this case a small rock. You can use any object, even a cell phone, wallet, or keys. As an alternative to this exercise, you can hold the object in your hand or place it on your lap. Please experiment with variations for enhanced effects.

Lie on your back and relax. Place the stone on your stomach and close your eyes. Focus all your attention on the sensation you feel from the stone on your stomach. Can you feel how heavy it is? Is it warmer or cooler than your skin? Notice the sensation of it moving up and down as you breathe. Can you feel the texture of the stone, smooth or rough? Keep your attention focused on the sensations. Move the stone around, to your arm or leg, and repeat the exercise.

Enhancing Attentional Skills

The famous Heart Sutra teaches that form is emptiness and emptiness is form. You can build skills of attention by using meditations on form or emptiness. Attention is enhanced by deliberately training the focus of attention (filling the mind by focusing on something, a form). It is also improved by removing the obstacles for an undistracted attention by opening the flow of consciousness without any object of focus (emptying the mind by focusing on nothing). Practice these exercises, first to focus deliberately on something and then to open and empty your attention.

Focusing Attention: Filling the Mind

Improving the focus of your attention on something can be done through many different modalities, and in fact, varying the methods is helpful. We offer focus through an image and a sound. You can also focus on a chant or on an enjoyable experience or memory.

Close your eyes and think of your favorite color. Picture it vividly, letting it fill your mind completely. Think of nothing else. Once you have pictured your color for several minutes, imagine that it becomes smaller and smaller, until it shrinks down to a single, concentrated dot. Then let it become larger and larger again. Practice this meditation regularly until you can picture your color at will.

To visualize sound, you can do a similar meditation using music. Play one of your favorite songs or pieces of music on a tape or CD, preferably quiet, peaceful music without excessive lyrics. Listen to it several times in a row. Pay close attention to all the details of the melody, the instruments, the rhythms. Then, turn off the music and close your eyes. Imagine that you can hear it playing in your mind. Stay with it, thinking of nothing else. Enjoy the music and the meditative experience that accompanies it. Also, try it with your eyes open. As you gain in skill, you will learn to not be distracted by external conditions.

You can do this exercise with any of the senses, such as by visualizing the sense of the rock you held on your stomach in the earlier exercise, or slowly eating a ripe piece of fruit and then recalling the sensory experience of the taste.

Allowing Attention to be Open

When the perfect man employs his mind, it is a mirror. It conducts nothing and anticipates nothing. Thus, he is able to deal successfully with all things, and injures none.

(Legge, 1962, p. 266)

Consciousness can become clouded over like a dirty mirror. Letting go of the continual stream of thoughts is a way to remove obstructions, allowing clearer perception to emerge naturally. Unlike the filling-the-mind exercises, these require an allowing attitude that opens the way for clarity to occur automatically. So, paradoxically, deliberately try to do these exercises, and yet allow yourself to respond spontaneously. If you embrace the paradox experientially, you will open new vistas and potentials.

Mirror Mind Meditation

Empty consciousness is like a mirror, just reflecting the world all around without adding any thoughts. So, you aren't trying to wipe away all thought, but rather to allow each cognition to simply come and go, like a reflection in a mirror. Don't add anything, but don't try to take anything away either.

Vividly visualize your mind as a mirror, clear and empty. Keep this image of a mirror reflecting nothing. If a thought occurs to you, see it as a reflection in the mirror, knowing it is not the mirror, only the reflection. Let the mirror clear again. Eventually fewer reflections appear, until your mirror mind remains clear.

Encouraging Emptiness

Pick a time of day when you are already feeling somewhat quiet with no immediate responsibilities, perhaps between clients, early in the morning, or at night just before sleep, and go with it. Sit or lie down and allow your thoughts to drift. Don't think about anything in particular. Try to remain quietly in the present moment. So, if you find yourself engaging in a thought, gently bring yourself back to just being quiet now as soon as you realize it. As you sustain the quiet, you may find that the flow of thoughts slows naturally, and you experience moments of no-thought, empty and peaceful.

Classic Zazen

The practice of Zazen is a long-established way to discover the no-mind of form and formless consciousness, empty of all thought while also being full of the present moment. Here we briefly review the instructions, but please refer back to Chapter 5 as well.

Breathe calmly and regularly. As you begin to meditate, clear your mind of all thought. When a thought does arise, notice it, and then dismiss it, returning to your calm, clear mind. By continuing to do this over time, you will eventually find that thoughts intrude less and less and that your concentration becomes natural and profound.

Attention to Action

Zen has an old saying that you should not permit the events of your daily life to bind you, but never withdraw yourself from them. The ability to choose to focus your attention on something of your choosing or to have your attention be open and clear can be brought into everything you do in your life. As the Zen masters taught, when eating, eat, and when sleeping, sleep. Don't add anything extra. Everything you do is an opportunity to be sensitively attuned, aware of what is, just as it is. You can bring a quality of awareness to all the basic physical activities of life: lying, sitting, standing, and walking. Everyone engages in these activities throughout the day, every day. But how often do you pay attention to what you experience when you are reposing in bed, sitting at the dining table, standing in line, or walking down the street? We don't usually notice such things unless they are a problem to us. For example, if your foot hurts, you naturally become aware of every painful step, but once it is better, you hardly notice walking. But you can train yourself to be aware in any situation. By turning attention mindfully to these fundamental body activities, you enhance your awareness in every aspect of life.

Lying Down

Lie down on your back on a padded floor or on a couch or bed, or on the grass outdoors. Close your eyes. Feel how your body meets the surface. Do you experience yourself sinking in, pressing down, or holding yourself away? Are your muscles tight, or do they feel relaxed? Is your breathing regular and calm, or labored and tight? Are your breaths shallow or deep? Pay attention to the sensations of your body and observe. Notice as many details as possible. Try not to just think about it or conceptualize; instead, feel and sense these things, from the inside. Do not try to put what you are feeling into words. Simply notice and let the feeling be, without interfering. Experience lying quietly with this heightened awareness for 5 or more minutes, up to 20 minutes or so. When you feel ready, gently stretch your legs and arms, and sit up.

Sitting

Sit on the floor or in a chair. Close your eyes. Hold your head upright so that your back is straight but not rigid. Do not strain to be straight, but do not slouch either. You should feel a free flow of air as you breathe gently, in and out. Allow your rib cage to move as you breathe. Pay attention to your body sensations. Do you feel comfortable or are you fighting to keep upright? Does your breathing feel constricted? Can you let go of effort, or do you need to tense a little? Try stretching your midsection slightly. Does this open the air passages? Perhaps you have been slumping forward without realizing it. Be comfortable. Accepting your posture is part of your body awareness, so let your body positioning be comfortable.

Standing

Take off your shoes. Move your feet around, scrunch your toes, and then lightly tap the bottoms of your feet to sensitize them. Now, stand up with your feet placed shoulder width apart, eyes closed, and arms hanging loosely at your sides. Breathe naturally and comfortably. Notice how your feet meet the floor. How wide do your shoulders feel? Sense how far it is from your feet to the top of your head. Pay attention to your skin. Does it feel warm or cool? Is there any tingling? Notice if you are tightening your muscles. Can you let go of unnecessary tension that is not involved in keeping your body upright? For example, if you notice uncomfortable tension in your shoulders, can you relax them a bit? Allow yourself to stand for several minutes, aware of your body posture as you do so.

Walking

Stand for a moment, as you did in the previous exercise, relaxed and aligned with gravity. Then, when you feel in touch with standing, take a step forward, very slowly. Feel your heel as it meets the floor, then the ball of your foot as you roll forward. Note how your balance shifts as you step. Let your arms swing naturally. Take another slow step, sensing carefully. Notice how you feel as you walk. Continue to walk, paying close attention to your sensations of motion, with comfortable breathing and relaxed steps. Try different paces, slow or fast, but without losing awareness.

All of the activities that you have experienced—lying, sitting, standing, and walking, are part of everyday life. Take a moment, here and there in the day—to turn your attention to these activities, as you did in the exercises. Sometimes, you may have time for just a brief, inward glance. Other times, you can perhaps spend several minutes sensing. With time, your habitual awareness will alter, as you engage attentively in the fundamental activities of living.

REGULATING EMOTIONS

In the Zen sense, all emotions make up the tapestry of who we are. When we let ourselves feel what we feel, mindfully aware, the emotion is altered, often becoming more comfortable and easy to handle. Research confirms this insight, finding that simply attending mindfully to strong emotions lessens their intensity and returns the nervous system to balance (Lutz, Brefczynski-Lewis, Johnstone, & Davidson, 2008).

Noticing Feelings Mindfully

As a therapist, you are probably able to notice what you are feeling. But do you take the time to do so mindfully? Time spent turning your attention mindfully to your emotional experience from time to time may give you new insights about the intensity and quality of your affect. And sustaining mindfulness meditation will help you to stay centered and balanced.

Give yourself a moment to sit quietly and turn your attention to what you are experiencing emotionally. As you begin to identify a feeling, notice all that goes along with it: your breathing rate and quality, and any accompanying sensations and thought patterns. Allow the feeling and simply notice whatever is there without thinking beyond it, just staying concentrated on the feeling and its accompanying sensations and thoughts just as they are. Don't pass any judgments on the feeling, simply notice and let it be as it is. Without doing anything except remaining aware of the feeling, you will notice that as time passes, your affect intensity lowers and your nervous system settles of itself. Do this meditation when having different emotions at varying intensities.

Regulating Emotion With Breathing Meditation

Breathing is a barometer of emotion. When we feel strong emotion, breathing is altered. You can use attention to breathing to help get in touch with feeling. And if you stay with the meditation, the feeling will begin to transform as breathing becomes calmer and easier.

Focus all your attention on your breathing. If you are having a strong emotion, your breathing may be heavier, deeper, or shallower than normal. Begin where you are, following the sensation of the air as it comes in through your nose, goes down into your lungs, and then out again through your nose. Don't alter your breathing; simply notice it. Feel your rib cage as it moves up and down with every breath. Stay focused on breathing and notice how your emotional reaction alters.

MAKING AWARENESS A HABIT WITH THE MINDFUL GLANCE

Bringing mindfulness into each moment begins with deliberate practice, but it eventually evolves into a habit to be aware. Practice the mindfulness exercises in Chapter 5. As you become comfortable with them, you can easily bring mindfulness into any moment. Here are a series of exercises to help you foster awareness of yourself, the mindful glance.

We have separated these into three exercises, but as you become more skilled, you can do a quick check of all three together. When you direct a mindful glance toward your sensations, thoughts, feelings, and actions, you awaken to your inner nature at that moment.

Take a mindful glance from time to time through your day. Do not force anything—simply notice. Over time, you will add an intuitive dimension to your functioning. You may be pleasantly surprised as your attention sharpens and awareness deepens—helpful skills for working with clients!

Mindful Glance to Body

Let your attention scan through your body noticing your body sensations. Do you feel tight in your muscles? Which ones are tight and which ones are relaxed. Let your attention move around your body but do not try to change anything deliberately. Allow nature to take its course. Tightness is often an unnecessary clenching of muscles. If you become aware of any areas you are tensing unnecessarily, gently let go if this feels natural to do, allowing your muscles to find a comfortable tonus needed for whatever you are doing.

Mindful Glance to Thoughts

Sit up and continue to allow your muscles to relax. Turn your attention to your thoughts. Follow the flow of your thoughts without influencing them. What are you thinking about? Do you flow from idea to idea, or are your thoughts clustered around a single concern? Notice the ideas and concerns but do not interfere. Simply try to be aware and allow your ideas to develop as they do.

Mindful Glance to Feelings

Intuitive feelings can also be a guide to deeper levels. Sit with your eyes closed. Relax your breathing. What are you feeling? Don't force a response, simply wait for one to occur to you. Do you feel calm and quiet? As you sit, perhaps you notice other feelings. Whatever you experience, allow your feelings to be.

Mindful Glance to Actions

Now turn your attention to what you are doing as you are doing it. Pay close attention to the activity, sensing each movement you perform. Notice every detail about it as you do it. If your mind wanders away from the task, gently bring it back as soon as you notice. Stay fully focused on the task until you have completed it.

Grasping Glance All at Once

Zen meditation teaches us to grasp the whole, and that we can do so in an instant. This exercise can be practiced anywhere, anytime. It may be easiest to begin doing it right after performing the mindful glance exercises.

So, in this moment, let your focus be open. Allow your attention to roam freely in this present moment without choosing one thing over another. Take in your sensory experiencing, thoughts, feelings, and actions together, unified here and now. Perceive everything and nothing in particular, all at once. With perception open and mind clear, you will have a wordless, nonconceptual experience, grounded and centered right now.

ENHANCING YOUR RELATIONAL SKILLS

From the very first encounter with the client, we have an opportunity to attune and use our awareness to perceive our clients more clearly than they might be seen in their typical interactions. We meet our clients where they are, encountering them in the here and now moment. In the Zen sense, each moment is open, with potentials for something new to happen. And when we bring ourselves fully to the present moment, our perception opens, and we can see the client all at once. The interaction is unique in this way—outside of the typical social context with its characteristic roles and limitations.

Therapy resonates with the true person, and can elicit the client's personality as a whole. As a meditational therapist, you respond from your own truth, as you experience within you what the client brings to the session. You facilitate the client becoming more unified from the very beginning. "Only go straight" as Zen Master Seung Sahn (1927–2004) often told his students (Seung, 1992, p. 6). Clients complain of suffering inner battles, conflicting fragments at war within. And yet, what a person says and expresses in body language, voice tones, and implicit meanings, along with the expressed interpretations of what is felt and thought, are all part of the present moment. This moment, the combination of suffering, battling fragments, is where we begin.

Mindful Mirroring

You can use the ability to make your mind like a mirror to accurately reflect the client, without interposing your own biases or opinions. This is a skill to be used with your expertise and knowledge, not instead of it.

Turn your mindful attention to your client. Begin with mindfulness of body, noticing how she is sitting, what she is wearing, whether her clothes are clean or dirty, matching or mismatched, too big or too small. Look for anything else about her appearance that you perceive. Do not make any assessments or judgments; simply open your awareness and observe. Then move on to notice her emotions, shown in facial expression and body language. Is she sad, happy, angry, or frustrated? What are the cues that you perceive, such as the quality or tone of her voice—is it loud or soft, strong or weak? Next, notice her thoughts. Listen to the content of what she is saying for clues. Finally, allow yourself to take in the whole person. What draws your awareness? You may find that in being mindfully aware of your client, you learn something new about her.

Reflecting the Client for the First Time

Use beginner mind to help you experience your clients more clearly. When we first meet people, we can perceive them without previous bias, just as they are in the present moment. Bring your beginner mind to the session.

Before the client arrives, meditate using one of the preceding exercises to clear your mind of extraneous thoughts and become present in the moment. Then, when the client enters the office, you can experience this person anew, as if for the first time. The ability to set aside all preconceptions and experience the other directly may reveal some aspects that you may have overlooked before.

Koan: Wu Tends the Sick

Kuei-shan asked Tao-wu, "Where are you coming from?" Tao-wu said, "I've come from tending the sick." Kuei-shan said, "How many people were sick?" Tao-wu said, "There were the sick and the not sick." Kuei-shan said, "Isn't the one not sick you?" Tao-wu said, "Being sick and not being sick have nothing to do with him at all. Speak quickly, speak quickly." Kuei-shan said, "Even if I could say anything, it would have no relation."

(Loori, 1994, pp. 215–216)

When looking at our clients, we get tempted to see them in terms of the problem. We might even start to think of them as their diagnosis. But in the Zen sense, we should look beyond the illness to the person. Ultimately, we go beyond being sick and not sick, since this is not what therapy is all about. In the daily life of sick and not sick, we are simply living our lives. People often take sides, identifying with one or the other, being neurotic or being healthy. Even the ego that worries about being sick or not sick is gone. Ultimately, all dualities can dissolve in the open clear moment.

Meditate on the client, beyond good or bad, sickness or health, and simply experience him as you are together, sharing in the session. Your clear, intuitive awareness shines through, to guide your work together.

CONCLUSION

Our training gives us great insight and understanding into how human beings suffer, and what we can do to help them. But there are also times in therapy to set all these learnings aside, to enter into the empty uncreated moment with the client, and just be there. Attunement, sensitivities, and intuition open. You communicate on the most profoundly spiritual level. And in this being-in-the-moment together, change happens.

Conclusion: Living Life as an Art

Compassionate harmony is our inner compass.
—(C. Alexander Simpkins & Annellen M. Simpkins)

Long ago, a monk was famous for his gardening skills. The king heard of his abilities and had him brought to his castle to plant a new garden. The monk agreed to do so if the king promised to follow his instructions. The king agreed. The monk asked that certain supplies be brought to the area. Then he told the king and his men to leave him alone. When the king and his men left, the monk sat down in the middle of the plot of land and began to meditate.

A few hours later, one of the king's men peeked in and saw the monk still meditating. Later that night the king's men looked again, but the monk was still meditating. Food was brought to the monk the following day, but he continued to meditate. Many days passed in this way. The king began to feel impatient. Finally, he could wait no longer. The king walked up to the meditating monk and said angrily, "I brought you here to create a beautiful garden, but all you have done for the past week is sit there!"

The monk said nothing and continued to meditate. Not accustomed to being ignored the king said fiercely, "I give you one more day to finish the task, and then I will kill you!"

The next day the king was amazed when he came in with his executioner. There before him was the most beautiful garden he had ever seen.

"How is it," asked the king, "that you sat for an entire week, doing nothing and then created this most exquisite garden in only one day?"

The monk replied in a quiet, absolutely calm voice, "You asked me to create a beautiful garden, but to do so I must first become One with the beauty of nature. Then the rest is easy."

Clients sometimes think that therapy just takes place in the therapy hour. Therapy may be the vehicle of healing, but the healing process is ongoing in every moment of every day. The Zen therapy way is to go about your everyday life as you do, but with a difference. Whatever you do is an opportunity to be awake and aware. "When you are concentrated on the quality of your being, you are prepared for the activity" (S. Suzuki, 1979, p. 105). Then the quality of your awareness is the activity itself. You do everything fully, so immersed in the moment that you are no longer self-conscious of how you are doing. Instead, you are just doing. This quality of activity brings a profound integration between thoughts, feelings, and behavior: you and your life, in harmony with the world.

This book has addressed the things we all can do, therapists and clients, to enhance the quality of therapy meditatively. As problems are being dealt with, clients find an ever-growing capacity to incorporate awareness into their being in the world. Problems are noticed and can be acted upon. New options open up as rigid patterns dissolve. And for therapists, the ability to be flexible and aware is an invaluable treasure as well, not just to access your sensitivities with clients, but also to enhance the quality of your satisfaction and fulfillment in your own life.

THE KOAN OF LIFE

I can't say where I am heading
As I journey over our infinite earth
And yet, with each step, I am at ease
(Paraphrased from Zen Master Dogen)

As you live each day without the fetters of complicated concepts, abstractions, beliefs, and worries, every day can be a good day, as Ummon said (from the *Hekiganroku*). But when Ummon said every day is a good day, he didn't mean good as opposed to bad. His meaning reaches deeper to the absolute quality of being expressing itself as it is. The koan asks, what is the true nature of this day, this hour, this moment?

> When the Dharma is truly, fully, and existentially understood, we find there is nothing wanting in this life as we live it. Everything and anything we need is here with us and in us. . . .
>
> (Shimano, 1995, p. 7)

The world and all that is in it expresses reality. Every therapy session, each moment in your life is a koan to be solved, an opportunity to learn about your deeper being. How you respond is your choice. You always have the option to respond with your most enlightened nature.

Personal Self to Universal Self

Let go of the limited concept of ego and self. By losing yourself in the actions of your everyday life you discover something more, your deeper true nature, Mind with a capital *M*. You discover this vast source of potential within and can live through it.

Your concept of self need not restrict you. Don't make anything extra, just start from the concrete, here-and-now moment and you will be grounded in deeper reality. We waste a lot of effort lost in abstractions, opinions, beliefs, and worries about all of these ideas, far removed from reality itself. But you don't need to get lost in these mental constructions. You are freed by staying close to what is right at hand. Start from what is here in front of you and express your universal self, at One with the world. Staying true to the universal self can extend the personal self beyond the confines of your taken-for-granted life. You gain strength and capacity to handle your life and can even reach out to help others.

Your meditative life is a full life, artistic and creative, passionate and emotional, calm and tranquil. You can live well in the everyday world with your everyday mind, meditating. Stay attuned to the profound essence of all things. At One with the universe, you can live a fulfilling life, adding your uniqueness to the whole.

Seize the moment
Before it has passed

The first opportunity
Is also the last
Each moment of time
In itself complete
And your life's potential
Is always unique!
(C. Alexander Simpkins)

Appendix: A Quick Tour Through the Brain

COMPONENTS OF THE NERVOUS SYSTEM

Begin Small: Neurons

The brain is made up of neurons. Neurons are the functional units in the brain and throughout the nervous system. There are more than 180 billion neurons with at least 80 billion involved in cognitive processes. Each neuron connects with hundreds of other neurons, and so we have vast potentials for an enormous amount of interactions occurring simultaneously (see Figure A.1).

Neurons have two main functions: They process certain chemicals within them, and they communicate with other neurons. This communication process of inputs, integration, and outputs occurs across the synaptic gap between neurons. When the gap is close enough, the electrical signal can simply leap across and keep going. But more often, the gap is too large for this to happen. With the larger gaps, the electrical signal is converted into a chemical, known as a neurotransmitter, and the neurotransmitters swim across the gap to then be converted back into an electrical impulse when they reach the other side (see Figure A.2).

We have a number of different kinds of neurotransmitters. Glutamate is an excitatory neurotransmitter that is found throughout the nervous system. GABA (gamma aminobutyric acid) is inhibitory and, like glutamate, is found everywhere in the nervous system. Certain neurotransmitters are more

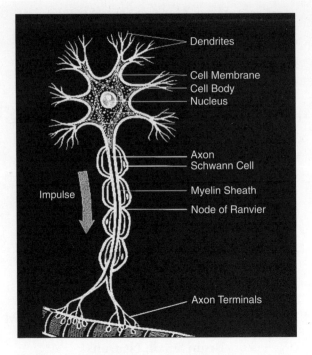

Figure A.1   The Neuron

specific in what they communicate. For example, dopamine is related to pleasure and reward. Serotonin involves emotionality and sleep patterns, norepinephrine influences alertness, and endorphins alleviate pain. The neurotransmitter system usually has everything it needs already built in. But when the neurotransmitters are out of balance, drug therapy and psychological treatments such as meditation, hypnosis, and psychotherapy can stimulate

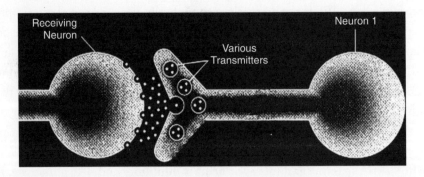

Figure A.2   Synaptic Transmission

or inhibit processes to stimulate a better balance. Medications for psychological problems such as depression and anxiety are just acting to stimulate the neurons to produce more of certain neurotransmitters or to block the action of other neurotransmitters.

The transmission across the synapse either activates the neuron to fire or deactivates it from firing. When neurons fire together repeatedly, these neurons tend to become wired together, known as Hebb's rule (Hebb, 1949), forming a stronger synaptic connection. This firing and wiring strengthening, known as LTP (long-term potentiation), explains, at a neuronal level, how learning and memory occur. It also helps to account for neuroplasticity.

The Central Nervous System and Peripheral Nervous System

All the neurons combined make up the nervous system, consisting of the central nervous system (brain and spinal cord) and the peripheral nervous system (autonomic nervous system, cranial nerves, and spinal nerves) (see Figure A.3). The peripheral nervous system extends through the whole body and communicates information to and from the central nervous system. The autonomic nervous system interacts closely with the central nervous system, often automatically and unconsciously.

The neurons of the autonomic nervous system include two key systems: the sympathetic nervous system and the parasympathetic nervous system. The sympathetic nervous system prepares the body for vigorous action. The parasympathetic nervous system acts as an opposite to the sympathetic nervous system's activations. So, when the sympathetic activation constricts blood vessels or inhibits digestion during exercise, the parasympathetic system relaxes vessel walls and stimulates digestion when the workout is over. Both systems work together to help foster appropriate responses. These systems of activation and deactivation are involved in emotions such as fear and anger, as well as participating in responses to stress and feelings of enjoyment. Together, these two systems maintain the control that keeps the mind, brain, and body in balance. Yoga breathing, postures, and meditations can shift the balance in the autonomic nervous system.

Brain Structures and Functions

The brain orchestrates the nervous system. It is often described in terms of its structures and functions. Unconscious processing tends to travel a short,

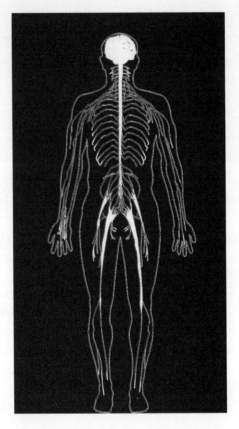

Figure A.3 Central Nervous System

subcortical path through the lower brain areas, known as bottom-up process-ing, which does not engage the higher-level-processing cortex. For awareness of emotions, sensations, and cognitions, the information usually travels a long path, sometimes called top-down processing, involving higher parts of the cortex (see Figure A.4).

Lower Brain Areas: Brainstem and Cerebellum

At the base of the brain is the brainstem, the transition between the spinal cord and the brain. This area is important in regulating vital body functions such as breathing, heart rate, and other automatic functions. These lower brain areas coordinate their action with many other regions of the brain (see Figure A.5).

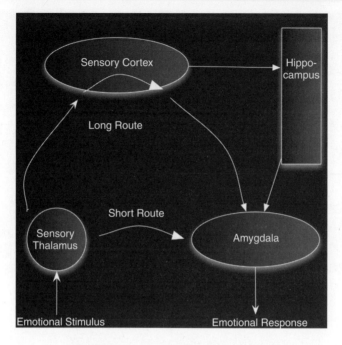

Figure A.4   Short Path and Long Path

The cerebellum (Latin for *little brain*), located at the back of the neck, has two hemispheres with functional sections in each, known as lobes. The cerebellum interacts closely with other parts of the brain through loops of interaction. It serves a variety of functions including the regulation of higher

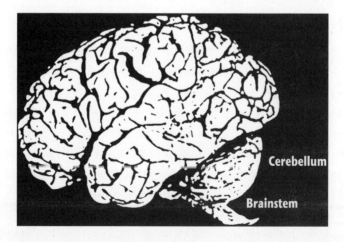

Figure A.5   Lower Brain

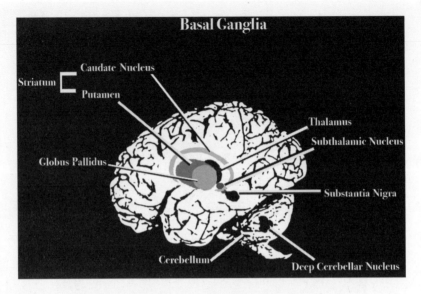

Figure A.6   Basal Ganglia

cerebral processes in motor planning, cognition, involuntary functions, and problem solving. It also regulates posture and the command of movement. We have all experienced the effort required to learn new movements, such as playing a sport or mastering a dance pattern. During the learning period, the cerebellum is active. Once movement control is mastered, the cerebellum becomes less active and other parts of the brain get involved.

Interior Brain Areas: Basal Ganglia and Limbic System

The region that spans the area from the brainstem to below the cortex in the interior of the brain is the limbic system, for emotions, and the basal ganglia, for voluntary movement and coordination.

The basal ganglia (Figure A.6) form a C-shape of four interconnected structures: the substantia nigra, the caudate nucleus, the putamen, and the globus pallidus. These structures are also involved in planning movement, performing movements in sequence, and maintaining learning. This area is also part of predictive control, attention, and working memory.

The limbic system (Figure A.7) has been given much attention for therapy, since it is intimately involved in regulating emotion, fear conditioning, fight or flight, and stress responses, as well as learning and memory. Many

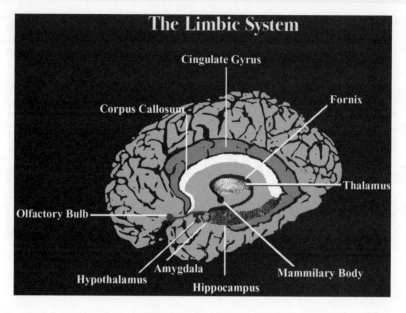

Figure A.7   Limbic

structures play a central role in the limbic system. The most central ones include the amygdala for emotions; the hippocampus for learning and memory; the hypothalamus for regulating many autonomic functions, including biological rhythms and stress; and the thalamus as a gateway for sensory information. Several other structures are considered important for some aspects of emotion, and they are the olfactory cortex, involved in the sense of smell, the pituitary gland regulating hormones, and the nucleus accumbens, important for reward, laughter, pleasure, addiction, and the placebo effect. Two cortical areas are also strongly linked to the limbic system: the cingulate gyrus for monitoring conflicts and the orbitofrontal cortex (part of the prefrontal cortex). All of these structures interconnect and interact together, although some contribute more to one function than to another. With so many varied brain structures all closely interacting functionally with each other as well as with higher cortical functions, it makes sense as to why emotions play such an important role in every aspect of living.

Higher Brain Areas: The Cerebral Cortex

The cerebral cortex (Figure A.8) is the outer layer of the hemispheres, with many convolutions, or *gyri*, and folds, or *sulci*. Folding increases the surface

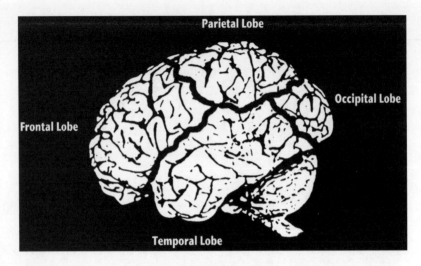

Figure A.8   Lobes

area of the cortex, so that more than two-thirds of the surface is hidden from view. The cortex is sometimes referred to as the higher part of the brain. Each hemisphere is divided into four lobes: the frontal, parietal, temporal, and occipital. The lobes monitor different functions, although they are all inter-related, interacting together. The fibers that connect the two hemispheres are called the corpus callosum, which helps the two hemispheres communicate with each other.

Frontal Lobe

The frontal lobe accounts for nearly one-third of the cerebral cortex. The prefrontal cortex is located at the front of the frontal lobe behind the fore-head. The fact that the prefrontal areas have extensive links throughout the brain shows how interrelated brain functions really are. Areas of the prefrontal cortex are involved in executive functions that include planning, higher-level decision making, sequencing, and goal-directed behavior. Independent thinking is processed in this area as well. Another part of the prefrontal cortex processes personality characteristics such as the experience of empathy, socially appropriate behavior, and emotional control.

The primary motor area of the frontal cortex is located in the back (posterior) area of the frontal lobe. It is important for control of movement. This area has a map of the body on it. Larger portions of the cortical map are devoted to areas that are used more, such as the hands and face. The nonprimary motor cortex, located in front of the primary motor cortex, includes a premotor area and a supplementary motor area. These areas are involved with movement and coordination in general, such as stance, gait, and initiation of voluntary movement sequences. Mirror neurons are located in the motor area of the frontal lobe as well. These neurons are involved in understanding and empathizing with the intentions and actions of others and help with social understanding.

One other important area located in the frontal lobe is the cingulate gyrus, also called the cingulate cortex. This area is involved in motivated behavior, spontaneity, and creativity. Complex behavior and attention, or conflict monitoring, are also processed in the cingulate gyrus. This area is primary during the emotional reaction to pain and in the regulation of aggressive behavior. It has also been found to play an important role in maternal attachment, as evident in behaviors like nursing and nest building in animals.

The Parietal Lobe

Behind the frontal lobe and close to the cingulate gyrus is the parietal lobe. This lobe is involved in sensation and perception of touch, pressure, temperature, and pain. Sensory information from the body is correlated there during perception or cognition of a sensation. The parietal lobe is activated when locating objects in space and mapping the relationship of the body to the world. The back (anterior) portion of the parietal lobe is the sensory strip. The body is mapped on the sensory strip for sensations, similar to how the primary motor cortex is where movement is mapped for the body.

The Temporal Lobe

The temporal lobe houses the primary auditory cortex. It is located near the temples and moderates auditory information. Wernicke's area, on the left hemisphere side, plays a larger role in understanding spoken language. Although most of the visual processing occurs in the primary visual areas in the occipital lobe, some visual processing is performed in the temporal lobes, involving perception of movements and face recognition.

The Occipital Lobe

The occipital lobes are located in the posterior region of the brain. Axons coming from visual input from the eyes pass through the thalamus and are directed to the primary visual cortex. The visual cortex is also sometimes called the striate cortex because of its striped appearance. Human beings rely on their vision quite heavily, and this is revealed in the complexity of this region of the brain. There are more than 32 zones for visual processing, differentiating different aspects of seeing, such as color, texture, and movement. All are located in the occipital lobes.

HOW THE BRAIN AREAS WORK TOGETHER

So, how do all of these brain areas function? Senses provide a window to the world. First, the receptor organs (such as the eyes, fingertips, nose, tongue, and ears) detect a stimulus. Each sensory system has its own pathway that sends the signal to the cortex. The signal registers on receptor fields for the particular sensory modality in a cortical map, located on the cortex. Maps can change, depending on what stimuli are experienced. Maps that are used more often tend to grow larger. Attention, regulated in the frontal lobe, is what helps to notice important stimuli and ignore others, such as attending to reading while ignoring the sound of rain on the roof.

Pathways

The central nervous system is a complex collection of structures and functions that are organized in pathways. Thoughts, feelings, and behaviors are intimately involved in the flow of these pathways, which are dynamic systems of interactions between brain structures and the flow of energy and neurotransmitters.

A number of pathways through the nervous system help coordinate the mind-brain-body balance. One pathway processes sensory input and has a special pathway to process painful stimuli. A reward pathway (Figure A.9) regulates positive emotions and drives toward fulfillment, satisfaction, and enjoyment. The fear pathway, also called the HPA pathway (Figure A.10), provides the capacity to respond to threat and then return to homeostatic balance. When overactivated, the fear pathway becomes a stress pathway.

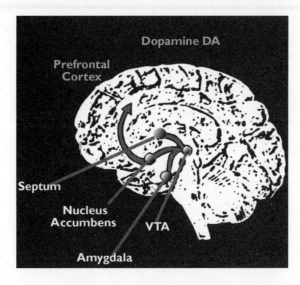

Figure A.9   Reward Pathway

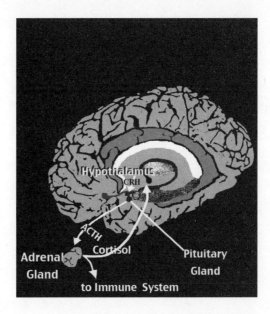

Figure A.10   HPA Pathway

Regulatory systems control the appetite and the sleep-wake cycle as well. When any of these systems are out of balance, disorders and problems tend to develop. All of these systems can be altered using the therapeutic Yoga techniques included in this book.

References

Abe, M. (1989). *Zen and western thought.* London, England: Macmillan Press Ltd.

Adler, K. A. & Deutsch, D. (Eds.) (1959). *Essays in individual psychology: Contemporary applications of Alfred Adler's theories.* New York, NY: Grove Press.

Ainsworth, M. D. S., Blehat, J. C., Waters, E., & Wall, S. (1978). *Patterns of attachment: A psychological study of the strange situation.* Hillsdale, NJ: Erlbaum.

Arana, D. (2006). The practice of mindfulness meditation to alleviate the symptoms of chronic shyness and social anxiety. *Dissertation Abstracts International: Section B: The Sciences and Engineering 67*(5-B), 2822.

Badawi, K., Wallace, R. K., Orme-Johnson, D., & Rouzere, A. M. (1984). Electrophysiologic characteristics of reparatory suspension periods occurring during the practice of the transcendental meditation program. *Psychosomatic Medicine, 46*(3), 267–276.

Badenoch, B. (2008). *Being a brain-wise therapist: A practical guide to interpersonal neurobiology.* New York, NY: W. W. Norton & Co.

Bartels, A., & Zeki, S. (2000). The neural basis of romantic love. *NeuroReport, 11*(17), 3829–3834.

Benson, H., & Wallace, R. K. (1972). Decreased drug abuse with transcendental meditation: A study of 1862 subjects. In C. Zarafonetis (Ed.), *Drug-abuse: Proceedings of the international conference* (pp. 239–252). Philadelphia, PA: Lea and Febiger.

Berne, E. (1996). *Games people play: The basic handbook of Transactional Analysis*. New York, NY: Ballantine Books.

Blofeld, J. (Ed.) (1994). *The Zen teaching of Huang Po*. Boston, MA: Shambhala.

Bowen, S., Witkiewitz, K., Dilworth, T. M., Chawla, N., Simpson, T. L., Ostafin, B. D., ... Blume, A. W. (2006). Mindfulness meditation and substance use in an incarcerated population. *Psychology of Addictive Behaviors, 20*(3), 343–347.

Bowlby, J. (1983). *Attachment*. New York, NY: Basic Books.

Bowlby, J. (2005). *A secure base: Parent-child attachment and healthy human development*. London, England: Routledge.

Braboszcz, C., Habnusseau, S., & Delorme, A. (2010). Meditation and neuroscience: From basic research to clinical practice. In R. Carlstedt (Ed.), *Integrating psychology, psychiatry, and behavioral medicine. Perspectives, practices, and research* (pp. 1910–1929). New York, NY: Springer.

Brewer, J. A., Sinha, R., Chen, J. A., Michalsen, R. N., Bubuscio, T. A., Nich, C., ... Rounsaville, B. J. (2009). Mindfulness training and stress reactivity in substance abuse: Results from a randomized, controlled stage I pilot study. *Substance Abuse, 30*(4), 305–317.

Brown, K. W., & Gordon, S. (2009). Toward a phenomenology of mindfulness: Subjective experience and emotional correlates. In Fabrizio Didonna (Ed.), *Clinical handbook of mindfulness* (pp. 59–84). New York, NY: Springer.

Brown, R. P. & Gerberg, P. I. (2005). Sudarshan kriya yogic breathing in the treatment of stress, anxiety, and depression: Part II-clinical applications and guidelines. *Journal of Alternative and Complementary Medicine, 11*(4), 711–717.

Cahn, B. R., & Polich, J. (2006). Meditation states and traits: EEG, ERP, and neuroimaging studies. *Psychological Bulletin, 132*(2), 180–211.

Cahn, R., Delome, A., & Polich, J. (2010). Occipital gamma activation during Vipassana meditation. *Cognitive Processing, 11*(1), 39–56.

Carson, J. W., Carson, K. M., Gil, K. M., & Baucom, D. H. (2004). Mindfulness-based relationship enhancement. *Behavior Therapy, 35*(3), 471–494.

Carter C. S., Grippo A. J, Pournajafi-Nazarloo H., Ruscio M. G., & Porges S. W. (2008). Oxytocin, vasopressin and social behavior. *Progress in Brain Research, 170*, 331–336.

Ch'en, K. (1973). *Buddhism in China*. Princeton, NJ: Princeton University Press.

Chiesa, A. (2009). Zen meditation: An integration of current evidence. *Journal of Alternative and Complementary Medicine, 15*(5), 1–8.

Cleary, T. (1993). *The flower ornament sutra: A translation of the Avatamsaka sutra*. Boston, MA: Shamabala.

Cochin, S., Barthelemy, C., Roux, S., & Martineau, J. (1999). Observation and execution of movement: Similarities demonstrated by quantified electroencephalography. *European Journal of Neuroscience, 11*, 1839–1842.

Conze, E. (1995). *A short history of Buddhism*. Oxford, England: Oneworld Publications.

Craig, A. D. (2002). How do you feel? Interoception: The sense of the physiological condition of the body. *Nature Reviews, Neuroscience, 3*, 655–666.

Craig, A. D. (2005). Forebrain emotional asymmetry: A neuroanatomical basis? *Trends in Cognitive Science, 9*, 566–571.

Craig, A. D. (2009). How do you feel now? The anterior insula and human awareness. *Nature Reviews, Neuroscience, 10*, 59–70.

Creswell, J. D., Way, B. M., Eisenberger, N. I., & Lieberman, M. D. (2007). Neural correlates of dispositional mindfulness during affect labeling. *Psychosomatic Medicine, 69*, 560–565.

Dalai, L., & Cutler, H. C. (1998). *The art of happiness*. New York, NY: Riverhead Books.

Damasio, A. R. (2000). *The feeling of what happens: Body and emotion in the making of consciousness*. Chicago, IL: Harcourt.

Damasio, A. R., Grabowski, T. J., Bechara, A., Damasio, H., Ponto, L. L., Parvizi, J., & Hichwa, R. D. (2000). Subcortical and cortical brain activity during the feeling of self-generated emotions. *Nature Neuroscience, 3*(10), 1049–1056.

Darwin, C. (1872). *The expression of the emotions in man and animals*. New York, NY: D. D. Appleton (Reprint, Chicago, IL: University of Chicago Press, 1965).

Davidson, R. J. (2010). Empirical explorations of mindfulness: Conceptual and methodological conundrums. *Emotion, 10*(1), 8–11.

Davidson, R. J., Goleman, D., & Schwartz, G. (1976). Attentional and affective concomitants of meditation: A cross-sectional study. *Journal of Abnormal Psychology, 85*, 235–308.

Davidson, R. J., Jackson, D. C., & Kalin, N. H. (2000). Emotion, plasticity, context and regulation: Perspectives from affective neuroscience. *Psychological Bulletin, 126*, 890–906.

Davidson, R. J., Kabat-Zinn, J., Schumacher, J., Rosenkranz, M., Muller, D., Santorelli, S. E., ... Sheridan, J. F. (2003). Alterations in brain and immune functions produced by mindfulness meditation. *Psychomatic Medicine, 654*, 564–570.

Davidson, R. J., & Lutz, A. (2007). Buddha's brain: Neuroplasticity and meditation. *IEEE Signal Processing Magazine, 176*, 171–174.

DeBerry, S. (1982). The effects of meditation-relaxation on anxiety and depression in a geriatric population. *Psychotherapy: Theory, Research, and Practice, 19*(4), 512–521.

Derrida, J. (1982). *Margins of philosophy*. Chicago, IL: University of Chicago Press.

Dumoulin, H. (1988). *Zen Buddhism, a history, Vol. 1*. New York, NY: Weatherhill.

Dumoulin, H. (1992). *Zen Buddhism in the 20th century*. New York, NY: Weatherhill.

Elias A. N., Guich S., & Wilson A. F. (2000). Ketosis with enhanced GABAergic tone promotes physiological changes in transcendental meditation. *Medical Hypotheses, 54*(4), 660–662.

Ellis, A., & Ellis, D. J. (2011). *Rational emotive behavior therapy*. Washington, DC: American Psychological Association.

Emerson, R. W. (1965). *Selected writings of Ralph Waldo Emerson*. New York, NY: Signet Classics.

Farb, N. A., Anderson, A. K. Mayberg, H., Bean, J., McKeon, D., & Segal, Z. V. (2010). Minding one's emotions: Mindfulness training alters the neural expression of sadness. *Emotion, 10*(1), 25–33.

Francis, D., & Meaney, M. J. (1999). Maternal care and development of stress responses. *Current Opinion in Neuobiology, 9*, 128–134.

Frank, J. D., & Frank, J. B. (1991). *Persuasion and healing*. Baltimore, MD: Johns Hopkins University Press.

Gage, F., Kempermann, G., & Hongjun, S. (2008). *Adult neurogenesis*. Cold Spring Harbor, NY: Cold Spring Harbor Laboratory Press.

Gage, F. H., Eriksson, P. S., Perfilieva, E., & Bjork-Eriksson, T. (1998). Neurogenesis in the adult human hippocampus. *Nature Medicine, 4*(11), 1313–1317.

Gallese, V. (2009). Mirror neurons and the neural exploitation hypothesis: From embodied simulation to social cognition. In J. A. Pineda (Ed.), *Mirror neuron systems: The role of mirroring processes in social cognition* (pp. 163–184). New York, NY: Humana Press.

Gay, E. (Ed.) (1989). *The Freud reader.* New York, NY: W. W. Norton & Co.

Gellhorn, E., & Kiely, W. F. (1972). Mystical states of consciousness: Neuro-physiological and clinical aspects. *Journal of Nervous and Mental Diseases, 154,* 399–405.

Goleman, D., & Goleman, T. B. (Eds.) (2001). The emotionally intelligent workplace. Hoboken, NJ: Jossey-Bass.

Gottman, J. (2011). *The science of trust: Emotional attunement for couples.* New York, NY: W. W. Norton & Co.

Gottman, J., & Levenson, R. W. (1992). Marital processes predictive of later dissolution: Behavior, physiology, & health. *Journal of Personality and Social Psychology, 63,* 221–233.

Gould, E., Beylin, A., Tanapat, P., Reeves, A., & Shors, T. J. (1999). Learning enhances adult neurogenesis in the hippocampal formation. *Nature Neuroscience, 2,* 260–265.

Graham, A. (1968). *Conversations: Christian and Buddhist: Encounters in Japan.* New York, NY: Harcourt Brace & World.

Grepmair, L., Mitterlehner, F., Loew, T., Bachler, E., Rother, W., & Nickel, M. (2007). Promoting mindfulness in psychotherapists in training influences the treatment results of their patients: A randomized double-blind controlled study. *Psychotherapy and Psychosomatics, 76,* 332–338.

Gross, J. J., & Levenson, R. W. (1993). Emotional suppression: Physiology, self-report, and expressive behavior. *Journal of Personality and Social Psychology, 64,* 6, 970–986.

Harvard Medical International. (2004). The benefits of mindfulness. *Harvard Women's Health Watch, 11*(6), 1–3.

Hayes, S. C. (2004). Acceptance and commitment therapy and the new behavior therapies: Mindfulness, acceptance, and relationship. In S. C. Hayes, V. M. Folette, & M. Linehan (Eds.), *Mindfulness and accepting: Expanding the cognitive behavioral tradition* (pp. 1–29). New York, NY: Guilford Press.

Hayes, S. C., Bissett, R., Korn, Z., Zettle, R. D., Rosenfarb, I., & Cooper, L. (1999). The impact of acceptance versus control rationales on pain tolerance. *Psychological Record, 49*(1), 33–47.

Hayes, S. C., & Feldman, G. (2004). Clarifying the construct of mindfulness in the context of emotion regulation and the process of change in therapy. *Clinical Psychology: Science and Practice, 11*(3), 255–262.

Hebb, D. (1949). *The organization of behaviour.* New York, NY: Wiley.

Heidegger, M. (1962). *Being and time.* San Francisco, CA: HarperCollins.

Heidegger, M. (2002). *Off the beaten track.* Cambridge, MA: Cambridge University Press.

Heider, F. (1958). *The psychology of interpersonal relations.* New York, NY: Wiley.

Heine, S. (1997). *The Zen poetry of Dogen.* Boston, MA: Tuttle Publishing.

Heller A. S., Johnstone, T., Shackman, A. J., Light, S., Peterson, M., Kolden, G., ... Davidson, R. J. (2009). Reduced capacity to sustain positive emotion in major depression reflects diminished maintenance of frontostriatal brain activation. *Proceedings of the National Academy of Sciences, 106*(52), 22445–22450.

Herrigel, E. (1971). *Zen in the art of archery.* New York, NY: Vintage Books.

Herrigel, G. (1958). *Zen in the art of flower arrangement.* London, England: Arkana.

Hirai, T. (1974). *Psychophysiology of Zen.* Tokyo, Japan: Igaku Hoin Ltd.

Hotzel, B. K. (2007). Differential engagement of anterior cingulate and adjacent medial frontal cortex in adept meditator and non-meditators. *Neuroscience Letters, 421,* 16–21.

Hugdahl, K. (1996). Brain laterality—beyond the basics. *European Psychologist, 1,* 206–220.

James, W. (1896). *The principles of psychology.* Vol. I & II. New York, NY: Henry Holt & Company.

Jensen, O., Kaiser, J., & Lachaux, J. P. (2007). Human gamma-frequency oscillations associated with attention and memory. *Trends in Neurosciences, 30*(7), 317–324.

Jha, A. P., Kropinger, J., & Baime, M. (2007). Mindfulness training modifies subsystems of attention. *Cognitive, Affective, and Behavioral Neuroscience, 7,* 109–119.

Johnson, S. (2008). *Hold me tight.* New York, NY: Little, Brown and Company.

Johnstone, T., van Reekum, C., Urry, H., Kalin, N., & Davidson, R. (2007). Failure to regulate: Counterproductive recruitment of top-down prefrontal subcortical circuitry in major depression. *Journal of Neuro-science*, *27*, 8877–8884.

Jung, C. (1978). *Psychology and the east*. Princeton, NJ: Princeton University Press.

Kabat-Zinn, J. (2003). Mindfulness-based interventions in context: Past, present, and future. *Clinical Psychology: Science and Practice*, *10*(2), 144–156.

Kabat-Zinn, J., Massion, A. O., Kristeller, J., Peterson, L. G., Fletcher, K. E., Pbert, L., . . . Santorelli, S. F. (1992). Effectiveness of a meditation-based stress reduction program in the treatment of anxiety disorders. *American Journal of Psychiatry*, *149*, 936–943.

Kerem, E., Fishman, N., & Josselson, R. (2001). The experience of empathy in everyday relationships: Cognitive and affective elements. *Journal of Social and Personal Relationships*, *18*(5), 709–729.

Khalsa, S. S., Rudrauf, D., Damasio, A. R., Davidson, R. J., Lutz, A., & Tranel, D. (2008). Interoceptive awareness in experienced meditators. *Psychophysiology*, *45*(4), 671–677.

Kohr, R. I. (1977). Dimensionality in the meditative experience. *Journal of Transpersonal Psychology*, *9*(2), 193–203.

Kornfeld, J. (1993). *A path with heart*. New York, NY: Bantam Books.

Korunka, C., Tement, S., Zdrehus, C., & Borza, A. (2010). Burnout: Definition, recognition and prevention approaches. BOIT: Burnout intervention training for managers and team leaders.

Kosfeld, M., Heinrichs, M., Zak, P. J., Fischbacher, U., & Fehr, E. (2005). Oxytocin increases trust in humans. *Nature*, *435*, 637–676.

Krishnamurti, J. (1949). Self-knowledge lies in the unfolding of relationship. Public speech. Retrieved from www.messagefrommasters.com/Shiva-Shakti/jkrishnamurtion_relationship.htm

Kubie, L. S. (1975). *Neurotic distortion of the creative process*. New York, NY: Noonday Press.

Lagopoulos, J., Xu, J., Rasmussen, I., Vik, A., Malhi, G. S., Eliassen, C. F., . . . Ellingsen, O. (2009). Increased theta and alpha EEG activity during nondirective meditation. *Journal of Alternative and Complementary Medicine*, *15*(11), 1187–1192.

Lamm, C., & Singer, T. (2010). The role of anterior insular cortex in social emotions. *Brain Structure and Function*, *214*(5–6), 579–591.

Langer, E. J. (1989). *Mindfulness.* Cambridge, MA: Da Cap Press.

Lazar, S. W., Bush, G., Gollub, R. L., Fricchione, G. L., Khalsa, G., & Benson, H. (2000). Functional brain mapping of the relaxation response and meditation. *NeuroReport, 11*(1581), 1585.

Lazar, S. W., Kerr, C. E., Wasserman, R. H., Gray, J. R., Greve, M., Treadway, T., . . . Fishi, B. (2005). Meditation experience is associated with increased cortical thickness. *NeuroReport, 16*(17), 1893–1897.

Lee, S. H., Ahn, S. C., Lee, Y. J., Choi, T. K., Yook, K. H., & Suh, S. Y. (2007). Effectiveness of a meditation-based stress management program as an adjunct to pharmacotherapy in patients with anxiety disorder. *Journal of Psychosomatic Research, 62*(2), 189–195.

Legge, J. (1962). *The texts of Taoism.* Vol. I. New York, NY: Dover.

Levenson, R. W. (2011). COGS 200 Seminar at UCSD, The cognitive neuroscience of motivation and emotions, January 21, 2011.

Linehan, M. M., & Dimeff, L. (2001). Dialectical behavior therapy in a nutshell. *The California Psychologist, 34,* 10–13.

Loori, J. D. (1994). *Two arrows meeting in mid-air.* Boston, MA: Charles E. Tuttle.

Low, A. (1995). *The world: A gateway: Commentaries on the Mumokan.* Boston, MA: Charles E. Tuttle Co., Inc.

Lutz, A., Brefczynski-Lewis, J. A., Johnstone, T., & Davidson, R. J. (2008). Regulation of the neural circuitry of emotion by compassion meditation: Effects of meditative expertise. *PLoS ONE, 3*(3), 1897.

Lutz, A., Greischar, L. L., Rawlings, N. B., Ricard, M., & Davidson, R. J. (2004). Long-term meditators self-induce high-amplitude gamma synchrony during mental practice. *Proc Natl Acad Sci 16,* 101, 46, 16369–16373.

Lutz, A., Slagter, H. A. Dunne, J. D., & Davidson, R. J. (2008). Attention regulation and monitoring in meditation. *Trends in Cognitive Science, 12*(4), 163–169.

Ma, S., & Teasdale, J. (2004). Mindfulness-based cognitive therapy for depression: Replication and exploration of differential relapse prevention effects. *Journal of Consulting and Clinical Psychology, 72*(1), 31–40.

Maslach, C. Jackson, S. E., & Leiter, M. P. (1996). *MBI: The Maslach burnout inventory manual* (3rd ed.). Palo Alto, CA: Consulting Psychologists Press.

Maslach, C. Schaufeli, W. B., & Leiter, M. P. (2001). Job burnout. *Annual Review of Psychology, 52,* 397–422.

McGuire, E. A., Gadian, D. G., Johnsrude, I. S., Good, C. D., Ashburner, J., Frackowiak, R. S. J., & Frith, C. D. (2000). Navigation-related structural change in the hippocampi of taxi drivers. *PNAS, 97*(81), 4398–4403.

McLellan, A. T., Lewis, D. C., O'Brien, C. P., & Kleber, H. D. (2000). Drug dependence, a chronic medical illness. *JAMA, 283*(13), 1689–1695.

Melamed, S. Shirom, A., Toker, S., Berliner, S., & Shapiro, I. (2006). Burnout and risk of cardiovascular disease: Evidence, possible causal paths, and promising research directions. *Psychological Bulletin, 132*(3), 327–353.

Michalak, J., Heidenreich, T., Meibert, P., & Schulte, D. (2008). Mindfulness predicts relapse/recurrence in major depressive disorder after mindfulness-based cognitive therapy. *Journal of Nervous and Mental Disease, 196*(8), 630–633.

Monterosso, J., & Luo, S. (2010). An argument against dual valuation system competition: Cognitive capacities supporting future orientation mediate rather than compete with visceral motivations. *Journal of Neuroscience, Psychology and Economics, 3*(1), 1–14.

Murata, T., Takahashi, T., Hamada, T., Omori, M., Kosaka, H., Yoshida, H., & Wada, Y. 2004. Individual trait anxiety levels characterizing the properties of Zen meditation. *Neuropsychobiology, 50*(2), 189–194.

Musashi, M. (1974). *The book of five rings: A guide to strategy.* Woodstock, NY: Overlook Press.

Newberg, A. B., & Iversen, J. (2003). The neural basis of the complex mental task of meditation: Neurotransmitter and neurochemical considerations. *Medical Hypotheses, 65*(3), 625–626.

Pagnoni G., Cekic, M., & Guo, Y. (2008) Thinking about not-thinking: Neural correlates of conceptual processing during Zen meditation. *PLoS ONE, 3*(9), e3083. doi:10.1371/journal.pone.0003083

Paulus, M. P., Rogalsky, C., Simmons, A., Feinstein, J. S., & Stein, M. B. (2003). Increased activation in the right insula during risk-taking decision making is related to harm avoidance and neuroticism. *Neuroimage, 19,* 1439–1448.

Paulus, M. P., & Stein, M. B. (2006). An insular view of anxiety. *Biological Psychiatry, 60,* 383–387.

Pashler, H. (1994). Dual-task interference in simple tasks: Data and theory. *Psychological Bulletin, 116*(2), 220–244.

Perls, F. (1969). *Gestalt therapy verbatim*. Lafayette, CA: Real People Press.

Pine, R. (1989). *The Zen teaching of Bodhidharma*. San Francisco, CA: North Point Press.

Porges, S. W. (1992). Vagal tone: A physiologic marker of stress vulnerability. *Pediatrics, 90*(3), 498–504.

Porges, S. W. (2011). *The Polyvagal Theory*. New York, NY: W. W. Norton & Company.

Portas, C. M., Rees, G., Howseman, A. M., Josephs, O., Turner, R., & Firth, C. D. (1998). A specific role of the thalamus in mediating the interaction of attention and arousal. *Journal of Neuroscience, 18*, 8979–8989.

Preuschoff, K., Quartz, S. R., & Bossaerts, P. (2008). Human insula activation reflects risk prediction errors as well as risk. *Journal of Neuroscience, 28*, 2745–2752.

Price, A. F., & Mou-lam, W. (1990). *The diamond sutra and the sutra of Hui-Neng*. Boston, MA: Shambala.

Rausch, S., Gramling, S., & Auerbach, S. (2006). Effects of a single session of large-group meditation and progressive muscle relaxation training on stress reduction, reactivity, and recovery. *International Journal of Stress Management, 13*(3), 273–290.

Reps, P. (1980). *Zen flesh, Zen bones: A collection of Zen and pre-Zen writings*. Rutland, VT: Charles E. Tuttle.

Ressler, K., & Mayberg, H. (2007). Targeting abnormal neural circuits in mood and anxiety disorders: From the laboratory to the clinic. *Nature Neuroscience, 10*, 1116–1124.

Rolls, E. T., McCabe, C., & Redoute, J., (2008). Expected value, reward outcome, and temporal difference error representations in a probabilistic decision task. *Cerebral Cortex, 18*, 652–663.

Rosen, H. J., & Levenson, R. W. (2010). The emotional brain: Combining insights from patients and basic science. *Neurocase, 15*(3), 173–181.

Schore, A. N. (2003). *Affect regulation and the repair of the self*. New York, NY: Norton.

Seeley, W. W. (2007). Dissociable intrinsic connectivity networks for salience processing and executive control. *Journal of Neuroscience, 27*, 2349–2356.

Sekida, K. (trans.) (1997). *Two Zen classics: Mumonkan and Hekiganroku*. New York, NY: Weatherhill.

Seung S. (1992). *Only don't know: The teaching letters of Zen master Seung Sahn*. Cumberland, RI: Primary Point Press.

Shannahoff-Khalsa, D. (2006). *Kundalini Yoga meditation: Techniques specific for psychiatric disorders, couples therapy, and personal growth*. New York, NY: W. W. Norton & Company.

Shaw, J. C. (1996). Intention as a component of the alpha rhythm response to mental activity. *International Journal of Psychophysiology, 24*, 1–2, 7–23.

Shimano, E. T. (1995). *Zen Word, Zen Calligraphy*. Boston, MA: Shambhala.

Simpkins, C. A., & Simpkins, A. M. (1998). *Zen around the world*. Boston, MA: Charles E. Tuttle.

Simpkins, C. A., & Simpkins, A. M. (1999a). *Simple Taoism: A guide to living in balance*. Boston, MA: Charles E. Tuttle.

Simpkins, C. A., & Simpkins, A. M. (1999b). *Simple Zen: A guide to living moment-by-moment*. Boston, MA: Charles E. Tuttle.

Simpkins, C. A., & Simpkins, A. M. (2000). *Simple Buddhism: A guide to enlightened living*. Boston, MA: Charles E. Tuttle.

Simpkins, C. A., & Simpkins, A. M. (2009). *Meditation for therapists and their clients*. New York, NY: W. W. Norton & Co.

Simpkins, C. A., & Simpkins, A. M. (2010a). *The dao of neuroscience: Combining Eastern and Western principles for optimal therapeutic change*. New York, NY: W. W. Norton & Co.

Simpkins, C. A., & Simpkins, A. M. (2010b). *Meditation and yoga in psychotherapy: Techniques for clinical practice*. Hoboken, NJ: Wiley.

Simpkins, C. A., & Simpkins, A. M. (2010c). *Neuro-hypnosis: Using self-hypnosis to activate the brain for change*. New York, NY: W. W. Norton & Co.

Singer, T., Critchley, H. D., & Preuschoff, K. (2009). A common role of insula in feelings, empathy, and uncertainty. *Trends in Cognitive Science, 13*(8), 334–341.

Slagter, H. A., Lutz, A., Greischar, L. L., Francis, A. D., Nieuwenhuis, S., Davis, J. M., & Davidson, R. J. (2007). Mental training affects distribution of limited brain resources. *PLOS Biology, 5*(6), 0001–0008.

Solomon, M., & Tatkin, S. (2011). *Love and war in intimate relationships*. New York, NY: W. W. Norton & Co.

Stevens, J. (1989). *The sword of no-sword*. Boston, MA: Shambala.

Sugiura, Y. (2004). Detached mindfulness and worry: A meta-cognitive analysis. *Personality and individual differences, 37*(1), 169–179.

Suzuki, D. T. (1969). *The Zen doctrine of no-mind.* York Beach, ME: Samuel Weiser.

Suzuki, D. T. (1973). *Zen and Japanese culture.* Princeton, NJ: Princeton University Press.

Suzuki, D. T. (1994). *The Zen koan as a means of attaining enlightenment.* Boston, MA: Charles E. Tuttle.

Suzuki, S. (1979). *Zen mind, beginners mind.* New York, NY: Weatherhill.

Takahashi, T., Murata, T., Hamada, T., Omori, M., Kosaka, H., & Kikuchi, M. (2005). Changes in EEG and autonomic nervous activity during meditation and their association with personality traits. *International Journal of Psychophysiology, 55*(2), 199–207.

Takuan, S. (1986). *The unfettered mind: Writings of the Zen master to the sword master.* Tokyo, Japan: Kodansha International.

Tanahashi, K. (ed). (1985). *Moon in a dewdrop: Writings of Zen master Dogen.* San Francisco, CA: North Point Press.

Tang, Y-Y., Lu, Q., Geng, X., Stein, E. A., Yang, Y., & Posner, M. I. (2010). Short-term meditation induces white matter changes in the anterior cingulate. *PNAS, 107*(35), 15649–15652.

Tang, Y-Y., Ma, Y., Fan, Y., Feng, H., Wang, J., Feng, S., . . . Fan, M. (2009). Central and autonomic nervous system interaction is altered by short-term meditation. *PNAS, 106*(22), 8865–8870.

Teasdale, J. (1983). Negative thinking in depression: Cause, effect or reciprocal relationship? *Advances in Behavior Research and Therapy, 5*(1), 3–25.

Teasdale, J. (1988). Cognitive vulnerability to persistent depression. *Cognition and Emotion, 2*(3), 247–274.

Teasdale, J. D., Segal, Z. V., Williams, J. M. G., Ridgeway, V., Lau, M., & Soulsby, J. (2000). Reducing risk of recurrence of major depression using mindfulness-based cognitive therapy. *Journal of Consulting and Clinical Psychology, 68*, 615–623.

Thich, Nhat Hanh. (1998). *The heart of the Buddha's teaching.* Berkeley, CA: Parallax Press.

Tory, P. B. (2004). A mindfulness-based stress reduction program for the treatment of anxiety. *Dissertation Abstracts International: Section B: The Sciences and Engineering, 64*(10-B), 5203.

Travis, F., & Shear, J. (2010). Focused attention, open monitoring and automatic self-transcending: Categories to organize meditations from Vedic,

Buddhist and Chinese traditions (in press). *Consciousness and Cognition*, *19*(4), 1110-1118.

Uvnas-Moberg, K. (1998). Oxytocin may mediate the benefits of positive social interaction and emotions. *Psychoneuroendocrinology*, *23*(8), 819–835.

VandenBos, G. R. (Ed.) (2006). *APA dictionary of psychology* (p. 26). Washington, DC: American Psychological Association.

Vinogradova, O. S. (2001). Hippocampus as comparator: Role of the two input and two output systems of hippocampus in selection and registration of information. *Hippocampus*, *11*, 578–598.

Voltaire, F. M. A. (1950). *Candide*. New York, NY: Penguin Books.

Waddell, N. (1984). *The unborn: The life and teaching of Zen master Bankei*. San Francisco, CA: North Point Press.

Waddell, N. (Trans.). (1994). *The essential teachings of Zen master Hakuin*. Boston, MA: Shambala.

Watson, B. (1993). *The Zen teachings of master Lin-Chi*. Boston, MA: Shambala.

Watts, A. (1973). *This is it*. New York, NY: Vintage Books.

Whitmyer, C. (1994). *Mindfulness and meaningful work: Explorations in right livelihood*. Berkeley, CA: Parallax Press.

Williams, M. G. (2010). Mindfulness and psychological process. *Emotion*, *10*(1), 1–7.

Witkiewitz, K., Marlatt, G. A., & Walker, D. D. (2005). Mindfulness-based relapse prevention for alcohol and substance use disorders. *Journal of Cognitive Psychotherapy*, *19*, 221–228.

Wundt, W. (1897). *Outlines of psychology*. (C. H. Judd, Trans.). Leipzig, Germany: Engelmann.

Yampolsky, P. B. (1971). *The Zen Master Hakuin: Selected writings*. New York, NY: Columbia University Press.

Yutang, L. (1942). *The Wisdom of China and India*. New York, NY: Random House.

Zhang, Y., Chen, Y., Bressler, S. L., & Ding, M. (2008). Response preparation and inhibition: The role of the cortical sensorimotor beta rhythm. *Neuroscience, 156*(1), 238–46

Zillmer, E. R., Spiers, M. V., & Culbertson, W. C. (2008). Principles of neuropsychology. Belmont, CA: Thomson Wadsworth.

Index

Abe, M., 57–58
Acceptance, 9, 17, 66, 82, 106, 110,
    128–131, 151, 170, 185
ACT (acceptance and commitment
    therapy), 9
Acumen for therapists, 209–222
  attentional skills, 213–218
  developing a habit of mindfulness,
    219–220
  emotional skills, 218–219
  interpersonal skills, 219–220
  mastery, 209–211, 223–224
  sensory awareness, 212–213
Addiction, 13–14, 30–31, 153–165.
    See also substance abuse
Affect, 10, 11, 21, 28–29, 104–105, 117,
    123, 177. *See also* Emotion
  arousal, 117, 123–126, 138–141, 177
  intensity, 10, 115, 117, 121, 126–127,
    194, 212–214, 218–219
  regulation of, 10–11, 27–28, 29–31,
    104–105, 117, 120, 122–128,
    172–176, 231
  valence, 117, 119, 121–122, 127–128,
    189–190, 236
Amygdala, 15, 28, 30, 104, 115, 118,
    137–139, 156. *See also* Emotion
Anger, 113–134
  anterior insula's role in, 115–116

changing thoughts about, 128
cognitive appraisal theory of,
    116–117
James' theory of, 114
letting go of, 131–132
regulating, 122–125
repairing angry relationships, 177,
    183–190
research on, 9
self-acceptance for overcoming,
    129–132
Zen view of, 68–69, 84–85,
    113–114
Anxiety, 135–152
  attention deficit disorder (ADHD)
    (*see also* attention), 16, 75, 101
  burnout, 196–97
  neurotransmitters, 228–229
  posttraumatic stress disorder (PTSD),
    26, 101–103, 137, 145, 146
  problems with interoception, 157–158
  in relationships, 178–81
  relaxing and calming, 123–125
  research, 15–16
  scales, 15
  training attention for, 101–104
  treatments for, 139–144
Attachment theory, 17, 173, 174–176,
    177, 178–180, 235